UNIVERSITY OF NOTRE DAME
WARD-PHILLIPS LECTURES IN
ENGLISH LANGUAGE AND LITERATURE

Volume 10

*Popular and Polite Art
in the Age of
Hogarth and Fieldi*

Popular and Polite Art
in the Age of
Hogarth and Fielding

Ronald Paulson

UNIVERSITY OF NOTRE DAME PRESS

NOTRE DAME   LONDON

Copyright © 1979 by
University of Notre Dame Press
Notre Dame, Indiana 46556

9 8 7 6 5 4 3 2 1 0

Library of Congress Cataloging in Publication Data

Paulson, Ronald.
  Popular and polite art in the age of Hogarth and
Fielding.

  (Ward-Phillips lectures in English language and
literature; 10)
  Includes bibliographical references and index.
  1. Arts, English—England. 2. Art, Modern—17th–
18th centuries—England. 3. English literature—
18th century—History-and criticism. 4. England—
Popular culture. 5. Fielding, Henry, 1707–1754—
Influence. 6. Hogarth, William, 1697–1754—
Influence. I. Title. II. Series.
NX543.P38   700'.942   79-63358
ISBN 0-268-01534-1

Manufactured in the United States of America

Contents

Illustrations

Preface

Popular subculture is, for the first half of the eighteenth century, the least unsatisfactory term for what has been designated in a later period "radical or working-class culture" and in an earlier "the popular heretical culture."[1] Each of these terms may describe a different aspect of "popular," but they share the sense of a substratum of society which has its own laws, ceremonies, and loyalties, and lives according to "an unwritten code, quite distinct from the laws of the land."[2] There is no easy line separating the subculture from the culture, and I think it will become evident that there are many discrete as well as overlapping vocabularies we can call subcultures. My main source is the art and literature of the period, which contain traces of a subculture from which we can infer a mass of people below the level of the classics-reading, property-owning, and voting interests, who dissociated themselves—in varying degrees—from most aspects of social and cultural conventions as they existed at the time, and as we now read them in books of history or literary history. When E. P. Thompson asks of the great age of peace and prosperity seen by J. H. Plumb through the eyes of Sir Robert Walpole, "Peace and Prosperity for whom?" and concludes, "I am at a loss to know who this was, beyond the circle of Walpole's own creatures"—he is looking up from the position of a subculture.[3]

My title, it will be noticed, involves a series of substitutions for Thompsonian terms: *popular* for *plebeian*, *polite* for *patrician*, and *art* for *culture*. Thompson's use of *plebeian* is reasonable applied to eighteenth-century England, given the Roman ethos (patrician/plebeian), but it presupposes the downward point of view of the patrician, which is precisely what Thompson's own insights into the subculture avoid.[4] I am looking aslant from the detached view (essentially Hogarth's) of a person somewhat outside high culture who regards *popu-*

lar as a wider base than either *plebeian* or *subculture*. *Art* is preferred
to *culture* as limiting this study to the work of a few individuals rather
than attempting to deal with the larger concept which is the rightful
preserve of the historian and anthropologist.

I examine some of the works that were "popular" in the sense
that they were read or seen by almost everybody; were part of the
consciousness of the learned or educated as well as of the uneducated; read or seen or talked about by so many people that we can say
they were taken for granted as part of the environment, landmarks or
public signs rather than only works of literature or art (although some
of them were that also, and some writers and artists increasingly tried
to make them so). I am therefore concerned with the effect, the
impress, and the use made of things seen or read or merely accepted,
but that went largely unnoticed. The verbal examples are those
printed texts that became proverbial: *Robinson Crusoe*, of course, but
also *Joe Miller's Jests* and Hoyle's *Treatise on the Game of Whist*,
which added to the language a "Joe Miller" (a joke) and "according
to Hoyle." The things seen include alphabet books and decks of
cards, and in the streets the symbols and symbolic actions of crowd
rituals, the signboards, the engravings in shop windows and on tavern
walls, and the armorial bearings on coaches.

Some of these were also innovating phenomena in that they
established (or at least indicated) structures of consciousness of a sort
that claimed to be (or were thought to be) both new and quintessentially English. "Hoyle's whist" was taken to be as English a contribution to European culture as Capability Brown's garden on the aristocratic level, Hogarth's engraved "progresses" as Hugo Meynell's new
form of fox hunting.

In all of the books to which I refer there is a strong sense of
oral tradition being caught or fixed in print. Jestbooks put into
writing what was supposedly oral tradition, and cookbooks certainly
have to come about as a result of cooking practice written down in
the form of recipes. There was, however, a tradition of written
cookbooks going back to Epicius, and elements of the oldest written
tradition mingle with eighteenth-century culinary discoveries or fashions. Cookbooks, depending on the audience addressed, were
sometimes arranged on the model of aesthetic treatises, meals like
pictures (baroque or neoclassical or picturesque), and William King
was expressing more of a truth than he probably realized in his

mock-georgic *Art of Cookery* (1708) when he modified the *ut pictura poesis* topos into *ut coctura poesis*:

> Poets and Pastry Cooks will be the Same,
> Since both of Them their Images must frame.
> Chimera's from the Poet's Fancy flow,
> The Cook contrives his Shapes in real Dough.

"Tables," he tells us, "shou'd be like Pictures to the Sight, / Some Dishes cast in Shade, some spread in Light."[5]

So these are printed works that represent a formulation of some current preverbal practice. Hoyle's *Treatise on Whist* was one of the best sellers of the century, but you would not call it any more a working-class book than Peter Beckford's *Thoughts on Hunting*, which formulated the practice of Meynell's fox hunting. Though everybody played cards (or so it seemed), whist as developed by Hoyle was initially a gentleman's game, and only people above a certain economic level were likely to read books on the subject. On the other hand, Hoyle's book embodies in words procedures which may have reached far down into the practice of the "inferior sort of people," whose popular game was taken up by their betters and then "improved" and formulated in Hoyle's book. The form of the book was, of course, inherently different from the form of the practice of card playing itself. The rules, however, like the angles and distances that are spread out and materialized into the visual result of a map, project their own distinctive structure of play.

These works also share the quality of being peripheral, and in the largest sense I hope they will raise the question of the peripheral or marginal in eighteenth-century English literature and art. Freud, among others, has made us aware of the fact that we may often find the significant, nuclear aspect of a work in a peripheral detail. Artists of the medieval tradition that continued in Bosch, Brueghel, and (in eighteenth-century England) Hogarth, often emblematized their meaning in just such a peripheral way. But I am also referring to the kind of object which is itself peripheral to the consciousness of eighteenth-century Londoners. Of course, it is to be acknowledged that (as with fox hunting) one man's periphery is another's center. I am impressed by the "margin oriented" anthropologists like Mary Douglas, Victor Turner, and Edmund Leach who look to the blurred borders of phenomena for significance. They reverse Durkheim's formulation of sacred/profane = center/periphery and see the secular center shading off into sacred or taboo borders.[6] And I gain some confidence from the fact that eighteenth-century scholars have already begun to explore this territory in their concern with the disorder that is repressed, or held barely in check, in the great, surely central works of Swift, Pope, and Fielding by what we used to think of as their common social norms. What is being held in check, rather than their shared norms, may offer a clue to the quality that in fact distinguishes them from each other.[7]

One aspect of the peripheral is the subculture, and another is the works I have so far mentioned, most of which—whatever their exact social status—would be considered peripheral by any literary or cultural historian of the period. But if we begin with the "popular," we have to end with the works of some major artists—primarily that interesting pair Fielding and Hogarth—and see how the peripheral elements function peripherally or centrally in their work, and indeed what can be considered peripheral and what central. This means that I am concerned with popular structures and their use in polite art— sometimes as a particular source, but also in certain cases as a sign of peripherality itself as a significant phenomenon.

"Art" is an aspect of "culture," and by "culture," as opposed to "society," I mean pretty much what Sidney W. Mintz has called "a kind of resource" as opposed to "a kind of arena"; in other words, "sets of historically available alternatives or forms on the one hand, and the societal circumstances or settings within which these forms may be employed on the other."[8] As I move along, I try to link the subculture and high-culture phenomena I am describing to the real contingencies defined by their social structures, circumstances, and settings at a given time. I deal with only a few nodes of time, clusters of events, texts, and circumstances around the years 1730, 1740, and 1750, which have seemed to me (and I chose them for this reason) the only sure places at which high and low, art and literature, can be seen coming together in a meaningful conjunction. I want to show in this period at least that while popular topoi and iconography cling to old, tried forms, they also embody an impetus for change that is of the greatest importance. All of my examples point toward the writing and painting of the 1750s, and not to anything that can be called a history of the time.

The "historically available alternatives" to which Mintz refers are not always easy to separate. Elements in the works of Hogarth and Fielding that appear to be subcultural introjections may well share their characteristics with certain assumptions of the dominant culture. I am not sure that historians have yet agreed as to whether there really was a "popular heretical culture" or a "radical or working-class culture," or only plebeian versions of the vocabularies of the Classical Republicans, the Eighteenth-Century Commonwealth men, and the Old Whigs. There may not be within reach a language of any particular subculture itself. Hogarth, with his subculture origins, may come closest to giving us this, but in general he merely reflects its existence in his representations of its various external forms. And insofar as we even discover a subculture there, its forms may only reflect those of the ruling class in an earlier time. Thompson has shown that the behavior of the crowd in eighteenth-century bread riots was based on the *Book of Orders*, the printed codification of emergency measures for scarcity made by the Elizabethan government.[9] We always have to remember Coleridge's salutary response to Wordsworth's claims for the natural language of the uneducated man. This language actually takes its power from the Bible, Coleridge remarks (quoting Henry More), and concludes:

> If the history of the phrases in hourly currency among our peasants were traced, a person not previously aware of the fact would be surprized at finding so large a number, which three or four centuries ago were the exclusive property of the universities and the schools; and, at the commencement of the Reformation, had been transferred from the school to the pulpit, and thus gradually passed into common life.[10]

One thing that Thompson—with George Rudé, Keith Thomas, Natalie Zemon Davis, and other historians—has shown is that popular rituals are usually conservative in form.[11] The example we all remember is the ballad hunters who penetrated the remotest parts of Europe's mountainous peasant areas to collect original, uncorrupted folk songs, and discovered corrupt versions of the melodies of Beethoven and Schubert. In our own time, Negro spirituals have been traced back to Anglican hymns like "Old Hundred."[12]

They may also be conservative in content—aimed, as Keith Thomas argues, at making life bearable.[13] To be precise, we would have to distinguish the subculture forms as something between com-

pensation and opiate (which more or less accommodates them to the
intentions of the dominant culture) from certain *counter*culture forms
which reveal not only difference from the main culture but rejection
of it, awareness of its weakness and rebellion against its innovations.[14] In treating these issues I have become involved in, as I
described, a critical phenomenon. In Gregory Batcock's words: "The
critic has, as it were, to paint the painting anew and make it more
acceptable, less of a threat than it often is. It is scarcely an exaggeration to say that the art of our time could not exist without the efforts
of the critic."[15] Batcock is describing contemporary art, but he could
as well be describing the main phenomenon I am concerned with in
eighteenth-century England. It is a reciprocal action: the subculture
tries to make its raw experience—its vulnerability—bearable; and the
culture tries to make the subculture gestures safe and unthreatening.
(Or it merely misunderstands their true import and reinterprets them,
putting forward a series of secondary motives that suit the dominant
culture's assumptions.) And occasionally an artist tries to incorporate
something of the subculture as a transfusion to revive English literature and art.

The extreme selectivity of my examples will be apparent. I deal
with no poetry, but only different forms (visual as well as verbal) of
prose. I hope my examples are as significant as I think they are, but I
have space for no more than a few of them and a sketching out of the
issues within the format of this book, which began as the Ward-
Phillips Lectures at Notre Dame University, delivered in April 1978.
I wish to thank my hosts and the University Press for their hospitality
and all the courtesies extended to me. To these four lectures, I have
added the remaining chapters as somewhat more elaborate cases of
the interaction of popular and high art. Parts of chapters 2, 3, 4, and
6 of Part II have appeared in print already in a different form, and for
permission to reprint them I wish to thank the editors and publishers
of *New Literary History; Tobias Smollett: Bicentennial Essays Presented to Lewis M. Knapp Modern Language Notes;* and *Augustan
Worlds: Essays in Honour of A. R. Humphreys.*[16]

Chronology

1728   John Gay, *Beggar's Opera*; Hogarth, paintings of *Beggar's Opera*; Pope, *Dunciad*; Fielding, *Love in Several Masques*; Defoe, *Tour thro' the Whole Island of Great Britain*; *Polly Peachum's Jests*.

1732   Hogarth, *Harlot's Progress*; Fielding's *Covent-Garden Tragedy* and other farces.

1735   Hogarth, *Rake's Progress*.

1739   *Joe Miller's Jests*; Hume, *Treatise of Human Nature*; Banier, *Mythology and Fables of the Ancients*; Hogarth's *Good Samaritan* and *Pool of Bethesda* finished and in situ.

1740   Richardson, *Pamela*, closely followed by Fielding's *Shamela*.

1742   Fielding, *Joseph Andrews*; Hoyle, *Short Treatise on the Game of Whist*.

1744.   Corbyn Morris, *An Essay towards Fixing the True Standards of Wit*; Newbery, *A Little Pretty Pocket Book*.

1745   Hogarth, *Marriage à la Mode*; Fielding, *True Patriot* and *History of the Present Rebellion in Scotland*.

1747   Hogarth, *Industry and Idleness*; first part of Richardson's *Clarissa*; Fielding, *Jacobite's Journal*; Smollett, *Roderick Random*; Joseph Spence, *Polymetis*; Thomas Blackwell, *Letters Concerning Mythology*.

1748   Cadogan, *Essay upon Nursing*; Fielding; *Tom Jones*; Cleland, *Fanny Hill*; Hume, *Enquiry Concerning Human Understanding*; Benjamin Martin, *Institutions of Language*.

1749   John Free, *An Essay towards a History of the English Tongue*.

1750   Hogarth, *March to Finchley*; William Ellis, *Country House-wife's Family Companion*; Rousseau, *First Discourse*.

1751   Fielding, *Enquiry into the Late Increase of Robbers*; Hogarth, *Beer Street* and *Gin Lane* and *The Four Stages of Cruelty*; Smollett, *Peregrine Pickle*; Francis Coventry, *Pompey the Little*; James Harris, *Hermes*.

I. Subculture Types

1. The Criminal

WITHIN A FEW WEEKS in January and February 1751 Henry Fielding published a pamphlet, *An Enquiry into the Causes of the Late Increase of Robbers*, and William Hogarth published six prints, *Beer Street* and *Gin Lane* and *The Four Stages of Cruelty*. In these words and images we have parallel attempts to deal with the same problem of crime among the urban poor in England at midcentury.

As historians have realized, the old image of Fielding as "democrat" and "radical social reformer" well ahead of his time was not earned by this pamphlet, or by its successor *A Proposal for Making an Effectual Provision for the Poor, for Amending Their Morals, and for Rendering Them Useful Members of the Society* (1753).[1] As Bow Street magistrate, of course, he wrote from a delimited, official point of view. At the heart of his argument he writes:

> In free Countries, at least, it is a Branch of Liberty claimed by the People to be as wicked and as profligate as their Superiors. Thus while the Nobleman will emulate the Grandeur of a Prince; and the Gentleman will aspire to the proper State of the Nobleman, the Tradesman steps from behind his Counter into the vacant Place of the Gentleman. Nor doth the Confusion end here: It reaches the very Dregs of the People, who aspiring still to a Degree beyond that which belongs to them, and not being able by the Fruits of honest Labour to support the State which they affect, they disdain the Wages to which their Industry would entitle them; and abandoning themselves to Idleness, the more simple and poor-spirited betake themselves to a State of Starving and Beggary, while those of more Art and Courage become Thieves, Sharpers, and Robbers.[2]

Fielding is concerned with "the very Dregs of the People" because when *they* aspire "to a Degree beyond that which belongs to

3

them"—try to "affect" (as in "affectation," the source in *Joseph Andrews* of the ridiculous) a state that is not proper to them—they sink into crime, which is dangerous to all the higher sort of people, however much they may themselves affect a yet higher state (in less overtly dangerous ways). What "the very Dregs" do, Fielding says, using key terms of his age, is "disdain the Wages to which their Industry would entitle them" and abandon themselves "to Idleness," thereby becoming criminals.[3]

As to the "superior part of mankind," as Fielding calls them, they cannot be legislated against like the poor, but may perhaps be reasoned with:

> And here I must again remind the Reader, that I have only the inferior Part of Mankind under my Consideration. I am not so ill-bred as to disturb the Company at a polite Assembly; nor so ignorant of our Constitution, as to imagine, that there is a sufficient Energy in the executive Part to controul the Oeconomy of the Great, who are beyond the Reach of any, unless capital Laws. Fashion, under whose guidance they are, and which created the Evil, can alone cure it.

We will have to wait, he acknowledges, "till they have Sense enough to be reasoned, Modesty enough to be laughed, or Conscience enough to be frightened, out of a silly, a shameful, and a sinful Profligacy, attended with horrid Waste of Time, and the cruel Destruction of the Families of others, or of their own."[4]

This sort of passage—which runs as a refrain through the *Enquiry*—marks the limits of Fielding's sympathy. It shows his awareness of the plight of the poor, but also his pragmatic approach to the problem at hand.[5] He points out, for instance, that one of the causes of the poor's thievery lies with the church wardens and overseers of the poor (discussed in his fourth section) who "are too apt to consider their Office as a Matter of private Emolument, to waste Part of the Money raised for the Use of the Poor in Feasting and Riot"—a point illustrated in Hogarth's *Industry and Idleness*, plate 8 (fig. 3) and implied in *The First Stage of Cruelty* (fig. 8) by the St. Giles insignia on young Tom Nero's arm and the absence of the St. Giles parish officers who should be looking after him.[6] In his fifth section, on receivers of stolen goods, Fielding goes after the middlemen who escape through loopholes of the law but are more criminal than (though not so immediately dangerous as) the thief—a theme that runs through his novels as well as Hogarth's prints.[7]

But however much he damns the various strata of the governing class, Fielding is offering small comfort to—and certainly not communicating with—the governed. He is, after all, with his genteel ironic tone, writing *to* the superior sort, not the inferior. Reading the pamphlet is beyond their scope, as its cost is beyond their means. And so he must employ his irony to get at the rich while proposing stronger laws for limiting the potentials for mischief in the poor, who *can* be affected by legislation. The laws must prevent the poor's excessive gin drinking and make them settle down to safe, industrious behavior.

In Hogarth's *Gin Lane* (fig. 7) the architectural and human decline is plainly the consequence of drinking gin, but there are no signs of crime, only terrible accidents and self-destruction. If we look around to see what led to the gin drinking, we find (besides the distiller) only the pawnbroker who permits, indeed encourages, these people to drink themselves to death. The only other hint is the distant church spire, which indicates an absence rather than an active cause. Hogarth has chosen the church of St. George's Bloomsbury, the one London church with a king on its steeple (George I), and has substituted by an optical illusion the pawnbroker's sign in the foreground for the cross. This fortuitous grouping materializes a sign of the conjoined authority of church, state, and pawnbroker. As the local representative of church and state, the pawnbroker allows the drinking to go on. Let me suggest that this peripheral detail, this "mistake" in the employment of compositional perspective (of the sort Hogarth ridiculed in *False Perspective*, fig. 20), would be seen by a naive viewer, unconcerned with laws of perspective, in a surer and more immediate way than by the reader of Fielding's *Enquiry*—and carries a message quite outside the range of Fielding's argument.

A church steeple is closer and more prominent in the pendant, *Beer Street* (fig. 6), and the king is manifested front-center in George II's printed *Address to Parliament*, which is being read by fat, prosperous tradesmen. The king's *Address* offers plans for the "Advancement of our Commerce," which in terms of the metaphor of fat/beer versus thin/gin means making them fatter. The two prints are as much about the absence or presence of royal/ecclesiastical authority as about the drinking of beer or gin.

The fact is that the government encouraged distillation and sales of gin in order to support the landed interest (encourage the production of spirits distilled from home-grown cereals) and provide itself with revenues. As one historian of gin has concluded, "the rise and decline of gin drinking can be related directly to taxation and legislation."[8] In 1743 Parliament repealed the 1736 Gin Act and adopted a more moderate one, drafted by a prominent distiller of the time. Lord Bathurst's argument was that since it was impossible to prevent the retailing of spirits, it would be better to license it instead, as this would reduce usage by increasing expense and also provide money for the European wars. The new law, known as the Tippling Act, increased the price of gin, granted licenses only to alehouse license holders, and forbade distillers to retail. But in 1747 the distillers petitioned for the right to retail, and the act was modified accordingly. Once this right was restored to the distillers, gin consumption, which had waned slightly since 1743, rose markedly; drunkenness increased, population declined, and in 1750 a commission reported that in some parts of London one in every five houses was a ginshop. Whether or not Hogarth had this information, he assumes some such situation when he includes the spire of St. George's in *Gin Lane* and juxtaposes with this print of the emaciated gin drinkers the prosperity of the fat merchants and the royal urge to greater commerce in *Beer Street*. The basic cause and effect relationship would be understood by the poor: not that beer drinking leads to prosperity and gin drinking to want, but the reverse. Rather, beer drinking is a product of prosperity and gin drinking of want.

Another pair of details is relevant. In the background of *Beer Street* a fat, encumbered upper-class woman is being crushed in her too-tight sedan chair (related to the fat beer drinkers in the foreground), and in *Gin Lane* a poor, emaciated dead woman lies in her coffin. Each woman has two attendants and a box to hold her. Such details may have been overlooked by the audience of responsible citizens to which Fielding addresses himself, but the poor would have seen them straightaway. And once the women are seen as a pair, the fat one becomes a cause of the emaciated, dead one, as do the fat, beer-drinking purveyors of essential commodities in the foreground.

The two plates convey an implied contrast between the state's paternalist duty to regulate on the old mercantilist basis and the new ideal of supply and demand in a free market ("advance our commerce," as the king's *Address* says) which wishes to regulate itself and determine its own level of profit and cost. "Whereas the first appeals to a moral norm—what *ought* to be men's reciprocal duties—the second appears to say: 'This is the way things work, or would work if the State did not interfere.' "[9] From the point of view of eighteenth-century bread rioters,˙this assumed the shape of the man (here the pawnbroker, but any merchant) who seeks private gain at the expense of his own neighbors, who accordingly can only riot or sink into gin and crime. For the poor man of this period, as Francis Place wrote, "none but the animal sensations are left; to these his enjoyments are limited, and even these are frequently reduced to two—namely sexual intercourse and drinking. . . . Of the two . . . drunkenness is by far the most desired" since it provides a longer period of escape and costs only a penny.[10] The people of Gin Lane could not have afforded beer; gin alone was within their competence.

Hogarth allows for a direct address to the poor, and this means that in a much more significant sense than is possible for Fielding he is showing them forced into their bad habits by the interests of the governing social structure itself. Fielding only questions an occasional particularly brutal law. Hogarth's visual images undermine the structure of authority itself. This is partly because there is in visual forms a greater potential for doubleness of interpretation of the sort Fielding solicits. Fielding must address only an audience of the superior sort, and irony is his only weapon against them (or method for instructing them). Hogarth can reach both groups directly, the poor as well as their betters. Both audiences can go to the visual image and take away the aspect each sees through his particular preconceptions. What the rich will see as peripheral irony, the poor will see as central.[11]

The Reward of Cruelty (fig. 11), by all odds Hogarth's most horrifying image, is an example of the way in which this second audience would have understood what the first would probably have only dimly sensed: I refer to the taboos surrounding human dissection. The popular beliefs that reverberate in this plate include the possibility of resuscitation after hanging, the magically therapeutic powers of a malefactor's corpse, and the ability of the spirit of the dead to return to the living. The notorious Tyburn riots of the years leading up to 1752, as Peter Linebaugh has shown, were essentially aimed at rescuing the victim's body from the dissectors—a concerted extralegal action by small groups of his friends, relatives, or fellow apprentices.[12] These represent a kind of class solidarity, a set of beliefs, unwritten and of the subculture but as reasonable as those with which we are more familiar, namely the views of the "better sort" of people who thought in terms of the legal system and believed in the medical utility and the penal retribution involved in the dissection of malefactors.

Hogarth makes his statement this time by portraying the chief surgeon in the pose of a magistrate in relation to the condemned malefactor. The Company of Surgeons has made off with Tom Nero's body from the gallows. Only a year later, in March 1752, did the law equitably settle the matter by making dissection a part of the official penalty the judge could impose upon certain, but not all, criminals. This law, the "Murder Act," was framed as an immediate response to the Penlez riots of 1749 (in which Fielding as Bow Street magistrate played an adversary role). It is not without significance that the dissector in Hogarth's picture has been traditionally identified as Dr. John Freke, the surgeon who was prevented from dissecting Penlez's body in the *cause célèbre* that followed his execution—and who did dissect many other criminals.[13] Looking back, we have to see the first *Stage of Cruelty* as defined by the absence of the St. Giles Parish officers, and the second by the very decided presence of the bulky lawyers who are in fact responsible for the collapsed horse which Nero is beating (they have crowded in to save a fare). Thus we proceed to the grimly threatening constabulary of *Cruelty in Perfection* and the surgeon-magistrate of *The Reward of Cruelty* (figs. 8–11), those representatives of the law, the forces from above for whom Nero—as is finally made explicit in his "reward"—serves merely as someone who is not (to use Fielding's phrase) "beyond the reach of . . . capital laws."

2. The Apprentice

ANOTHER OF HOGARTH'S BEST-KNOWN IMAGES is of the Tyburn execution itself, of "Tyburn Fair" or the "Theater of Tyburn," which has been called "the ritual at the heart of London's popular culture."[1] This image, with its parallel in the lord-mayor's procession, concludes Hogarth's first series of overtly popular prints back in 1747, the story of two apprentices, *Industry and Idleness* (figs. 4–5).

The apprentice is an especially useful example. In the first place, one easily defined entity is that large "adolescent subculture" of the London apprentices, which possessed the set of ideals imposed upon them by their masters as well as their own subset of ideals which they jealously nourished themselves and carried with them into the outside world as journeymen and small artisans: ideals deeply hedonistic and antiauthoritarian, associated with youth and summed up in those two outlets of sex and drink. They are also a good example because in 1734 Samuel Richardson published a typical *Apprentice's Vade Mecum*—typical in that from its prohibitions we can infer the positive characteristics of the subculture. The *Vade Mecum* is a printed series of admonitions, couched (as befitted their author) in prudential terms, written from the point of view of the master, and summing up the patriarchal relationship of apprenticeship. One-third of the pamphlet is devoted to the evils of the theater (excepting *The London Merchant; or the History of George Barnwell*, of course, Lillo's admonitory tragedy about a bad apprentice), and much is said about the evils of drink and fornication.[2]

The apprentices were an unruly bunch of adolescents, closely related to those youth clubs Natalie Zemon Davis has written about in medieval France, who were constantly seeking the sports (dice or cards) and plays, the mumming and dancing, the singing and drinking and lovemaking they were officially forbidden. Their attention

9

was, however, less focused on the old man marrying (buying) the young girl of their own age (celebrated in the ritual of the charivari) than on their own relationship to the master, their surrogate father. They were notorious for the jokes they aimed at the master or his wife, based on hatred of his power but focused on his wealth and bourgeois sensibility. Many hinged upon the fantasy of marrying his widow or his daughter and assuming paternal control of the shop. There are accounts of the verbal joke slipping into the verbal threat, as with the apprentice who "did threaten [his master] in an unusuall manner, and often swore he would be his death, and would crush his head against the table, with many such like provoking expressions," which occasionally led to the action itself.[3] Apprentices frequently ran away and all too often rioted—in fact were considered a likely nucleus for any mob action. They constantly had held up to them by such writers as Richardson the polar opposites of Dick Whittington and George Barnwell, the apprentice who became lord-mayor and the other one who let his sexual drives lead him to ruin and the gallows. Hogarth does the same in his series of twelve plates (the number itself designated a popular series) celebrating an industrious apprentice named Francis Goodchild, who *does* marry the master's daughter, and lamenting an idle one named Tom Idle who flubs all his opportunities.

I have dealt with this series in very great detail in *Emblem and Expression* and will not do so again. But my argument there was that despite the change toward a consciously popular form, toward simpler designs and messages—the simple contrast of industry and idleness (those terms we have already encountered in Fielding's *Enquiry*)—Hogarth retained his basic allegiance to his audience of "the superior sort" who could be relied upon to follow "the pleasure of the pursuit" ("a kind of chase") into its subtlest ramifications.[4] I referred to Hogarth's understanding of the Renaissance poet's "veil of allegory" which presupposes two audiences, one the general body of readers and the other "readers of greater penetration." I showed how this play, with such emblems as Blind Justice, such conventional iconography as left = evil and right = good, and the biblical verses appended beneath the designs, led to an ironic undermining or undercutting around the fringes of primary difference. In the last pair of plates the apprentices, who have respectively occupied left (Idle) and right (Goodchild) sides of the scene, are nearly indistinguishable from each other and their respective rewards. Goodchild has moved left-ward into exactly the same space as the criminal Idle whom he condemned to death in plate 10.

The question I am raising is whether the essential experience of *Industry and Idleness* is arrived at through sophisticated inference drawn by the "readers of greater penetration" who were the elite of Hogarth's audience, who read down, or by a "working-class audience" who immediately perceived a meaning that questioned the whole social system? This audience consisted of neither the connoisseurs familiar with Ripa, Alciati, and the great tradition of Renaissance art nor the masters (represented by Richardson's *Vade Mecum*) who bought the sets of prints for their apprentices, often as Christmas presents, and hung them around the shop walls as admonitions. (Apprentices could not have afforded to buy the prints themselves.) When the apprentice looked at Francis Goodchild in plate 4, with his master in his counting house juxtaposed with an emblematic print of Opportunity taking Time by the forelock, he saw at once a young man who in an earlier plate had courted his master's daughter and here clutches his keys and moneybag as if they were his own.[5]

Let us take as our example plate 6 (fig. 2), where the industrious apprentice has married his master's daughter. The shop sign of the firm already reads "West and Goodchild" (and in another, alternative state, "Goodchild and West," the junior partner having usurped the senior's place),[6] and the ballad singer is celebrating Goodchild's marriage with "The Ballad of Jesse or the Happy Pair," which the apprentice-reader, I believe, would have applied to Goodchild and his master as well as to Goodchild and his bride. The apprentice sensibility—for whom the "Goodchild and West" state was made—would go straight to the cynical, subversive meaning. The master's sensibility, by contrast, would read the plate "straight," as part of a happy success story.

As to the learned reader, the man with that "sound book learnedness into which our old public schools continue to initiate their pupils":[7] he would probably have meditated on the ballad of "Jesse or the Happy Pair." There appears to have been no such ballad, but the word *Jesse* in Hebrew means wealthy, and what one remembers of the biblical Jesse is his genealogy (given twice in the Old Testament) and his son David, who married Michal, his master's daughter. Out of this marriage a distinguished tree was to grow—the Tree of Jesse, the outcome of which was Jesus.[8] This is the meaning the master (or Goodchild, for whom the ballad is produced) would have read. But the learned reader would also recall that Goodchild and David are both apprentices; David, originally engaged in a lowly capacity as harper to King Saul, becomes his master's close companion, best friend to his son Jonathan, and lover of his daughter (in each case a "happy pair"), and finally "takes over the business" as king of Israel. The title of Hogarth's plate is a reminder that the wife, being the master's reward to his servant for faithful service (David slew double a hundred Philistines for his dowry), is a sort of "seal of approval" and will be an important factor in the servant's advancement. The story of Saul's delays in delivering up Michal may also hint that the master used his daughter as bait to get the apprentice to work harder in his interests.[9]

But there are yet other Saul–David implications loosed by the pursuit of "Jesse": for example, Saul's anxiety over the fact that David is destined to replace him as king continues to grow after the marriage, leading to attempts on David's life and to his own eventual ruin. By a complex process, based on a thorough knowledge of the Bible plus the principles of literary allusion gained by reading the Augustan classics (Milton, Dryden, Swift, and Pope), the educated reader arrives at a series of ironies that tend to undercut the obvious comic-strip contrasts of the Goodchild success story.

What we notice, however, is that the main difference between the ends reached by the "readers of greater penetration" at the top and the apprentices and artisans at the bottom is the speed of transit. Both join in arriving at a reading and a set of assumptions at odds with those of the master. But the apprentice enjoys an immediacy and intensity of response quite different from the "pleasure of pursuit," which is a kind of mystification or muffling, defined by John Berger as "the process of explaining away what might otherwise be evident."[10] It does not occur to the penetrative reader to take sides.

In plate 8 (fig. 3) I suspect that the apprentice, without need of mediation, sees the gluttonous dignitaries around the table in the light of the poor petitioners waiting vainly outside the door, and the empty place at the table allowed to remain so rather than be used for one of them.[11] Neither the master nor the "reader of greater penetration" would in all probability notice this aspect of the picture. The latter might remark the gross merchants and ask why Goodchild is so tiny and distant in the scene of his triumph; he might see Hogarth's subtle satire as working in both ways. But the unsophisticated audience of apprentices sees it instantaneously as about the life of sheriffs and aldermen, exploiters in whose bosom Goodchild has now lost himself. And then, when this audience looks at the emblem of Blind Justice in the form of the posturing Alderman Goodchild passing judgment on his late fellow apprentice in plate 10, it sees straight to the judicial eyes, averted from the skulduggery going on in the background with the connivance of the law itself, because this is the way it thinks. As an alderman, Goodchild can only pass judgment according to the laws of ruling-class society—a set of laws as remote in many ways from the poor apprentices as the Ten Commandments of the Old Testament.

Among other things, *Industry and Idleness* leads us to conclude that Hogarth associates the visual language of images with the subculture; the language of words—at least of written, inscribed words like those of the Ten Commandments—with the dominant or master's culture. The popular print showing Opportunity catching Time by the forelock pinpoints the actual relationship being established between apprentice and master, getting at a truth that is elided by both the pious words of the reading matter Francis Goodchild posts on his wall next to his loom and the pious words from the Book of Proverbs (and Leviticus) that are etched beneath the designs. These biblical maxims constitute the voice of authority. The pictorial and popular images, depending on how we regard them, either shine through or subvert the words of the official text (even, as in the case of Opportunity, the picture's official, or master's, meaning).

Goodchild, we notice in the first plate (fig. 1), has a well-preserved copy of the *Prentice's Guide* and a ballad of Dick Whittington; in plate 2 a hymnal, in 4 his master's *Day* (or Record) *Book*, and in 6 (fig. 2) he is patronizing literature in the form of "The Ballad of Jesse or the Happy Pair." Even the shop sign of "the Happy Pair," "Goodchild and West," is strictly verbal, not the usual visual image which Hogarth associates with shop signs, which might have shown David and Saul (or Jonathan). In plate 10, as alderman, Goodchild has his bailiffs employ both a Bible and a letter of sentence, which amount to the same thing since it is by the standards of Old Testament law that Goodchild sentences Idle to death for stealing a watch. It is not surprising to see that Goodchild collects and preserves texts.

He respects the word, which is the law, and senses the advantages in making the most of language and books. In every plate in which he appears, he holds or is in close proximity to an open book of some sort; and he even keeps his eyes cast downward in the direction of the biblical texts beneath the designs, as if "reading" or referring to them. (His eyes are always averted from what goes on around him—from what he has to *do* to succeed.)

Idle, by contrast, is as antitextual as he is antisocial. By his failure he represents the fact that utilization of language is synonymous with social success, and in particular the language of the written law. In the first plate, his copy of the *Prentice's Guide* has disintegrated through neglect (or active defacement) and he has only the ballad of Moll Flanders, a rogue heroine; in 3 he uses as a resting place, and covers with his body, the "text" of the gravestone which might otherwise present him with a useful moral, *Ubi sunt* or *Memento mori*. In 5 he lets his indenture—that most precious document of commercial London—float away on the water, and all the while he ignores the repeated warnings of the biblical passages beneath him, focusing his eyes on something in *this* world.[12] If Goodchild is an effective utilizer of language, and thereby rises to a societal command of it as an administrator of the law, then Idle, through cutting himself off from the word, sinks to the bottom of the heap and further.

The ironic conclusion comes in plate 11 (fig. 4), where poor Idle at last becomes, in his final moments, a reader and even a generator of texts. We see him intently reading the Bible and listening to the pious exhortations of the Methodist preacher, while a woman in the foreground hawks "The Last Dying Speech & Confession of Tho. Idle."[13] His story, by being verbalized, has been transformed and "made useful" in just the way his body is being made an exemplary punishment by the law. Both have been domesticated in the structure of official Christian society. Idle has become an anti-Whittington, to be avoided by those apprentices seeking success. The printed "Dying Speech" (whether written by him or, more likely, foisted on him by some hack writer) forces Idle into the societal role of the "Repentant Criminal."

In short, society gets its way with the most recalcitrant of deviates. But there is a final irony, which is the fact that the visual images of Hogarth's prints were themselves destined to be used as written, prescriptive words on the walls of shops like that of West and Goodchild.

One other figure in plate 11 should be identified: the "ordinary" of Newgate Prison. As Peter Linebaugh has recently shown, Hogarth places the clergyman of the Established Church, cut off from Idle and his Methodist comforter in a closed carriage, on the same vertical, almost at the center of the picture, with the hawker selling the "Dying Speech of Tom Idle."[14] They are the only two figures who look directly at the viewer, for they offer the alternative versions of the story of the condemned criminal. The ordinary of Newgate, in his printed *Accounts* of the criminals under his spiritual charge, represented the polite view of crime. His *Accounts* were the official version of the "dying speeches" hawked by this subculture woman; they sought to tame and domesticate the energy and disorder of the subculture figure of the criminal by presenting his conduct as behavior which inevitably led to the gallows. In the first part of the *Account* he described the basic facts of the trial, and he followed this with citations of the biblical texts he preached to the condemned and synopses of his sermons. The rest consisted of a narrative of the malefactor's life and crimes, leading up to an account of the hanging itself. The narrative was often sensational and salacious far beyond the demands of the moral: for the ordinary's *Accounts* were his chief source of income, and he had to make them exciting to compete with the many rival accounts by hacks who attempted to break his monopoly.

Here, in one graphic image, Hogarth shows the two accounts juxtaposed: the admonitory words of society, enclosed in the carriage, cut off from the condemned man, giving him no consolation, and in his own plates reflected in the biblical verses which would have reminded viewers of the ordinary's pious quotations—and, looming in the foreground, the wide-mouthed plebeian vender, perspectively dwarfing the ordinary, as the raucous popular voice. Even in his literary domestication, Idle survives in two versions with two different meanings, one polite and the other popular.

These visual subculture images set up a substitute code, "an unwritten popular code" like the ritual of wife-selling E. P. Thompson has described as used by the poor who have no access to the actual legal code of divorce, which required an act of Parliament and could be utilized only by the rich and influential.[15] They also show that there is one way of reading or viewing for the educated audience of Fielding's *Enquiry* and another for the essentially visual/aural cul-

ture of the uneducated "inferior part of mankind."[16] The latter tends
to identify completely with one position and commit himself to a
fairly literal (from his point of view) reading. Perhaps he sees con-
cretely and naively in terms of persons and events close to him,
rather than in abstractions. But we are not comparing the perception
of a civilized man and a child or savage; only people with different
sets of organizing schemata and assumptions about what "reading" is
about. If we examine the materials the apprentices and journeymen
perused, beginning with popular prints, we see that these were images or series of images that deal with immediately contemporary
events—murders or political upheavals—and were arranged in terms
of cause and effect, that universal "custom" which so exercised David
Hume. But *their* cause-effect structure was built on a single adversary
relationship between a lone deviate and the inescapable force of
constables, magistrates, and executioners. The subculture heroes
were the deviates—Moll Flanders, celebrated in Tom Idle's ballad, or
Captain Macheath, whose picture the Harlot keeps on her wall.

Both figures—apprentice and whore—are totally individualists,
one by choice and the other by profession. It would appear that if
Goodchild breaks the apprentices' group solidarity in one way, Idle
does in another. But this is to miss the point of the subculture's
choosing its heroes from the outcasts and loners who have become
"enemies of society." To judge by the Tyburn riots, the group comes
to the rescue of the lone malefactor from its midst—once he has paid
his penalty; all that matters is that he is one of them. He does not
lose his identity as poor apprentice or simply as poor criminal. Goodchild does: he is now a master. In a sense, the two groups of apprentices and masters, ballad sellers and Newgate ordinaries, fight for the
soul of Tom Idle to retain him as subculture hero or translate him
into "Repentant Criminal."

Look once again at the first plate of *Industry and Idleness* (fig. 1)
and ask: Why is Idle placed in the shadow, away from the light of the
window, and without a wall to support him and the inspiring proverbs that may improve his mind (only a post on which to fit his ballad
of Moll Flanders)? Do his tattered clothes indicate his own carelessness or are they rather the consequence of his master's disapproval—
or his master's carelessness or disdain (responsible, as he is, for the
well-being of his surrogate children, as the churchwardens are for
Tom Nero)? Do Goodchild's neat clothes point to his own care or his

master's partiality to him? The sophisticated audience would of course see this scene as emblematic of the two apprentices' situations, a single cause of all that follows in the series. But a more literal audience, identifying with apprentice against master, might see it as an effect of some initial deviance. If you are a poor boy who lacks the favor of his master, the ability to please him, perhaps even industry, and have a dark station in the shop, then you are doomed to fall victim to your oppressive state of affairs, never to rise—indeed to descend ever lower.

Even Goodchild's name has weighted things in his favor. Is he good because his name inclines others to expect good of him and treat him well, or is he named (allegorically) to correspond to his good character? Have others been prejudiced against Idle by his name and so discouraged him that he has taken on the qualities which his name assigned him? Or, as the sophisticated audience would assume, is the name an indication of what he essentially *is*, an emblem of him? We know the answer to this question if we are the poor of eighteenth-century London. Recall the joke in *Joe Miller's Jests* (no. 96) of the shoeshine boy going to church and being asked his name by the parson. He replies, "Rugged and Tough," to which the parson huffily returns, "Who gave you *that* Name?" "Why the Boys in our Alley, reply'd poor Rugged and Tough, Lord d——mn them." This is a bowdlerized version (further bowdlerized in later editions by the omission of "Lord d——mn them") of jokes like the modern one about the girl and her little brother who arrive at a country school. "Your name?" asks the teacher. "Snotnose McGee," replies the girl. "None of your impertinence, you hillbilly. You go right home and tell your mother to teach you some manners." The girl turns to her little brother. "Come on, Shitass, if she don't believe me, she'll never believe you."[17] The name has been imposed by the social milieu—in the sense of fathers, guardians, neighbors, and the rest—and Tom Idle is helpless within it. His gambling, drinking, and whoring take the form of an apprentice's escape from the specific entrapment of the shop.

As I shall show in the second half of this book, Hogarth the public man, the governor of hospitals and benefactor of the poor, supports the centrality given the parable of the Good Samaritan by Latitudinarian divines in mid-eighteenth-century England. But in his most potentially radical work the parable that begins to emerge is that of the talents (Matthew 25). This is the one New Testament subject cited in the biblical quotations beneath the *Industry and Idleness* designs: Plate 4, showing Goodchild being given charge of the master's countinghouse, prints the words on the "good and faithful servant" but projects over the whole series the unstated situation of the other, "the wicked and slothful servant." Indeed, Hogarth's allusion to the parable of the talents is a neat example of the way he questions the status of a central, therefore dominant, concept or document by revealing what it leaves out—what it represses. Thus what is shown, by the juxtaposition of images, is that Tom Idle is in essence the servant who is given a *single* talent, against the more generous allowance of five and two to the other servants. He starts at a disadvantage, and moreover he does nothing more blameworthy than to return to the lord that which was lent him (his ugliness, idleness, bad name). The lord refuses to accept his attempt at mitigation and orders that the single talent of this "wicked and slothful servant" be taken away and given to the servant who now has ten talents (Francis Goodchild): "For unto every one that hath shall be given, and he shall have abundance: but from him that hath not shall be taken away even that which he hath." And the "slothful" and "unprofitable" servant is cast "into outer darkness: there shall be weeping and gnashing of teeth." The following verses (32 ff.) extend the contrast to the Last Judgment separation of sheep from goats, right hand from left, on which Hogarth builds the spatial contrasts between his apprentices.

What characterizes Hogarth's position as subversive is his refusal to take a biblical parable on its own terms (or the terms of its official commentators) as a religious truth—and so as a paradox. It is evidently the policy of the kingdom of heaven that the rich are to get richer and the poor poorer. The servant fears his lord is "a hard man," and he *is* ("thou oughtest therefore to have put my money to the exchanger, and then at my coming I should have received mine own with usury"). Hogarth sees from the servant's point of view rather than (as the parable expects) from the lord's, from which the fact that one servant receives five talents, another two, and a third only one is of absolutely no importance.

The subculture assumptions come pretty clear in Hogarth's distrust of authority figures and the refusal to see from their point of view. Everywhere in his prints are the oppressive shadows of fathers, judges, physicians, magistrates, lawyers, teachers, and in particular clergymen. It is the Church of England ordinary of Newgate who rides ahead of Idle in his closed coach, and only a fanatic Methodist Samaritan who accompanies the condemned man during his last moments.[18] In the first plate of *A Harlot's Progress* (back in 1732) the clergyman was deciphering the address of the bishop of London (Walpole's agent for ecclesiastical preferment) while ignoring the poor country girl who is being lured into prostitution: precisely the same paradigm used in *Beer Street* and *Gin Lane* twenty years later. In the second plate, a painting on the wall shows Uzzah trying to steady the Ark of the Covenant, which is falling. But Uzzah is breaking the law, for he is not a Levite, and only Levites can touch the Ark. In the biblical text he is struck dead by an angry Jehovah. Hogarth characteristically omits the hand of God and substitutes a human priest, a keeper of Jehovah's law, who is stabbing Uzzah in the back. In the last plate the hand of the clergyman is under the dress of the prostitute next to him, instead of officiating at the Harlot's wake.

From all of his prints and paintings it is plain that Hogarth associates the law with the Old Testament, the Ten Commandments, and the harshness of eye-for-an-eye justice. Old Testament subjects appear enclosed and forbidding as pictures on the walls, painted copies after dead masters, serving to urge on the living to brutal punishments for the least transgression to themselves. When Hogarth undertakes a history painting himself, it is of a New Testament subject and illustrates Charity (as in *The Good Samaritan* and *Pool of Bethesda*).[19] But his subversion of Old Testament stories leads me to wonder also about his parodies of New Testament subjects, including the way he relates his life of a Harlot to print series of the life of the Virgin. M[ary?] Hackabout appears in the compositions of Mary the Mother in the Visitation, the Annunciation, and the Death of the Virgin—and her funeral is a parody of the Last Supper. Are these merely inverted parodies, like Milton's Satan, Sin, and Death of the Holy Trinity or Pope's Dullness holding Cibber's head in her lap of a pietà? Are they projections of the Harlot's imagination in which a Mary Magdalen thinks of herself as the *other* Mary (as Hudibras' Quixotic imagination is represented by Hogarth in graphic terms as baroque processionals and battle scenes; or as Mr. Peachum in the *Beggar's Opera* paintings assumes the pose of Christ in a *noli me tangere*)? Or are they in some ply popular sense a naturalization and reduction of sacred materials to a joke—the refusal to see paradox?

Even if Hogarth's popular audience did not recognize the images of Dürer's *Life of the Virgin* or his *Passion* behind the *Harlot's Progress*, it is possible to suppose that the impulse, taken from the popular tradition, carries over into allusions recognizable only as ironies by "readers of greater penetration." This way of describing A *Harlot's Progress* was verbalized in Thomas Paine's famous sentence: "Were any girl that is now with child to say, and even to swear to it, that she was gotten with child by a ghost, and that an angel told her so, would she be believed?"[20] If, in this frame of mind, you look for a father of the Harlot's child (in the position of Christ in her "last supper"), you will find the only sign of him in James Dalton's wig box atop her tester bed in the scene in which the magistrate breaks in to arrest her, as the angel entered in the Annunciation (fig. 16). If you want to see a genuinely popular version of Dürer's *Life of the Virgin* and *Passion*, perhaps you could not do better than look at the plates of Hogarth's *Harlot's Progress*.

Paine was essentially the great spokesman of working-class anticlericalism, the final avatar in revolutionary Europe of the beliefs of the radical sects which flourished among the poor long after they had been officially wiped out or absorbed. Christopher Hill has defined the "popular heretical culture" in precisely these terms, as a set of assumptions derived from a "radical underground" of Ranters, Anabaptists, Familists, going back to the Lollards but still surviving after the Commonwealth—who rejected root and branch the traditional distribution of power and privilege, the traditional social hierarchy, and the authority of the Established Church.[21]

Of course, Paine also drew (as his title *The Age of Reason* admits) on the authority, if not ideas, of the Enlightenment *philosophes*. As Lawrence Stone has shown, the upper classes were independently coming around to the same distrust of selected patriarchal structures, in particular "the authority of the clergy, the scriptures and moral theology."[22] A fact which does much to explain Hogarth's unique position in his period is that a lower-class subculture set of values and an evolving upper-class set (called Deism and philosophical atheism) were converging, and this is probably why he was able to hold both polar audiences in thrall. The aristocracy and the lower orders, of course, traditionally shared an irreverence for laws civil and ecclesiastical that curbed personal liberty (loose living, sexual excesses, drinking, and swearing); and this pitted both groups against the real *other*, the respectable middle class of masters (who were also both visible and safe surrogates for the remote authority at the top). Gentlemen had their models in Restoration rakes and libertine philosophy, which regarded such activity as an escape valve from the responsibilities of a ruling elite. The apprentice's "libertine" acts (up through rioting) were equally escapist, but from the oppressive weight of the society in whose functioning he had no part whatever.

Hogarth, we have to remember, expressed his radicalism only in images, never in words. In words, he spoke for either the aristocratic cognoscenti or the masters. When he wrote of *Beer Street* and *Gin Lane*, he said they were presented as a contrast "where the invigorating liquor [beer] is recommended in order to drive the other [gin] out of vogue." In Beer Street "all is joyous and thriving. Industry and Jollity go hand in hand." At the same time he explained that the *Stages of Cruelty* was made specifically "in hopes of preventing in some degree that cruel treatment of poor Animals which makes the streets of London more disagreeable to the human mind, than any thing whatever, the very describing of which gives pain."[23] It has been apparent from the evidence of *Industry and Idleness* (its treatment of Idle and its own use by masters) that the structure Hogarth embodies includes society's inevitable desensitizing of the visual-aural impression of subculture energy and subversion—a phenomenon that includes Hogarth himself. But it is also relevant, given our model of the apprentice, to recognize their own dichotomy of the *apprentice* who grows into a *master*.

Hogarth was a part of that group that demonstrated that class was to some extent a matter of age, and as a man passed from one age to another he also passed from one class to another, though retaining traces (sympathies, antipathies) of the earlier and younger. Hogarth was the apprentice who did become a master, retaining a psychomachy of the two levels or aspects of himself in *Industry and Idleness*, where he gave Goodchild his successful career (originally his own name William) and Idle his face and probably his secret proclivities. He was the particular case of an apprentice who never completely abandoned his apprentice's assumptions—the emotional feel of deprivation but also of youthful energy and natural forces restrained by ordinary "custom." He also retained the assumptions of

Bartholomew's Close where he was born—a Dissenting community (his birth was recorded in a Dissenters' register), in a neighborhood sheltering radical discontent.[24] He looked up from the position of the apprentice and journeyman—at best the small artisan—a role he never quite lost the terrible insecurity of, any more than of the debtors' prison in which his father (a Latin scholar of pretensions) languished and he himself lived his adolescence. Just below was the abyss of the lowest order of society—the porters, sailors, chair men, day laborers, street sellers, and casual workmen.

This point of view was based on hostility to the gentry and capitalists, stock jobbers and middlemen, the "respectable" and "pious." Hogarth shows in all of his work the subculture's traditional attitudes toward "them," "their" morality, and "their" authority in all its forms, while touting the myth of the "free-born Englishman." His circumventing the middlemen, as he was careful to make clear, did not make him one of them. He distinguished himself as independent artisan (one who makes his own product but also sells it) from the print seller on the one hand and the aristocratic connoisseur—even patron—on the other. For Hogarth, this meant being a "free-born Englishman," but also to some extent sharing a common cause with the very greatest aristocrats and the king (as in his apparent apostasy to them in 1763). It meant not losing touch with the radical tradition which goes back to the Ranters and Seekers, whose violent oaths and sexual freedom were reactions against the gentility of the Puritan middle class, as well as a strange linking up with aristocratic mores.

It is not extravagant to see Hogarth as himself the apprentice (and, with his father, the malefactor) who chooses as his first metaphoric equivalent a whore, whom he genteelizes with the biblical "harlot," and uses as a subculture heroine—the subject of many popular print series—in order to produce a story about the subculture's attempt to survive by finding common cause with the culture proper. The Harlot does this by trying her best to be a "lady" and even, perhaps, a genteel version of the Virgin Mary. Fifteen years later, when he produces overtly popular prints, Hogarth chooses a genuine apprentice as his hero, who refuses to seek any common cause with society, and proves powerless to withstand the societal embrace which, after punishing him, turns him into a safe culture sign.

We can conclude that Hogarth implicitly questions the whole structure of authority in his society, but never directly, because his center is always the subculture hero, the harlot or rake or apprentice who makes the hedonistic choice and suffers the most exemplary punishments. He is in effect dramatizing the situation of the subculture, and incidentally addressing it as one apprentice to another. His prints are more about the subject of the absorption of the vital subculture energy into the fabric of society, and the ironies engendered thereby, than anything remotely resembling a call to arms of the masses.

And yet in his popular prints—but in fact beginning with *A Harlot's Progress*—Hogarth established what appears (at least in retrospect) to be a visual equivalent of Paine's "new political language" that created a "mass readership" in *Common Sense* and *Rights of Man* (1776 and 1791).[25] If the art Hogarth despised was aimed at flattering, sublimating, and diverting, the kind he advocated tries to release and focus consciousness against that dominant official art and even against the official social structure, its analogue. Hogarth's art, from his subscription ticket to *A Harlot's Progress* on, was an outsider's art that (to use Marcuse's term) stimulates revolutionary consciousness, while Fielding, we have seen, remains on the side of the dominant society, even when he is aware of its failings, looking at it from inside.[26] That Hogarth elicited nothing like the immense and violent response to Paine's "new language" is because there was no French Revolution to consolidate or to act as context for Hogarth's utterance; and because Hogarth's visual language, though it did not allow the reader to overlook elements, placed on the periphery what Paine placed squarely in the center. Moreover, Hogarth was never advocating overthrow; he was only materializing a folklore which served the radical tradition as a kind of graphic version of John Wilkes and served himself as a way of taking art back to lost sources of energy. Both as politics and as aesthetics the subculture stimulated in Hogarth a nostalgia for the past, not a longing for the future: it sought a restoration of ancient liberties for the reformer and of native art unsullied (apparently) by Continental sophistication for the artist.

3. The Crowd

HOGARTH'S MARCH TO FINCHLEY (1750) (fig. 12) illustrates the "crowd ritual" or "urban ceremonial" to which I want to turn next. But it also provides a bit of contemporary evidence for the different readings I have supposed for Hogarth's kind of visual work. Almost as soon as he had finished the painting, which he had destined for a wall in the public galleries of the Foundling Hospital, and before he had published the engraved version (which would reach a much larger public), Jean André Rouquet published an authorized pamphlet in French explaining the painting—and this was promptly translated into English. Rouquet's reading is for the connoisseurs—in particular the French market—and it says that *The March to Finchley* is subversive of conventional ideas of art. It is too new, Rouquet ironically remarks, and bears too great a resemblance to the objects it represents; it lacks the signatures of smoke, varnish, and dirt that endear paintings to most collectors. Moreover, it seems to advocate a kind of disorder and pokes fun at all conventional history paintings by showing contemporary soldiers behaving in unheroic ways instead of as the troops behave in Le Brun's *Victories of Alexander* or Laguerre's *Marlborough's Victories*. To complement Rouquet's pamphlet, we have the story of George II's automatic reaction when he was shown the print: "Does the fellow mean to laugh at my guards?" He saw straight to the popular point of the picture, that Hogarth was ridiculing the royal grenadiers.[1]

What I am concerned with in this painting, however, is the visual significance of the crowd and of Hogarth's friend John Wilkes. They became acquainted in the 1750s following the publication of the popular prints and *The March to Finchley*, just after Hogarth produced his most celebrated images of the crowd. Their friendship and later angry break make one of the strangest episodes of Hogarth's life. When the showdown with Wilkes came in 1763, in the manner of the break between Burke and Fox over the French Revolution, it could have been the result of Hogarth's horrified realization of what Wilkes really portended, or only of their disagreement over a specific issue of war or peace, Pitt or Bute. But it drew the line between Hogarth and the radical tradition that grew out of the Wilkite riots and processions. I suspect that what they shared up to that point was an appreciation of the subculture assumptions I have been describing, which both of them held, in however ambivalent a way.

We immediately associate both men with the visual quality of the public parade or spectacle, the massing and movement of symbolic crowds, the Saturnalia or carnival overcoming Lent. Somewhere within the crowd is the figure of Wilkes, the peripheral subject of the crowd and the source of its energy. The Wilkes of 1763–70 and of the 1770s is both Tom Idle, the malefactor on his way to Tyburn, and Francis Goodchild, the lord-mayor on his way to the Guildhall. As the two figures merge in Hogarth's last two plates, until they are physically superimposable, so Wilkes, being carried aloft or his coach drawn by the crowd, is on the one hand the martyr of the governing system and, on the other, the crowd's "monarch and ruler" and the person of whom they chanted "God save great Wilkes our King" and posted handbills on church walls urging parishioners to pray not for the monarch but for "Wilkes and Liberty." The Wilkite processions conducted him (personally or in effigy—if nothing else, represented by a hieroglyphic "45" for the crucial "revolutionary" issue of his *North Briton*) to and from prison, and then, when he was elected lord-mayor, to and from the Guildhall.

The images we first think of in Hogarth's prints relate to the alternative endings of *Industry and Idleness*. Besides the kermis of flowing drink and sexuality in *The March to Finchley* (or a Saturnalia of soldiers), there is the crowd burning the Rumps at Temple Bar (fig. 14) at the Restoration, and repeated in 1680—both times carried out in fact by apprentices. There is the celebration of Restoration Day in the fourth *Time of the Day*. The clanging meat cleavers in the sixth plate of *Industry and Idleness* (fig. 2) are not far removed from a charivari. The *Skimmington* (fig. 13) celebrates cuckolded husbands and unfaithful wives, and *Southwark Fair* is a Saturnalia.

Much scholarship has gone into the purpose, origins, and construction of crowds in recent years. One fact that has emerged is that an early model was the medieval demonstrations of youth groups (young bachelors) and apprentices, who marched and made symbolic gestures (or carried symbolic objects) against what, from their point of view, were the basic disorders or disparities: the old man marrying the young bride and the wife domineering over (or cuckolding) her husband.[2] The crowd, to judge by its origins, is characterized by its youth and maleness; its animus against old age, as carnival against Lent, is focused against the tyranny of the old master or father. It is perhaps useful to recall that, in imagery at least, revolutions (e.g., the French) have usually seen themselves as a force of energy embodied in sexually potent male youth.

There is also the crowd's inebrious quality. When Wilkes is locked up in prison, the crowd waylays representatives of the government, forces them out of their coaches, and makes them enter the nearest tavern and drink royal toasts to Wilkes, one bumper after another (sometimes to the number of forty-five) until everyone is drunk. Released from prison, Wilkes is greeted with houses lit up and bonfires set, bells rung, and fireworks set off as in celebration of a national victory. The figure of Wilkes himself is a strangely familiar one (celebrated in Hogarth's caricature of 1763). He is as close as one can come without makeup to a Lord of Misrule, the mock king of the Saturnalia when slaves ruled their masters. The characteristics everyone noted of this Punch figure were his physical deformity (his ugly, cockeyed face—the contrary of the ideal quality associated with aristocratic icons), his sexual potency, and his persistent violation through destruction, not appropriation, of property.

The English "crowd ritual" inherited by Wilkes (and Hogarth) can be interpreted in different ways. (1) The lower orders appropriate the symbols and rituals of authority, as they chair *their* heroes or light bonfires for them (as the nation does for its king or military heroes), much as they invent their own legal forms for their extralegal activities. Or (2) the ruling class institutionalizes plebeian license, offering the lower orders a release from their everyday restraints. From the official point of view, there are acceptable ways of letting off steam, such as parades on certain calendar days, and unacceptable ones, like drinking, whoring and, ultimately, thieving, murdering, and rioting. The difference depends on whether the official calendar festivals are used by and for the ruling class, or taken over by the lower orders and made into their own, tendentious expression.

When the Wilkite crowd carries out a mock execution on Tower Hill with effigies of Lord Bute, the princess dowager, and the Fox brothers, beheaded by a chimneysweep and burned as an acting out of the populace's memory of the true duties of a just judge, it is, in effect, making Goodchild and Idle one. This is what E. P. Thompson has called plebeian "countertheater," as opposed to the "theater" of the ruling class who represented their paternalism by mimed gestures such as appearances at church, opening of festivals, dispensing largesse at Christmas, and wearing ceremonial attire. "There is a sense," says Thompson, "in which rulers and crowd needed each other, watched each other, performed theater and countertheater to each other's auditorium, moderated each other's political behavior. This is a more active and reciprocal relationship than the one normally brought to mind under the formula 'paternalism and deference.' "[3] The plebeian crowd rituals were countertheater in the sense that they acted out, rehearsed, or mimicked actions against their betters, but did not actually "live out" their actions. They burned effigies, not people.

The question is whether (and to what extent) this countertheater was a "rehearsal" in the sense of a threat of action to follow or merely in the sense of an exorcism, a stoic coming to terms with one's own impotence. Let us say it was an act like that of the little boy Freud describes in *Beyond the Pleasure Principle*, who compensated for his mother's being away "by himself staging the disappearance and return" by playing a game in which he repeatedly threw away toys and retrieved them.[4] The repetition stressed the departure, the distressing part of the experience, over the return. But as another version of the game showed, the boy could also use the departure phase to celebrate or fulfill a wish about the *absence* of his *father* (and so "his sole possession of his mother"). The throwing away can, therefore, be construed as either an attempt to "make oneself master of the situation" in the only way possible, or a threat or simulated act of revenge on the "other."

The story of the crowd in Hogarth's youth and early manhood was of the government's inability to control the Tory-Opposition pageantry by merely humoring or absorbing it. The medieval religious festivals, such as Corpus Christi, had been secularized into "national" celebrations, which by the end of the seventeenth century were politically partisan, Whig or Tory. While intended by the governing ministry to dissipate dissent and consolidate authority, they could and did get out of hand, as when Tories turned a Whig celebration, say of William III's birthday, into parody. As is quite clear in Hogarth's "Night," the fourth *Time of the Day* (1738), the contiguity of George I's birthday and Restoration Day (28, 29 May) allowed for the anti-Hanoverian crowd to celebrate in a subversive way. There is no question that Jacobite symbolism was used in the 1720s and '30s as a means of popular dissent; but its use was as theatrical as the chairings and bonfire lightings in that it did not follow that the people who used them were Jacobites. Some imagery of dissent was needed and the "lewd Jacobite gesture" was the image "most calculated to enrage and alarm the Hanoverian rulers."[5] One result was that the political calendar, now an occasion for rioting along party lines, was gradually dropped, and the Riot Act (known as a "Hanoverian proclamation") and even force were employed from time to time. Suppressed, the old and generally rebellious as well as the contemporary and partisan political feelings went underground or sought expression in the conventional forms that remained—the lord-mayor's processions, the hustings of general elections, or Bartholomew (or Southwark) Fair. Fielding complains in his *Enquiry* of these "Saturnalias."[6]

Another way these subversive feelings survived was in the representation of crowd rituals in Hogarth's prints. He represents not just the crowd but the idea of countertheater, emphasizing the imitation of polite forms with graphic equivalents from the tradition of Continental art. Thus the *Skimmington* crowd (fig. 13) arranges itself into a parody of a baroque processional like Carracci's *Bacchus and Ariadne* (Rome, Farnese Palace), and the *Finchley* crowd into here an anti–*Marlborough's Victories* or "Choice of Hercules," there a Madonna and Child or Good Samaritan group. We shall see in a later chapter that he depicts the upper levels of society as also living according to a metaphor of theatricality.

In the midst of Hogarth's crowd, often off-centered, is a figure surrounded or held up by the crowd as a kind of effigy. In the *Skimmington* it is the hen-pecked, cuckolded husband with his shrewish wife, riding backward on a horse, who are the subject of the procession; it is the hated Puritans being burned in effigy, along with the rumps of beef for the Rump Parliament; and of course the criminal and the lord-mayor in *Industry and Idleness*. There is a festival figure of deep ambiguity: king and criminal, carnival and Lent, savior and scapegoat, whose reverberations Hogarth seems to be trying to recapture.[7]

There remains only the question of whether the parody of the ruling class in, say, "God save great Wilkes our King" assimilates itself to the official tradition or is a mode of subversion. Is it a comic coexistence of cultures or a replacement of a false one with a true? Hogarth's *Skimmington* may leave the matter in doubt: he is subverting, replacing, but at the same time drawing strength from the great tradition of art. The Wilkite crowd, like the crowd of the subculture, was loyalist, not revolutionary, in the sense of desiring overthrow and reconstitution; they only wished to regain what they considered lost freedoms from pre-Norman England, when laws had not yet been corrupted by the continental invaders. Not an altogether *un*revolutionary stance this, since it meant returning to a *grand*father and resisting the father, the present king and government. The stated policies of the Wilkites were coexistence and amelioration; and yet their iconography makes one wonder whether Wilkes is to be seen as coexisting with or replacing George III. The phenomena to notice are the way the subcultural material derives from a return to precultural sources, and the fact that it is not a replacement, a substitution, so much as an addition to the laws or customs of the time, one that fills the interstices of a culture made for and by the ruling class. And it is generally tolerated within the free interpretation of the laws, which though extremely rigorous were loosely administered. Wilkes was not tolerated, though he at length became lord-mayor, repudiated the Gordon riots, and ended his days chatting amicably with George III.

One of the many popular rituals represented by Hogarth was the hustings, which Gwyn Williams has called "the English mob institutionalized"[8]—the place and occasion where they could respond to the candidates' speeches with everything short of their votes (which were possessed only by those qualified for the franchise by a forty-shilling freehold). It is important to Hogarth that the ceremony of chairing the member is carried out primarily by the crowd, not by the electors themselves. He does not quite show—though it is just around the corner—the crowd (as it often did) tearing the hustings apart with hatchets, crowbars, and their bare hands, pulling it down and carrying off the boards in triumph. But he does show them carrying off in triumph—all they have of triumph—the victor of the election, preceded and followed with banners, up and down the main street of the town, another hero-scapegoat; and his position in their love-hate grasp is clearly precarious.

The hustings, indeed the whole set of four *Election* prints (1754–58), describes a characteristic process. The candidate is first the aristocratic outsider who, in the first scene, stands by, unavoidably aware of the crowd with its banners—related to the outsider who stands just outside the kermis scenes Svetlana Alpers describes in Dutch paintings.[9] Once he is the successful candidate, he is absorbed by the crowd, made an effigy. In the same way, Hudibras skeptically eyes the skimmington, but he has himself become part of the Saturnalia in *Burning the Rumps at Temple Bar*, riding now as an effigy in the procession. And this is what happens to both apprentices, who at the end have become effigies in their respective processions.[10] The final image is of the subculture hero barely under the wraps of society's own forms, and the irony is that society's version of the hero—the Hudibras or the successful candidate or the Industrious Apprentice—is also reduced to an effigy and absorbed in the popular procession. The processes are parallel, and we could say much about the ambiguity of the effigy itself. The man has in any case lost his own identity and been turned into a reductive sign, Idle into an admonitory Malefactor, Goodchild into Lord-Mayor and Success, as well as Blind Justice. As a sign, the M.P. or lord-mayor is the object of a popular procession, out of his own control, forced to act out this role for them and reminded of their potential capacity for unseating him.

At length the effigy becomes—or is turned into by the crowd—an idol, as in the Pittite crowd Hogarth portrays in *The Times*, plate 1 (1763), worshiping William Pitt's image exalted on stilts (and, in an alternative state, substituted for with the image of Henry VIII, king-as-tyrant). By this time the crowd has become for Hogarth a force of the irrational, like the mob congregation of *Credulity, Superstition, and Fanaticism* (1762), partly at least because he sees it directed by an individual who is not *of it*. It has lost its main function "of more or less spontaneous popular direct action," resting upon "articulate popular sanctions" of the sort I have described, and that appear in earlier Hogarth crowds.[11] Hogarth now seems to detect "the deliberate use of the crowd as an instrument of pressure, by persons 'above' or apart from the crowd"—and to anticipate what the unsympathetic would refer to as the Wilkite mob with its idols of Wilkes, "Wilkes and Liberty," and "45," which may have been as much Wilkes's representation of the crowd ritual as Hogarth's *Skimmington* and *Burning the Rumps at Temple Bar*.

4. The Signboard and Its Painter

I HAVE BEEN ARGUING IMPLICITLY that it was what the mass of Londoners *saw* that mattered. They probably never saw a painting. (If they did, it would have been in only a few places, such as St. Paul's, Greenwich Hospital, St. Bartholomew's Hospital, and the Foundling, and would have required an act of will.) But they did see the symbols carried by the crowd, itself performing symbolic actions, and they saw the signboards and shop signs that cluttered the streets of London. They also saw engravings (including engraved copies of paintings), painted arms on coach doors, decks of cards, and other common images. They did not go anywhere to see these objects, which were simply present in their environment, so obvious as to be virtually invisible. These images were absorbed and made part of a fundamental way of seeing, not only by those who saw nothing better (or different) but also, to a degree, by those who did.

I wonder what a Londoner felt if he stopped and considered, instead of once again merely passing, a sign of the "Good Woman" on a tavern. Such a sign is represented in Hogarth's *Times of the Day: Noon* (fig. 17), and two versions of it were hung in the Sign Painters' Exhibition of 1762 (nos. 3 and 55). The woman is headless; that is, has no tongue, is no longer the conventional "scolding woman," the shrew, that popular effigy of the skimmington. In retrospect, as your sense of the sign accumulates, you may realize that this is a man's sign, in front of a man's tavern, and that to him a woman is not just what is omitted in the sign—head, tongue, mind—but what is included, that is, a body. This becomes the subliminal image of woman for one basic impulse in man, expressible at this popular level of consciousness: the *"good* woman" is all body, without head, tongue, mind, or spirit.

It was no doubt for this reason that Hogarth juxtaposed the

31

"Good Woman," in his representation of it, with a "John the Baptist's Head" on a charger, inscribed "Good Eating"—the woman's equivalent fantasy of her husband (or rather the man's fantasy of the woman's fantasy). This signboard design also hung in the Sign Painters' Exhibition (no. 33). It is only in the context of these signs for tavern and eating house that we come to see the strange kite hanging off the roof of the Huguenot chapel across the way as the sign of the church: a mode of ascension into the sky.[1] In this case Hogarth has set up three parallel signs, as he has contrasted the opposite sides of the street on a Sunday noon. Two actual signboards lead us to assimilate the third object into the same category.

How significant signboards were to Hogarth can be seen not only in his representation of them in so many pictures but in the symbolic gesture of his cooperation in the Sign Painters' Exhibition of 1762. A great many of the signs exhibited there can be seen *in situ* within his scenes, where they serve as the subculture equivalent of those old-master paintings he shows hanging in the rooms of the "great" and the would-be "great."

The March to Finchley (fig. 12) is structured on shop signs. On the left is the sign of "Adam and Eve" (Sign Painters' Exhibition, no. 6 in the passage), which was believed to derive from the arms of the Fruiterers' Company. Hogarth uses it as the sign for a nursery (i.e., as a Garden of Eden, as a place where children are cared for, or plants). On the right is the "King's Head" (no. 13 in the large Passage Room; another, no. 42, is in the Grand Room), here placed in conjunction with a brothel so as to seem its sign. The cats on the brothel roof make an additional sign, like the kite on the church roof, recalling the old joke about the child who watches a pair of cats in coitus topple off the roof of a brothel and tells the madam, "Your sign just fell off." These signs establish meaning through their juxtaposition with each other and with the buildings. In the lower right-hand corner the hen and chickens (no. 6 in the Passage Room—a popular sign with haberdashers, mercers, and linen drapers) become a materialized sign. The baby chicks, wandering about looking for their mother hen, who has been stuffed into the haversack of one of the foraging soldiers, serve as a sign for the whole scene of troops milling about in disorder instead of marching off to defend England against the invading army of the Young Pretender.[2] The hen and chickens are subsumed in a larger sign, a parody of a Good Samaritan composition, of the sort that could be seen by Londoners in Hogarth's paintings on the great staircase of St. Bartholomew's Hospital.

All of these various kinds of signs serve as an "armature" for the crowd, which is the picture's representational subject: people who are quite obviously not following the model of regimentation of the Hanoverian army, or of the "progress" (so called) of a harlot or rake, or the children of *Marriage à la Mode* who perform like puppets in a show they did not make—following in each case the moves of their aristocratic models. Hogarth places in the center of his picture the popular folk image of the crowd that corresponds to the sign of Adam and Eve, on one side, and of the promiscuous Charles II on the other, which thereby designates the scene Saturnalia, in opposition to the thin lines of soldiers marching off to war in the distance. I take the image of the mother and child on a cart in the middle distance to sanction, in some sense, the chaos of the foreground: in this context less a Madonna and Child than simply a sign of the mother–child relationship that is established in the "Adam and Eve" at the left and dissolved in the confusion signified at the right by the row of whores in their windows and the chicks searching in vain for their mother hen. (All those lost chicks suggest why Hogarth destined the painting for the Foundling Hospital.) In the same way, the tree in the Adam/Eve sign relates to the actual trees in Hogarth's engraving—the one on the Adam/Eve side blooming and leafy, the one on the brothel side bare and dead.[3]

The March to Finchley represents a particularly full employment of the whole range of environmental signs, shading off into emblem and the popular (or sophisticated) religious images of the painters. It is plain from this example that the first principle of the signboard is its basis in the verbal pun. Two cocks are a sign for Cox, or a hat and a tun (a rebus) for Hatton. In *Spectator* no. 28 (2 Apr. 1711), on shop signs in London, Addison takes the example of Mr. Bell, who uses the sign of a bell for his alehouse—but which, he adds, "has given Occasion to several Pieces of Wit" on the pun of bell–belle.[4] He explains the sign of the "Bell-Savage," showing an Indian standing beside a bell, in relation to the beautiful woman found in the wilderness known as *la belle sauvage*. Hogarth, in *A Harlot's Progress*, plate 1, places the sign of a bell against the wall of a tavern so that it appears directly above the head of the bawd Mother Needham (bawds, Addison says elsewhere in his essay, ought *not* violate decorum by operating at the sign of the "Angel"); hanging just over her dowdy head, it suggests the verbal pun *belle*.

But as a more purely visual pun, the sign anticipates the obscene coat of arms of the Harlot that hangs among her funeral decorations in the final plate: "azure, *parti per shevron*, sable, three fossets [faucets], in which three spiggots are inserted, all proper."[5] The image of faucet and spiggot or bell and clapper is carried further in the "frail china jars" that are the broken teacups of plate 2 (fig. 15). Out of the signboard principle of the punning visual equivalent Hogarth projects a powerful, yet almost subliminal, image which dominates (in, of course, a peripheral way) *A Harlot's Progress*. It is, at the same time, a literary emblem, carrying memories of cracked crystal, the china scene in *The Country Wife*, John Crowne's lines "Women like Cheney [china] shou'd be kept with care, / One flaw debases her to common ware," and Belinda's honor as a "frail China jar."[6]

"Shop sign" is a better word than signboard because it designates a personal or professional emblem, like Goodchild's (or Idle's) name, the equivalent of a street number that identifies one's house. It is not unrelated to heraldic signs or the *impresa* as a personal enigma to be deciphered with all the urgency of a Rumplestiltskin. The shop sign derives either from the name of the proprietor or from his occupation: from the implement of his trade (measuring rule for a surveyor, urinal for a physician, knife for a cutter), the source of his product (bunch of grapes for a pub), the object served (hand for a glove maker), the product itself (stocking for a hosier), or the part for the whole (a nail for a carpenter).

Therefore, what the examples of the "King's Head" outside the brothel and the Harlot's escutcheon indicate is, first, the whore's need for respectability and, second, the close relationship between popular signs and the heraldic arms of the nobility. They share the origin of their graphic forms in profession and name, in fact and in identity, but turned into the accidental resemblance of a pun. The Ferrer arms consist of a shield *vairé*, and some families of the name adopted the horseshoes of a farrier. Fletcher employs an arrow (*flèche* or *flécher*) or arrowhead (*fléchière*), referring to the employment of a fletcher, an arrow maker. Fox family arms carry foxes and foxes' heads, Lyons arms carry lions, Trotter a horse, and Oakes acorns. Indeed, the escutcheon and the shop sign are merely two forms, one high and the other low, of a single attempt at self-identification, which can be traced back to examples in ancient Rome. Larwood and Hotten, however, refer to it as quintessentially English—"that cockney custom of punning on the name, so common on signboards."[7] And it is clear that Hogarth took it as a paradigmatic expression of the English, a painterly equivalent of his pug and his own plebeian manners. Against his parodies of the "dark masters" of painting must be placed his remark to his pupil Dawes that signboards—which he liked to walk around London observing—were "specimens of genius emanating from a school which he used emphatically to observe was truly English,"[8] and also his participation in the Sign Painters' Exhibition.

For another fact emphasized by Addison in *Spectator* no. 28 on signboards was that there is an analogy between the arts of sign painting and history painting. Addison launches a lighthearted attack on signboards, urging Londoners to "clear the City of Monsters," and outlines his version of the Augustan need to rationalize irrational modes that was also set forth about the same time in a more systematic way by the third earl of Shaftesbury.[9] Recalling Horace's *De Arte Poetica*, he laments the fact "that creatures of jarring and incongruous Natures should be joined together in the same Sign." This practice, he explains, was often the result of merging shops, of marriages, and the like—and (he might have added) rebuses, like the bolt and the tun for Bolton. But each sign is an example of the familiar monster of Horace's famous passage, which—it is useful to remember—also includes the doctrine of *ut pictura poesis*. On the contrary, says Addison, we should use or develop "a Sign which bears some Affinity to the Wares in which it deals." Probability (Shaftesbury's criterion) demands that we rationalize those improbable combinations that began as erroneous puns. The willful separation of word from thing led to the catastrophic, independent progress of the word, ever further removed from truth and reality, uncorrected by the image.[10]

Bonnell Thornton, in his essay in *The Adventurer* no. 9 (5 Dec. 1752), developed Addison's remarks into a poetics of sign painting. Originally a sign expressed the occupation of its owner—hand and shears for a tailor, hand and pen for a writing master, hen and chickens for a poulterer are Thornton's examples. But then there appeared the sign of the publican who, not content with a bunch of grapes, must have a hog in armor, a blue boar, black bear, green dragon, or golden lion—pretentious heraldic devices from the upper classes. Or worse, he might (here Thornton returns to Addison's argument) have above the door of his tavern an angel, a lamb, or a mitre. He urges that "some regard should . . . be paid by tradesmen to their situation; or, in other words, to the *propriety of place*," and he projects a historical process of the independent origin of the shop sign, the subsequent emulation of heraldic devices of the great, and a debasement from which he hopes the original vitality can be recovered.

Thornton's etymology projects a scenario parallel to Hogarth's for English art history. Thornton's periodical *The Student* had published an essay on *The March to Finchley* in 1751 and he had become Hogarth's friend. In his essay of 1752 he laid the groundwork for the exhibition of 1762 and probably helped Hogarth formulate his own ideas on the subject, which meant rationalizing his practice of the preceding two decades. Hogarth uses, for example, the impropriety described by Thornton when he juxtaposes the "Adam and Eve" sign with the Cain-Abel fight going on below it. He is probably recalling the pugilist James Figg's academy, later taken over by George Taylor, which used this sign. Here young gentlemen were taught boxing, cudgelling, and the use of the short and broad sword for self-defense and display.

Thornton, in turn, may have been looking at Hogarth's image of the shabby sign painter who (besides the unnecessary pawnbroker) is the one derelict in *Beer Street*. The painter's visionary gaze keeps him at some distance from the pathetic, but in graphic terms he derives from the thin intruder in Brueghel's *Fat Kitchen* (*Cuisine Grasse*). The hungry artist, like his prototype, is rejected, reduced in this society to the painting of shop signs.[11] He is adding beneath the sign of the "Barley Mow" (which reappears as no. 37 in the Sign Painters' Grand Room) a sign of a gin bottle, the only spirit bottle he can afford as a model.

What Thornton wrote emphasized both the sad plight of the English artist and the possibility of a genuine English art based on this "truly English" genre. He speaks in the person of a sign painter, Philip Carmine:

I am at present but an humble journey-man sign-painter in Harp-alley [where the sign painters' shops were]: for though the ambition of my parents designed that I should emulate the immortal touches of a Raphael or a Titian, yet the want of Tast among my countrymen, and their prejudice against every artist who is a native, have degraded me to the miserable necessity, as Shaftesbury says, "of illustrating prodigies in fairs, and adorning heroic sign-posts."

Thornton's picture, like the Sign Painters' Exhibition itself, is deeply ambivalent. This is the aspiration of an untalented upstart who thinks he is a painter and—justly—ends painting only signs. It is also the plight, as Hogarth saw it, of even the talented painter, if he is English, in a time of degenerate patronage of foreigners. And we must remember at least two of Hogarth's reasons for being so interested in the Sign Painters' Exhibition in 1762.

In the first place was the fact, which would have been of extreme significance to him, that signboards were on their way out. From 1762 onward, legislation was passed to flatten them against the walls of the shops; the streets were numbered, and another function of the shop sign lost; and by the nineteenth century they had become quaint antiquarian objects.[12]

Perhaps more important, Hogarth connected sign painting with the slurs upon his (and his father-in-law's) title of Serjeant Painter to the King, which he held after 1757, and which caused him to be called by his enemies (with some justice, given the duties of the job) a "sign painter," one who decorated royal coaches with coats of arms. Certainly Hogarth's ambivalence can be seen in the timing of the exhibition, which specifically coincided with the mercantile-oriented exhibition of the Society of Arts, but also with that of the Society of Artists, where he had exhibited the year before. The newspaper squibs claimed that only the Society of Arts, with its emphasis on premiums for the best paintings of poultry and fish, was being satirized. But exhibits like *The Rising Sun* by a painter described as "a modern Claude Lorrain" and the responses published in the newspapers are proof that the Exhibition of Sign Painters was taken as a commentary on the Society of Artists as well.[13]

Hostile caricatures and newspaper jibes connected Hogarth with the exhibition. But one object in the exhibition was his own portrait on a signboard, the "Hogarth's Head" (as it had appeared over the doors of two different print shops in London since the early 1750s), and this was accompanied by a parody of his "Line of Beauty," a "Crooked Billet."[14] The totemic significance of the shop sign to Hogarth is unmistakable in this juxtaposition and in two related facts: his own choice for a shop sign over the door of his house-studio in

Leicester Fields was not the pug he employed in his self-portrait but a
"Van Dyck's Head," which in June 1751, after his disappointment at
the price brought by his *Marriage à la Mode* paintings, he had taken
down. We are not told with what he replaced it.[15] The Sign Painters'
Exhibition was a defiant return to popular art—his last exhibition, as
it proved. It was an exhibition that for Hogarth was part joke, part
acceptance of the view of his art propounded by his enemies, and
part a genuine conviction that signboards represented a native English art form to which English artists must return if they were to
have any hopes of freeing themselves from the fetters of Continental
traditions of religious and mythological painting.

Hogarth may have known that there was not only the distinguished example of Watteau's *L'Enseigne de Gersaint* but signboards
painted by Chardin and, in the seventeenth century, by Karel Fabrit-
ius and other Dutch masters. Nevertheless, the sign painter's profession was a fine case of the conflict between craft and art, popular and
elitist artifacts, or low and high cultures. As an "artist" you were
somewhere on a scale that rose from the plumber, who cast lead
statues and decorated lead cisterns, to the plasterer, who did elaborate
stucco design, and the carpenter, who did fine wood carving, to the
coach painter, who was approaching the status of official recognition
as an artist. The herald painters, who painted emblems and coats of
arms on coaches of the great were paid more and accorded more
prestige than the body makers, smiths, and trimmers of the carriages.
But there was often a narrow line separating the one from the other.
M. D. George writes euphorically: "It was that golden age when the
artist was a craftsman, and the craftsman an artist. Coach-painting
and sign-painting were both trades and arts."[16] But this could also be
seen as a confusion of social identities; and Hogarth's theme in his
print series of the search for and confusion (or loss) of identities can
be seen as a direct reflection of his own situation.

These are the forces and counterforces that were summed up in
the Sign Painters' Exhibition that opened 20 April 1762. It seems to
have consisted mainly of actual signs, or rather signs borrowed from
shops or from the stock of sign painters in Harp Alley.[17] They were
all standard, recognizable signs, a readily understood vocabulary, and
it is remarkable just how small the iconographic repertory was and
how many signs were repeated with variations. It soon becomes clear
that the real signs were either touched up or mixed with imaginary

signboards to produce a new meaning. Significance depends on the contiguity or relationship between signs more than on the signs themselves. Nos. 53 and 54 ("by Sheerman") were two old signs of the "Saracen's Head" and "Queen Anne."[18] Hogarth is supposed to have written under the first "The Zarr" and under the second "Empres Quean" (i.e., the czar of Russia and Maria Theresa, queen of Hungary), and painted their tongues lolling out and their eyes turned toward each other, and over their heads a wooden label, "The present State of Europe." This sort of reciphering through juxtaposition runs through the exhibition, with "The Three Apothecaries' Gallipots" as a companion to "The Three Coffins" and "King Charles in the Oak" to "The Owl in the Ivy Bush."[19]

I will single out only those that are related to Hogarth, whose work appeared exclusively in the Grand Room under the thin disguise of the name Hagarty. Hogarth has reciphered them as a personal iconography. He makes each his own shop sign, an emblem of an aspect of his art and life, a recapitulation of his career and favorite motifs, as if to re-create a shop sign to replace his lost "Van Dyck's Head." He begins with the ironic joining of the "Hogarth's Head" with the "Crooked Billet, formed exactly in the Line of Beauty" (its "Companion," nos. 1 and 2). No. 5, "The Light Heart" (sign for a vintner), shows a heart outweighed by a feather on a pair of scales (the catalogue of the exhibition quotes Ben Jonson's *New Inn* as its source). I would be surprised if Hogarth is not alluding to his notoriously ill-received painting in the 1761 Society of Artists' Exhibition, *Sigismunda*, which was criticized for the overly bloody heart of Guiscardo being held by the grieving Sigismunda.[20]

If no. 5 exposes the self-reflexive nature of the exhibition in the Grand Room, nos. 19 and 20 give an example of a nuclear structure of the Hogarthian composition. These are the signs of "Nobody" and "Somebody," or as the catalogue puts it, "Nobody, alias Somebody" and "Somebody, alias Nobody." The catalogue describes Nobody as "the Figure of an Officer, all Head, Arms, Legs and Thighs," and Somebody as "a rosy figure with a little Head and a Huge Body, whose Belly swags over, almost quite down to his Shoe-Buckles. By the Staff in his Hand it appears to be intended to represent a Constable.—It might also have been mistaken for an eminent Justice of Peace." The sign itself was used in the seventeenth century (for a ballad printer in the Barbican),[21] and the Nobody–Somebody tradition is an old one. Nobody is always the Tom Idle sort of hero and Somebody the Francis Goodchild (as with a somewhat different import, Gin Lane and Beer Street). In Hogarth's version, Somebody always carries the signs of authority.

Even without the catalogue's description we would recognize these figures as the frontispiece and tailpiece of Hogarth's MS. journal, the *Five Days' Peregrination* of 1732 (figs. 18, 19). There, Mr. Somebody is the antiquarian, surrounded with antiquarian objects, whereas Mr. Nobody is hung with knives, forks, spoons, glass, and bottle—all implements of the table. Somebody is the representative of "knaves or fools, in coat or gown"—what Fielding, Gay, and Hogarth thought of as "the great." The "jolly Nobody" is one "Who during his life does nothing at all / But eat and snore / And drink and roar, / From whore to the tavern, from tavern to whore, / With a laced coat, and that is all."[22] Somebody is the one who gets the credit, Nobody the underdog who, though he only eats and drinks, sees or embodies the truth of life—the patrons, constables, and clergymen versus artists, harlots, and apprentices. If we look back at the example with which we started, *Noon* (fig. 17), we see that Hogarth has divided the composition between Somebodies and Nobodies: between the sign of the "Good Woman" (Somebody) and "John the Baptist" (Nobody, as a sign for an eating house) and between the two sides of the street—the eaters, drinkers, and lechers on one side, the respectable pious churchgoers on the other, with their sign of the stranded kite.

In no. 28, "The Logger Heads," with the inscription underneath "We Are Three," Hogarth has again chosen a paradigm of his *modus operandi*. The two loggerheads within the design suppose—come to life only through—the third loggerhead, who looks at it *and* reads the inscription. And this tells us quite a bit about Hogarth's process in the exhibition: he has taken a well-known sign used by scriveners, which signified their secretarial silence and discretion,[23] and made it his own, a sign of his particular craft and of how a native English picture can function in relation to its audience. Nor does the process end here. The exhibition catalogue is augmented by the learned annotation of the *St. James's Chronicle* (written by Thornton and/or Hogarth), which cites the origin of "Logger Heads" in "the old Joke" and mentions Shakespeare's allusion "to this sign in his *Twelfth Night*, where the Fool comes between Sir Toby Belch and

Sir Andrew Aguecheek, and, taking each by the Hand, says, 'How now, my Hearts, did you never see the Picture of We Three?' "[24] This is Scriblerian annotation, of the sort with which Pope decorated his *Dunciad*, but it also draws attention to the origin of "Logger Heads" in folk art and to the use made of them by the national playwright, Shakespeare. In short, it indicates the alternative aspects of the exhibition: a parody of pretentious "high art" and art commentary, but also the promulgation of a native English art.

From the beginning of his career (going back to his paintings of *The Beggar's Opera*),[25] Hogarth toyed with these alternative responses to the problem of what an English artist could and should paint. On the one hand he tried to produce a "modern moral subject" which was English and contemporary; on the other he continued to parody the baroque conventions of the Continent, which was the "high art" of the academies. The signboards of the 1762 exhibition survive only in the description of the exhibition catalogue and the *St. James's Chronicle*, but from other works it is possible to see how Hogarth thought signboards could offer an example to contemporary artists. Although it served as "a Design [made] without the Knowledge of Perspective," illustrating Joshua Kirby's *Brooke Taylor's Method of Perspective Made Easy* (1754), the print known as *False Perspective* (fig. 20) is in fact a kind of signboard. It is purely emblematic, without either narrative or interpersonal relationships, constructed out of elements of shop signs such as "The Complete Angler" and a "Swan and the Half Moon" (Sign Painters' Exhibition, nos. 2 and 3 in the Passageway). The perspective errors are used to engender puns, to show not only how *not* to draw but, in a sense, *how* to draw—how to make a different set of relationships by using a different set of rules. I think Hazlitt's remark is significant, about "a phantasmagoria . . . with as little attention to keeping of perspective, as in Hogarth's famous print for reversing the laws of vision."[26] There is a sense in which Hogarth's print *is* a phantasmagoria, with its aim to reverse the laws of vision.

For Hogarth is not only making fun of clumsy "artists" (as he was of the clumsy signboard painters) but celebrating the joy of the naive eye that looks at signboards, and perhaps the world, not from single-point perspective but with an episodic and egalitarian contemplation of each object for itself, a far different phenomenon from the grading and differentiation of elements within a painting advocated by Reynolds and the academic tradition. The naive eye allows one to see pure relationship, unhampered by conventions of verisimilitude or iconographic purity. For example, Dufresnoy (and his translator Dryden) takes the position in his *Art of Painting* that we should always look to the center of a canvas for its subject. The single protagonist should be "in the midst of the picture." But when we look at the center of any plate in *Industry and Idleness*, we see nothing—certainly no heroic subject, but no protagonist either, for both apprentices (vs. Dufresnoy's single hero) are off to one side or the other. There is always something *un*important in the middle—a loom or pipe organ, the sea and a gallows, a cat and dog—while the people are peripheral.

An independent sequence of objects in the Hogarthian scene is one expression of this principle, of which "False Perspective" is a schematic representation on the way to the signboards of 1762. Hogarth, in his usual way, is both imitating bad perspective and trying to extend the range of art, laying a theoretical groundwork for the sign painters' solution and the possibility of other forms of popular art that do not adhere to rules. I have no doubt that this print has enjoyed its popularity not because it exposes clumsy art of a sort, but because the old crone who leans out a window with a candle and lights the pipe of a traveler on a distant hill—or the swan in the middle distance who is the same size as a dog in the foreground and a distant horse—supplies the pleasure of naiveté at the same time that she provides the insecurity of disorientation. These two sensations, summed up in the "Three Logger Heads," go hand in hand in Hogarth's art.

At another extreme, Hogarth draws upon the structure of the signboard's aristocratic alternative, the escutcheon. The first scene of *Marriage à la Mode* (1745) parodies both the coat of arms and the group portrait of the aristocratic family. The family tree itself is present, emerging from William the Conqueror's entrails, and laid out in terms of the crazy family relationships of the earl's stock and the stock of the rich merchant who is bartering his daughter. As "supporters," the earl and his heir frame the merchant and his daughter, who in heraldic terms make a quartering of the earl's shield; and the earl's own armorial markings—a gouty foot and his coronet—reappear in the sore on his son's neck and the stamp on all

the objects in his possession (including a pair of dogs, chained together like the young couple). The fourth scene, however, is the
crucial one (fig. 21), by which time the family has split into separate
fragments, the old earl is dead, his son off with a mistress, and the
new countess appears with her lover, a lawyer named Silvertongue.
They are presented as vested supporters, one *sejeant* and the other
couchant,[27] on either side of a gloomy escutcheon. The escutcheon
is her mirror, divided *per bend ombre*, a blank centerpiece, denoting
an empty past, an empty future. (In the painting it is divided bend
sinister, presumably for reversal in the engraving, in which the lines
of shading represent heraldically *gules*, the color of the blood that is
shed in the next scene.) The decoration beneath forms a crest with a
casque, the *garde visure* empty and placed *affrontée*. The drapery
around the mirror suggests a fringed and corded *mantelle*, the objects
in the wife's hair a coronet *triumphant*, and Silvertongue's paper a
ragget motto.

The whole picture emerges from this key, as the first scene did
from the family tree. The auction objects, laid out directly beneath
the mock escutcheon, serve as an additional, a comic heraldic motto.
The sequence is virtually a summation of the six scenes of *Marriage
à la Mode* in miniature: a round vessel and a bowl with a Rape of
Leda plus an Actaeon (the horns suggesting the cuckolded status of
the countess's husband) lead to a deformed progeny, which dimin-
ishes in size until it ends in a mouse. (In the last plate, the surviving
heir is crippled and deformed, with the father's and grandfather's
patch on its neck.)

The heraldic aspect is also present in Hogarth's self-portrait with
his pug (1745), (fig. 24), with its indication of quartering and com-
partmentalizing of himself, a supporter and a crest of his palette, the
Line of Beauty, and paintbrushes. When he revised the engraving
into *The Bruiser* (1763), (fig. 25), he replaced his portrait with the
familiar shop sign of "Bear and Ragged Staff,"[28] although the usual
version showed the bear muzzled, collared, and chained. (In Hogarth's version, Charles Churchill–as–bear, the enemy to all he
stands for, is quite free to do harm.) The "Bear and Ragged Staff"
shop sign had originally been the crest of Richard Neville, earl of
Warwick, but I have no doubt that Hogarth uses its shop sign incarnation. He continually plays with the dual possibilities that shop
signs are a corruption of heraldry and that heraldry is an over-

sophistication of the basic shop sign which embodies the identity of a man in the only meaningful way, through his occupation.

Reynolds' *Lord Heathfield* (National Gallery, London) is an example of a portrait as escutcheon. Heathfield, governor of Gibraltar, is a solid, squat body rising out of the bottom of the picture space in the shape of the Rock of Gibraltar, carrying in his hands the keys to the fortress he defended, and not very different from the arms granted by Charles II to Colonel Carlos, who hid him in the oak tree at Boscobel after the defeat at Worcester: "*Or*, issuing from a mount in base *vert*, an oak tree proper, over all on a fess *gules*, three Imperial crowns also proper," or the arms granted to Colonel Newman, through whose efforts Charles escaped through the gate of Worcester: "*Gules*, a portcullis imperially crowned *or*."

The heraldic shield, however, contained two dimensions—or layers—of definition, one by honor (as with Heathfield's "Gibraltar" and keys) and the other by blood. The shield goes back to the tunic worn over armor to identify the knight to his king and to his own soldiers in the field; the original signs referred only to his name, and then to this were added the augmentations of honor, his wife's arms (if she brought lands with her), and the increase of rank. All of these are embodied in family group portraits like Van Dyck's Pembrokes at Wilton or Reynolds' Marlboroughs at Blenheim, with the formal pattern based on a model (even when it deviates from it) of blood relationships, not unlike the one Hogarth lays out in the first plate of *Marriage à la Mode*. The parallel becomes much more compelling in the conversation picture, that characteristic eighteenth-century English form, which also in a way derives from Dutch genre scenes with their proverbs, jokes, and puns. What I have always noticed about the "conversations" of Hogarth, Devis, Zoffany, Stubbs, and even Gainsborough is their extremely schematic compartmentalized character (often the result of architectural interiors). Some figures (or groups) are divided *per pale*, others *per fess*, and we note the importance of vertical as well as horizontal demarcations. The composition of early Hogarth conversations, for example, was a triangle (sometimes apex-up, sometimes down) that heraldically derives from a shield *per chevron*; and the same can be said for many of Zoffany's families.[29]

The basic fact about English conversation pictures of families, as of heraldry, is that the individual is defined in terms of a past: "By the use of a certain coat of arms, you assert your descent from the person to whom those arms were granted, confirmed, or allowed."[30] First comes the self-domination, often in the form of a pun, as we have seen; then the metonymy of weapons for a soldier, wool sack for a wool merchant, or keys for a keeper (as with Heathfield). Then the escutcheon parts company with the shop sign and begins to add indications of family or blood lines. The past thereafter appears in a different sense on an escutcheon than on a shop sign; nor does the shop sign ordinarily grow, change, and complicate itself. The complex formal pattern of the shield, which is the marshaling of arms, indicates sovereignty, dominion, alliance, descent, or pretension— formally expressed by dimidiation, impalement, quartering, or superimposition. These formal additions or quarterings are made for one of two reasons: for augmentation of honor or inheritance. You quarter the arms of your wife or ancestresses from whom you acquired your lands. If your wife is not a heraldic heiress, the two coats are impaled; if she is, the arms of her family are placed on an inescutcheon superimposed on the center of her husband's arms (as in Hogarth's parody, where he puts a merchant's daughter in that position in *Marriage à la Mode*, plate 1). This then becomes a quartering for the next generation, which can—with the luck of marrying heiresses—lead to extremely complex patterns of quartering and impalement, representing elaborate family relationships.[31]

In the totally schematized shield resides the essence or conceptualization of a family; "every quartering exhibited means the representation in blood of some particular person";[32] and it is the artist's function to re-create the concrete reality that has been abbreviated. But if the conversation picture which flourished in the 1720s and '30s is an attempt to flesh out a conventional structure, it is also an attempt to secularize it and make probable (in the sense of Shaftesbury's arguments about the iconography of history painting in his *Tablature of the Judgment of Hercules*), demythologize, or literalize—however one chooses to regard it—the heraldic shield. Perhaps most obviously this is a making bourgeois of aristocratic arms; by which I do not mean that conversation pictures were all commissioned by the bourgeoisie, but that abstractions are related to real wives and intermarriages, children and ancestors, animals and family estates. However, what we most often think of as the English conversation picture does assert the presence of the self-made man and emphasizes augmentation of honor, though supported where possible by ancestral portraits, but more often by portraits of people he would *like* to be related to, by objects, property, and demarcations that imply blood lines of descent and augmentations of inheritance (sometimes honor also) which do not exist.

The version of the escutcheon that passes into the group portraits of Hogarth and Zoffany employs family portraits and busts, heirlooms, and other objects to convey these emblematic connotations: they place the sitters in relation to their past if they have one; and if not, then in relation to their possessions and collections, which project a pseudo past of Roman heroes on the one hand and of English heroes and distinguished families on the other (the monarch, the duke of Marlborough, Sir Robert Walpole). The sitter is in effect portrayed inventing a past to suit his achieved station.

Having related the shop sign to the aristocratic coat of arms, and shown the ways in which an artist could reconcile or contrast the two modes, we can also relate it to the effigy carried by the crowd in its "urban ceremonials." Both are attempts to return to an older, more stable time through the traditional signs of names and professions; both draw upon the solidarity of a cohesive group which we have called a subculture. Both also represent the process of appropriating the symbols and rituals of authority—whether heraldic signs, coronations, or chairings—and filling them with a political meaning of their own. But, as Hogarth's practice shows, while these signs embody an original vigor which is native English, untainted by sophisticated traditions, they are also reductive of human nature. They have lost something and therefore have to be explained in various ways.

The object of bringing the shop signs together is, in Hogarth's terms, to recover the original significance, or, failing that, to discover a new one. We begin by admitting that the original Bell behind the "Bell" (or "Belle") sign is lost. So there is the signboard "Bell" itself "in nature," on a street, haphazardly juxtaposed with other signboards—vigorous but subliminal. An example of popular iconography, it is also collaterally related to the aristocratic heraldic vocabulary with its similar linguistic principles, but without its exclusive emphasis on blood lines. Either sign can be taken as a degeneration or sophistication of the other, but once the sign has become a stereotype it can no longer designate the person or profession or house, but has meaning *only* in relation to other escutcheons or shop signs. The

"Bell" shop sign then appears within the scene of Hogarth's prints, juxtaposed with other shop signs, other kinds of signs, which create new meanings quite independent of the lost original ones.

Hogarth is not, in other words, arguing (as Blake would) that art is a purging of error, a revealing of truth hidden under deluding surfaces, but that art consists of a junkshop of old forms such as signboards that can be given new meaning by juxtapositions and transitions. He distinguishes between the old delusive aristocratic forms in which Blake was also interested and the old native English or popular forms that remain but are almost invisible, unnoted and unacknowledged (though not unloved), and even marked for destruction. He cannot make up his mind between the delusive and the "real," and so he tends to use, in his best work, both "high" and "low" materials.

At length the signboard, which has been taken into Hogarth's prints as one part of a sign system, is finally removed from nature altogether and juxtaposed with other signs in a picture gallery exhibition. This makes the signboard "art" and draws attention to its maker as "artist." The individual signboards appear in exhibition as a series, arranged according to transitions (ordinarily in groups of two or three), touched up, and revised into something that often returns to the original self-reference of the sign-as-name or occupation, though in this particular case assimilated to the artist Hogarth.

The signboard at this stage exists also in terms of its verbal description in catalogue and newspaper: for us it exists *only* in this way, since no sign from the exhibition has survived. This fact is significant because the art adumbrated here is basically a conceptual one, and so a verbal account is nearly sufficient, in fact allows us to summon up the visual experience in a way that may improve upon the artifact itself. (Nothing interesting in a painterly way was being done in the signs; they do not become Jasper Johns's targets or flags.) The point being stressed is the artist's need to assimilate his art to a subculture characterized by simplicity and natural vigor. The process is used equally to absorb a subculture object and to make it new and viable, as at the end of the century Wordsworth attempts to make use of naive poetry (then adding a preface to explain what he is about).

I find it extremely suggestive that Hogarth should have begun his career painting conversation pictures and ended it with an exhibition of signboards in which he shows a way to get back to the primitive sources of English art. His final response was predictably ambivalent: his last print, *The Tailpiece*, scatters its surface with the detritus of signboards (all of which could have been found in the Sign Painters' Exhibition) and their verbal puns, including a "World's End." This well-known sign (no. 21, Grand Room, in the exhibition) can be traced back as far as the mid-seventeenth century, usually marking the last house in a built-up area or along a road—or a pub or "ordinary" to indicate the last place for obtaining drink or food in the area. The sign, in its most usual form, showed a fractured globe against a dark background with fire and smoke issuing from the fissure. Hogarth first represents this sign a year after the Sign Painters' Exhibition in *The Times*, plate 1, where it appears above the door of the house that allegorically represents Europe and which, like the sign, is itself in flames. Less than a year later (April 1764), in *The Tailpiece*, he shows it with its label "The World's End" in a context where it means precisely that. It has also become his final shop sign, marking the end of his volume of engravings and his career, the last in a series of substitutions that began with his "Van Dyck's Head" and approached the end with the replacement of his face by Churchill's bear-face in *The Bruiser*.

Hogarth has once again absorbed the popular sign into his own sophisticated, ultimately personal structure of meaning without sacrificing its popular effect. The sophistication he has wrought is then absorbed into the popular image of the next generation. At 459 King's Road in London is a World's End pub and distillery, built around 1790, which originally marked the end of old Chelsea village. The traditional sign of the burning world is replaced by Hogarth's own image of Father Time and his scythe from *The Tailpiece*, sitting by a signpost with "Finis" written on it, a raven perched on its horizontal bar, and a skull at its base.

5. The English Dog

In the great Dispute between South *and* Sherlock, *the former, who was a great Courtier, said, His Adversary reasoned well, but he Bark'd like a Cur: To which the other reply'd, That Fawning was the Property of a Cur, as well as Barking.*

Joe Miller's Jests, no. 230

ANY STUDY OF "THE ENGLISH DOG" must begin with William Empson's essay of the same name in *The Structure of Complex Words*, where he argued that a conventional formula word like "dog," denoting mean or low, picks up a second, more "hearty" sense as "a half-conscious protest against the formulas, a means of keeping them at bay."[1] He shows the word changing from the derogatory to the "hearty" sense in the course of the eighteenth century. I wish to explore the way in which the word "dog" is different from, a repression or domestication of, the visual image. I will not go back over the ground Empson has covered (e.g., the sound and orthography of "dog" as the converse of "God") but would draw attention to the fact that "dog" originally denoted a large native English breed, as opposed to a hound or *hund* or *chien*.

I begin with the word as defined in 1736 in Nathan Bailey's *Dictionary*: "a Mongrel or Mastife, a Creature well known: Also an Andiron." The creature (so "well known") is eminently metaphorical. "Dog" as an andiron implies a transference of such canine qualities as strength and fidelity. An andiron physically resembles a dog, but it also patiently supports or holds up the logs which warm its master. But if an andiron can be described favorably in terms of "dog," a man cannot: Bailey's list of derivatives makes "dog" the vehicle for metaphors about man, who is *dogged* ("sullen, surly, crabbed") or the writer of doggrel ("pitiful Poetry; paultry Verses").

49

The derivatives in Samuel Johnson's *Dictionary* (1755) are more extensive: a *dog-trick* is "an ill turn; surly or brutal treatment"; *dog-cheap*, "cheap as dogs meat; cheap as the offal bought for dogs"; *dog days*, days in which the dog star rises, "vulgarly reputed unwholesome"; *doggish*, "churlish; brutal"; *doghearted*, "cruel; pitiless; malicious as in Lear's doghearted daughters"; and *dogfish*, "another name for a shark." Even *dogfly* is defined as "a voracious biting fly," whereas the *OED*, which corrects some of Johnson's anticanine references, informs us that dogflies are in fact "British flies troublesome to dogs."

Johnson's definition of "dog" is "a domestic animal remarkably various in his species. . . . The larger sort are used as a guard; the less for sports." The added category, "for sports," refers to a more favorably regarded dog, the hunter, and reflects the metaphor that gained ground during the Restoration (but which Johnson does not acknowledge openly) of "gay young dog" for a rake. By his third sense of the word, however, Johnson has reached the common meaning of "a reproachful name for a man": "*To give or send to the* Dogs: to throw away; *To go to the* Dogs, to be ruined, destroyed, or devoured." He does not acknowledge, nor need he, the other side of the metaphor, the dog himself, whose miserable life is reflected upon.

His fifth sense is an important one: "for the male of several species; as, the dog fox, the dog otter"; "dog" always refers to a male and "bitch" to a female—a distinction which doubtless contributed to the rise of "young dog"—as it was said, for example, of the future prince regent on his first appearance as a baby in Hyde Park in 1763: "God bless him, he is a lusty, jolly, young dog truly!"[2] Only in the twentieth century has "dog" come to refer to an unprepossessing female, a complete turnabout of the older usage. But this is probably explained by Johnson's sixth sense of "dog" (which we saw in dogfish or dogfly) as "a particle added to anything to mark meanness, or degeneracy, or worthlessness; as dog rose"—rather as the Houyhnhnms added the epithet Yahoo to a word "to express any thing that is evil." In short, as an epithet "dog" signifies either maleness or meanness, sometimes both.

Johnson's dog is simply a part of man, his baser or less fortunate, less conscious, largely male aspect. Empson refers to the difference between Johnson's dictionary definition of *dogged* as "sullen;

sour; morose; ill-humoured; gloomy" and his use of it in conversation, referring to the duke of Devonshire as having a "dogged veracity." Nonetheless, a "dogged veracity" is not only the strength of an andiron but an animal stolidity. When Johnson says, remembering Harry Hervey's kindness to him as a young man, "If you call a dog Hervey, I shall love him," we should recall the context of his remark: "Hervey was a very vicious man. But he was good to me. If you call a dog Hervey, I shall love him."[3] Hervey was the summation of doggishness to Johnson: vice-ridden but good to *me*; a dog is that part of us we despise and try to control but also have to acknowledge. As with one's tendency to indolence or to be excited by the bosoms of young actresses backstage ("I'll come no more behind your scenes, Davy," he told Garrick), one fiercely represses and yet retains a sneaking affection for the vice.

The two animals that most often serve in eighteenth-century England as vehicles for the tenor "man" are the ape and the dog, and they cover the two aspects of man he is least happy about: *to ape* is to imitate or mimic one's betters; and *to dog* is to stubbornly and stupidly follow one's natural instinct, whether for sycophancy (following close for scraps dropped) or fidelity to a master.[4] Johnson is one who finds it harder to forgive the dog; but moralists in general were more uneasy about the ape, who so physically resembles man. The dog is, happily, all animal. Indeed, the ape is an image which can be corrected by that of the dog, who, quite the opposite, does not hide or disguise but flaunts his lower nature; as Empson puts it, "the dog blows the gaff on human nature," exposing what we would like to conceal.

The dog, we should not be surprised to learn, is a device of the satirist in the eighteenth century. Pope's sense of dog, both more conventional and less personal than Johnson's, is summed up in the dog's collar inscribed "I am her Highness' Dog at Kew / Pray tell me sir, whose dog are you?" This cheeky dog shows some of the cynic's self-awareness, for part of the literature of the dog (not reflected in the dictionaries) was Diogenes' answer to the question why he was called a dog: "I am called dog because I fawn on those who give me anything, I yelp at those who refuse, and I set my teeth in rascals."[5] The central poem for Pope is his heroic epistle "Bounce to Fop," in which his own dog Bounce, the rough country dog, a large and masterful Great Dane (in fact a bitch), addresses herself to the courtly

spaniel Fop, who belongs to the king's mistress, and whom Bounce
has accidentally injured by an unguarded flick of her tail. "We country Dogs love nobler Sport, / And scorn the Pranks of Dogs at Court."
Fop is the fawning flatterer who, when you forget her for a moment—"Snap!" she bites you, while as to Bounce:

> The worst that Envy, or that Spite
> E'er said of me, is, I can bite. . . .
> Fair Thames from either ecchoing Shoare
> Shall hear, and dread my manly Roar.[6]

Pope, in short, employs two dogs. Even Bailey distinguished
mongrel from mastif: we are dealing with different, or to be more
precise antithetical, breeds of dog rather than merely changing attitudes or ambiguous concepts of "dog." There is the lapdog or snivel-
ing spaniel: a slavish flatterer, related to Shakespeare's spaniels melting candied sweets in their mouths, and ultimately Sporus, like
"well-bred Spaniels [who] civilly delight / In mumbling of the Game
they dare not bite." Then there is its polar opposite, the Great Dane,
who is derived from the rough, mongrel cynic-dog, "doggedness,"
and the dog-as-andiron, often a watchdog.

There was at least one sense, Pope saw, in which the dog could
serve as a foil to man—an ideal to which man failed to live up.
"Histories are more full of examples of the fidelity of dogs than of
friends," he wrote to Cromwell.[7] If it was not Pope himself, it was a
member of his circle who added the tablet commemorating Signor
Fido to the Temple of British Worthies in the garden at Stowe.
Signor Fido is praised for his "Fidelity," but at the very end of the
inscription it is admitted that he is not (cannot have been) a man:
"Reader, this Stone is guiltless of Flattery, for he to whom it is
inscrib'd was not a Man, but a Grey-Hound." But also, of course, in
the context of the British worthies, the dog is a *vanitas* emblem, a
reminder of even the greatest man's animal component.

The great anthology of proverbial canine lore and repertoire of
dog turns in the first half of the century was Francis Coventry's
Pompey the Little (1751). This life of a lapdog is a satire on man
which extends Pope's dog collar to the collars worn by knights of the
Garter, Bath, and Thistle and does variations on the old dog/fidelity
topos. Coventry uses the dog as Pope does, less as a metaphor for
man or an aspect of man than as a yardstick against which to measure

and judge him, often as an active satirist based on the dog's ability to show his contempt by raising his leg.

There are not a great many other dogs represented in the novels of the period. Robinson Crusoe remarks of his life on the island, "It would have made a dog laugh," and he says his dog was a pleasant and loving companion, but he has much more to say about Robin his parrot, a better alter ego because he can speak words that sound like Crusoe's conscience. There are no dogs where one would most expect to find them, in the Shandy family (I suppose they are not *needed*); there is no dog either to attack or defend Pamela or Clarissa. I would single out as the two significant dogs in fiction, expressing the two sides of the iconographic coin, Mr. Edwards' old, blind dog Trusty in *The Man of Feeling* (1771) who dies of sorrow when the family is evicted from its ancestral home—a scene of many tears derived from Ulysses' faithful dog who dies of joy on his return to Ithaca; and Tabitha Bramble's alter ego, the infamous Chowder, who cannot be coped with by Matthew Bramble and is bested by the apparently even lower creature, Humphry Clinker. The test question is: What animal do we turn to as our alter ego? Mr. Edwards' dog was on the wave of the future, pointing toward many Victorian dogs faithful unto death. Chowder represents the eighteenth century and the dog's intransigence in the face of man, not usually so frankly admitted.

The dictionary of the graphic tradition is Cesare Ripa's *Iconologia*, in which the dog appears front-center only as emblematic of the sense of smell, sharing the spotlight with a man smelling a flower. He is peripheral: as an incidental background figure he makes frequent brief appearances. In the elaborate illustrations of the 1758–60 Hertel edition a dog is included in the emblems of Flattery and Envy; but also more hieroglyphically in the emblem of Justice (he lies at Justice's feet, representing Friendship), Memory (he is supposedly known for his memory), Enmity (he is a natural enemy of the cat), and Obstinacy (he perseveres in following a scent). Most interesting, however, he is shown in the background of Impiety, not himself impious but devouring Jezebel for *her* impiety: "Evil was Jezebel's sole creed, / 'Till dogs upon her flesh did feed." This is the role of the active punisher as agent of nature or divine retribution; but also, ambiguously, the creature who is willing to eat unclean things, and (another form of impiety) the lowest of subjects devouring his monarch.

The earlier visual tradition had made much of the dog's fidelity and domesticity. In medieval and Renaissance tomb sculpture the dog was shown at the foot of the effigy of the wife, as in Van Eyck's *Arnolfini* (London, National Gallery), and in other paintings of interiors with happily wedded couples of families he served as a fleshed-out andiron.[8] But if he appeared in domestic situations that emphasized his fidelity, he also made appearances that drew upon his animal nature, his insistent maleness, and his biblical associations with unclean things and carnal appetite. Artists included him in brothel and tavern scenes to represent unchastity and gluttony (animal appetite), as in Carpaccio's *Women on the Balcony* (Venice, Correr), and, more delicately, as the lover's surrogate in paintings of nudes in their boudoirs (Titian's *Venus of Urbino* in the Uffizi and Watteau's *Lady at Her Toilet* in the Wallace Collection; best, Fragonard's *Le Guinblette*, showing the dog hoisted in air between the lady's outspread legs).[9] Pope is drawing on this tradition when he has Shock share Belinda's bed and lie in her lap in place of a lover.[10]

The dog begins to take on an independent existence in Hogarth's conversation pictures of 1729–35. These groups of families or friends have a dog who ought to be an emblem of the sort he was in Van Eyck's *Arnolfini*, but in fact Hogarth also draws on the second tradition I have mentioned, and upon a third, which is emphatically popular and probably best known by Rembrandt's dog having a bowel movement in the foreground of his etching of *The Good Samaritan*—as a touch of vulgar realism, a reminder of our common humanity, in the presence of Bible stories that tend to be prettified out of existence. A far more delicate version can be seen in various Watteau *fêtes champêtres*, the immediate progenitors of Hogarth's conversation pictures. The dog in the Berlin *Dancing Couple* compromises the idyllic mood by exposing to the viewer his prominent sexuality; the dog in the shop sign he painted for Gersaint (Berlin), picking over his fleas and licking his sores (a kind of Lazarus outside the rich man's gate), establishes one referent of a spectrum of nature and art, which includes the plebeian man lounging outside the doorway of the picture gallery, and the dressed-up connoisseurs within, with the mirrors, painted pictures, and mythological subjects in which they try to see themselves.

Finally, there is also the cynic-dog, the mongrel who snarls at Hudibras in Hogarth's early print *Hudibras Sallying Forth* (1726): the dog is both parody of Hudibras the snarling cur, and nature's response to and exposure of this same Hudibras as hypocrite. Always at one extreme is the dog and at the other the ape.

And so in a conversation picture like *The Wollaston Family* (Leicester Art Gallery), the dog is part of the family that is giving a fashionable party: but he is parodying the host, his master—his paws up on a chair, the cause of the one small spot of disorder (the mussed rug), in proceedings dominated by art and order. When the family has no dog of its own, or sometimes when it does, Hogarth introduces his own dog, a pug named Trump, as a kind of artist's signature. In *The Strode Family* (London, Tate) (fig. 22) he is in the right foreground, now balanced by the dog of the family his master is painting: as in "Bounce to Fop," he glares at the family's dog, an effete creature whose relation to the family (and distance from the artist and his dog) is shown by the bit of meat before him on a plate. The dog that represents nature in a world of art also represents the artist who, unseen, is painting the picture. (When Hogarth paints his own version of *The Good Samaritan*, [11] the dog is not defecating as in Rembrandt's—or, as in Bassano's in the National Gallery, London, engaged in licking up the wounded man's blood—but is himself wounded and licking his wound parallel to his master and *his* wounds. I would not want to deny that Hogarth's self-association with the dog carries over to a fellow feeling with the wounded man.)

The dog Trump of *The Strode Family* appears much enlarged in Hogarth's self-portrait (engraving published in 1745) (fig. 24). The purpose was to produce an emblematic image of himself as artist to be used as frontispiece of his collected engravings. His pug stands to the side as a heraldic supporter, as a muse or a personification of Fame, and in fact as his own dog, as a friend. Here are all the associations of "dogged," "watchdogs," and "andirons," as well as Bounce's "I can bite." But the distancing contrast between Pope and Bounce (as to sex and size) has become a parallel, even a physical resemblance: Trump is the spitting image of Hogarth, an alter ego not unlike Tabitha Bramble's Chowder.

This dog represents a dimension of Hogarth's idea of art which had appeared in *The Distressed Poet* (1736) (fig. 23) in the dog who enters the open door of the poet's garret and gobbles his last chop: a salutary combination of impertinence and carnality, opposed to the poet's poem "On Riches," his map of "Gold Mines in Peru," and the gentleman's sword he affects. A dog appears in Dutch "Dissolute Family" paintings (e.g., Steen's, Apsley House) as another example of the family's dissoluteness, or a natural consequence of it. But Hogarth's dog—it is important to distinguish—is an outsider who is entering to commit an outrage, to bring this family to its senses by invoking the threat of the satirist (another outsider) to expose and punish. Hogarth, quite different from Samuel Johnson or even Pope, is singularly unashamed, even proud, of the doggish quotient in himself—necessary, he says, in an artist in these times. At length, in the revision of the self-portrait into *The Bruiser* (1763) (fig. 25), the pug takes on a more active attribute of the cynic-dog, making water on Charles Churchill's *Epistle to William Hogarth*. For Hogarth, I think, who knew his dogs, this is not only a sign of contempt but a sign of self: the dog has found the traces of another animal (the bearish Churchill) and so leaves his own mark to say: I was, am still, here. Hogarth has removed *himself* from the picture, replacing his own portrait in the oval with that of Churchill, the author of the vicious personal attack on him; and the pug's gesture is, among other things, a sign that Hogarth is, in his most essential aspect, still very much present. [12]

This Hogarthian dog continued to function as an outcast agent of disruption in conversation pictures of the 1760s and beyond. [13] In a very different kind of painting, Thomas Rowlandson's *Kew Bridge* (c. 1790, Huntington) (fig. 26), the dog frightens a horse, producing rebellious vibrations that reach to the edges of the picture and include a carriage overturning short of a toll-gate barrier. This dog, whose catalytic effect is often to throw young men and women into each other's arms (as in *The Exhibition Stare-Case*), joins the Hogarthian theme, the dog as natural law, with the gallantry of the boudoir tradition and the male principle as sheer carnal appetite. He is often part of a crowd—in but not of it, always peripheral but its catalyst, the element of energy that stimulates the crowd to action. [14] In short, he is the Wilkes figure amidst the crowd. Wilkes himself wrote a couplet, "Epithet on the Lap-Dog of Lady Frail":

> At thieves I bark'd, at lovers wagg'd my tail
> And thus I pleased both Lord and Lady Frail. [15]

This can be interpreted to sum up the dog as simultaneously satirist and sycophant; but it can also stand for the dog (or Wilkes) as savage to malefactors but sympathetic to lovers, as both agent of nature and sexually oriented male principle.

I have already noted that English imagery sympathetic to the French Revolution took the form of youth, energy, sexuality (the "young dog") against aged fathers. The dog as a subversive agent is a familiar prerevolutionary figure who in Rowlandson's Whiggish circle continues to disrupt during the 1790s. But he was not picked up by the real revolutionaries; any reader of Burke's *Philosophical Enquiry into the Origin of Our Ideas of the Sublime and Beautiful* (1757) will see why. Dogs, as opposed to lions, tigers, and horses, are friendly and affectionate, but since "love approaches much nearer to contempt than is commonly imagined," we caress dogs but use the word to describe what is most despicable—a "common mark of the last vileness and contempt in every language."[16]

Thus while Goya uses a pair of dogs in *Capricho* 27 as Hogarth does in *Rake's Progress* (plate 5) to mock the human lovers, in the *Tauromaquia* (25) the dogs are present merely to bait the sublime bull, while the man—the bullfighter, on a horse—turns his back. The bull—in Spain, the Spanish people, or revolutionary energy—is the subject; the dogs are only hints or warnings on the sidelines. In England the point is that he is peripheral to his master. While the French Revolution and its supporters were associated by the English with tigers and other Burkean sublime beasts, the bulldog was firmly attached to his master, the English John Bull.[17] As early as the 1720s this breed had been treated in a special way: "Our Forefathers not only reposed an intire Confidence in the Fidelity of these Creatures," writes the Opposition journal, *The Craftsman*, "as *domestick Guardians*, but took them likewise as a Sort of *Companions* Abroad, to Participate with them in their Sports and rural Diversions." *The Craftsman* is attacking the Walpole ministry by referring back to the "generous *English Bull-Dog*" as "that antient genuine Race of *true-bred English Bull-Dogs* . . . excelling in Fight; victorious over their Enemies; undaunted in Death . . . But much I fear that few of *that Race* are now surviving."[18] But his subversive streak is held well under control, and in political cartoons of the late 1720s, contemporary with Hogarth's early conversation pictures, such a dog is shown straining at the leash, trying to get into the fight between those heraldic animals the French cock and the English lion—but he remains peripheral, off to the side, trying to assist the royal symbol.[19]

Sydenham Edwards, in his *Cynographica Britannica* (1800) (the first book in English devoted to dogs since *Of English Dogges*, the 1576 translation of *De Canibus Britannicus* of 1570), argues that the bulldog family has the best claim to being a native English breed—a fighting dog for which "Great Britain has always been famous" (he recalls its role in bull and bear baiting). This was the English dog, in which at the end of the century Edwards summed up English values in the midst of the revolutionary progress of Napoleon, telling how England had been "long eminent for her Dogs and Horses, now preferred in almost every part of the world," due to climate, breeding, education, and maintenance. By this time he is a good friend to man, indeed analogous to the good hearty Englishman of the Hogarthian breed (his subversive streak bleached out):

> The dog may be considered as, not only the intelligent, courageous, and humble companion of man, he is often a true type of his mind and disposition; the hunter's dog rejoices with him in all the pleasures and fatigues of the chace; the ferocious and hardy disposition of the Bull-dog may commonly be traced on the determined brow of his master; nor does the Dog of the blind beggar look up to the passing stranger but with suppliant eyes. [20]

Edwards, however, is referring not only to the staunch Hogarthian bulldog but also to the aristocratic shape of the hunting dog. By 1756 a satiric print shows a pack of dogs—no longer the single companion—barking *"pro Patria non sibi,"* "No French Chicanery," and "No Foreign Intrusion" as they pursue the French fox after their master Tom Steady, the fox hunter at the sign of the Heart of Oak in Antigallican Square. [21]

What has happened by the 1750s is that the pack of hunting dogs has become an English trademark—a pack of hounds each on his own line but all with a common purpose. This was a good symbol for Englishmen, especially aristocrats on a hunt, accompanied by members of the lower orders, who were not, however, allowed to wear the dazzling red hunt costume or go in for the kill. For if we look in vain for a book on dogs between 1576 and 1800, the reason is that the accounts of dogs were confined to books on hunting. To step back and look at the period as social history is to see that the two chief animals (vs. the dog and ape of the iconographical tradition) were the dog and the horse, with the horse far more written about.

There are dozens of books on horses and horse breeding from the 1720s on. If the Spaniards used the bull as their symbol of the forces of nature in travail, the English used the horse (witness Stubbs's great paintings of horses attacked by lions of the 1760s, as well as his monumental *Grosvenor Hunt* of 1763).

The actual importance of the eighteenth-century English dog must be detected from portraits like the one of Sir Robert Walpole (at Houghton), who commissioned the painter to paint him not as M.P. or first lord of the Treasury but as ranger of Richmond Park with his hunting dogs around his feet, a riding whip in his hand, and the hunt proceeding behind him. The hunt was the *locus* in which the horse was for keeping the man above and away from what the dog had to do. The dog, an extension of the man, was for flushing out and bringing the game to bay, the horse for riding after it. The dog was a surrogate for the hunter-as-killer, carrying out the dirty work. The horse was a swift and statuesque mount, a setting, a pedestal for the human hunter. (As the farmers who rode along, in the *Craftsman*'s words, were "a Sort of *Companions* Abroad, to participate with them in their Sports and rural Diversions.")

The hunting breed *par excellence* emerged in the sleek, aristocratic shape of the foxhound, a cross-breeding of the terrier and the bloodhound or southern hound, for both stag and hare were being replaced as beasts of chase by foxes—an animal, like the wolf, known only as a beast of prey before the end of the seventeenth century. Before the 1750s the fox was pursued by the clever, scent-conscious, but relatively slow hare hounds.[22] It was the accomplishment of Hugo Meynell, the Capability Brown of the English hunt, to change fox hunting from a slow, all-day affair to a hunt that allowed gentlemen to go much faster on their horses, sleep later in the morning and get up at noon to hunt, conduct a much shorter hunt, and create a more glamorous self-image. He did this by breeding a fast, reckless hound—another example of English breeding along the line of its famous horses. By the 1770s and '80s, Meynell's fox hunting was in the ascendant, reflecting attitudes like those embodied in Reynolds' portraits, which were developed for the same class of gentlemen. The ideal was based on racing on horseback behind a pack of hounds and observing their speed and flexibility as they tracked the fox; great speed was involved, and some competition as to who would reach the kill first, and not a little danger to the rider.[23]

The ritual was developed, as I have said, by one man, Hugo Meynell, and the process was completed by its formulation on paper by Peter Beckford in *Thoughts on Hunting* (1787), the Hoyle or Miller of hunting, which established the myth of fox hunting and its quintessentially English quality.[24] It could be argued that fox hunting was taken over by the aristocracy from an originally essential activity of the farmer, ridding his land of foxes to save his livestock. But I cite this rather as an example of the aristocratic parallel to the process we shall be following: a new game is invented, then formulated as a paradigm in a book that becomes proverbial. In the process, the aristocratic version of the dog, at least for men, is formulated too.

It is quite a shift from the lapdog and the mumbling spaniel, whose historical nexus was the court and the royal family's many dogs, to the hunting hound. But it is a thoroughly domesticated dog which (in its aristocratic alternative to Hogarth's plebeian pug) is an extension of his master's channeled desires—indeed, as Pope shows in *Windsor Forest*, an acceptable ritualizing of the part of him that loves war and carnage. The pack of hunting dogs appears in literature, quite as distanced as Bounce and Fop are by epistolary conventions, in the dogs that attack Parson Adams and do combat with Joseph Andrews. It is mock-heroic combat; we never get close to them.

Are any real, as opposed to iconographical, dogs represented in eighteenth-century English art? With the hunting dog, we are still within a convention of portraiture, but the painter at least conveys a fact of social history, as the sitter demands his setting—and as hunting changes from stags to fox and the dogs from larger to smaller and faster. But recalling Pope's brother-in-law, who resisted the Black Laws for poaching on the royal preserve of Windsor Forest, we might see a clear social distinction between "His Highness' Dog at Kew" and the "lawed dog" of the forest's inhabitants.[25] A "lawed dog" was one whose three foreclaws had been chopped off to keep him from hunting deer and poaching on the royal preserves (which meant those hunted by Walpole and his associates); inhabitants could keep hunting dogs only if they were "lawed." There are, needless to say, no representations in eighteenth-century art or literature of "lawed dogs."

In *Joseph Andrews*, Mr. Wilson's daughter's spaniel is shot by a young squire, the son of the lord of the manor, who has sworn "he would prosecute the Master of him for keeping a Spaniel"; and the dog, Fielding informs us, "whom his Mistress had taken into her Lap, died in a few Minutes, licking her Hand." The "lawed dog" may be in the background here, but this is a sentimental, conventionalized scene.

Only Hogarth's dogs remain dogs in their suffering. The tormented dog in *The First Stage of Cruelty* (fig. 8) is intended to indicate that Hogarth has seen something of the sort on the streets of St. Giles's Parish.[26] The dog himself is conventional only in that dogs "live a dog's life"—but this is perhaps rather exotic treatment even for the parish of St. Giles. The particular form of cruelty has been derived from a Callot *Temptation of St. Anthony*, where it is done to one of the damned by a demon.[27] The iconographic source may be Hogarth's way of saying this is an infernal scene, and the boy is a demon. The dog's return for revenge or philosophical meditation in *The Reward of Cruelty* (fig. 11) is certainly conventional—once again Jezebel's dog devouring unclean things.[28]

It tells us something about the eighteenth-century Englishman's concept of reality that a dog stood for so many different things. Two aspects he fiercely repressed: the wretchedness of the dog's lot (as opposed to his equivalent, the man's) and the subversiveness of his actions—the aspect of the downtrodden as well as the rebellious. Both of these are concealed under the hearty British bulldog and the pack of sleek foxhounds. Moreover, the dog is always off to one side, at the edge of the picture or to the side of the human figure; or he does not immediately catch the eye. In fact, you often (as in Rowlandson's *Kew Bridge*) detect the disruption and then look for the cause—and then find the detail, the dog.

These were largely unverbalized aspects of man in eighteenth-century England, made safe in the image of a household pet. In other words, "revolutionary" representation did not yet take a straightforward form; it indicated repression, or it sublimated, softened, and evaded unpleasant social facts. Certainly it symbolized and made metaphors which could distance the facts, instead of copying what was plainly to be seen. The dog tells us something about the average Englishman's detachment in metaphors from real social evils—which we can even see in Edmund Burke's dealing with the French Revolution as an aesthetic phenomenon, a theatrical tragedy with Marie Antoinette as heroine. The dog must be regarded as a prerevolutionary symbol, still domestic, engendering violence in small upsets that are far removed from Stubbs's horses and lions and Goya's bulls, even from the official bulldog and foxhound.

The conflict between the perceptual and conceptual dog resolves itself into the official English line taken by the dogs that join the most favorable senses of both: for John Bull, the Hogarthian, plebeian bulldog, and for the aristocracy, the sleek, swift, foxhound. Thus the dogs we have been concerned with reveal something of the unacknowledged underside of eighteenth-century life—the peripheral. The dog is *the* peripheral figure *par excellence* in eighteenth-century English art and literature, perhaps in the English consciousness. Except that he—unlike other peripheral figures, for example the artist in *Beer Street*—while peripheral, acts as catalyst on the crowd or as agent of disruption; the artist is peripheral in that he withdraws from the crowd and the action, unless he is the Hogarthian artist-as-pug who is in the thick of the action. Then he demonstrates how it is precisely the peripheral that supplies the force of energy that changes or disrupts an ordered (or apparently ordered) setting. Once actual revolution takes place, however, or even before, the forces of what is usually called ruling-class society take charge of the dog, and render him totally apolitical by placing him in categories of aesthetic and sympathetic response. Mr. Edwards' old, blind Trusty or Landseer's faithful grave-watcher becomes the model.

The ultimate category, I suppose, was the picturesque, which Gainsborough represents in his *Dogs Fighting* (Kenwood House), where the dogs are observed in combat by an analogous pair of boys. On the model of Hogarth's dual audiences, the boy with the light hair is rooting for the light dog, and the boy with the dark hair is sympathizing with the dark dog. "Among dogs," Uvedale Price informs us in 1794, "the Pomeranian and the rough water dog are more picturesque than the smooth spaniel or greyhound."[29]

I shall conclude this chapter with a passage from Ann Radcliffe's *Mysteries of Udolpho* (1794), where we will hardly recognize the Hogarthian/Rowlandsonian dog, though he is still vestigially present. Emily was sitting in her dead father's study when

> she saw the door slowly open, and a rustling sound in a remote part of the room startled her. Through the dusk she thought she perceived something move. The subject she had been considering, and the present tone of her spirits, which made her imagina-

tion respond to every impression of her senses, gave her a sudden terror of something supernatural. . . . and, distinguishing something moving towards her, and in the next instant press beside her into the chair, she shrieked; but her fleeting senses were instantly recalled, on perceiving that it was [her dog] Manchon who sat by her, and who now licked her hands affectionately.[30]

* * *

As a postscript I should perhaps add that the other figure Hogarth uses to inject life and nature into stuffy systems of social order is the child—the equivalent of the dog moved a step further inside the family. For if the dog is the one animal who is both inside and outside the family, the child is the animal who is totally inside but not yet grown to adult responsibilities. So the child offers eighteenth-century artists from Hogarth to Blake an agent of disruption who is also innocent (as safe as "man's best friend"). In *The Cholmondeley Family* (1732, Marquess of Cholmondeley) the adults sit or stand around a table looking formal, but in the next room, compartmentalized, are the two boys creating havoc. In this case the dog is unnecessary and so lies sound asleep, but often the child and dog cooperate to discomfit or parody the adult activities. In the drinking/carousing scenes where the adults themselves are no longer pretending but falling and knocking over furniture, the child is not needed, and the dog is asleep (e.g., *Midnight Modern Conversation*, Yale Center for British Art). It would seem that the child and the dog can put in question the order of the human/adult world by disrupting it or by mimicking it (like the subculture, dressing up in ruling-class costumes), without in either case really threatening it. In the more precarious time of the French Revolution, Blake's piping and leaping babes, who burst their swaddling bands, are regarded as genuine threats by parents and clergymen, and so are fiercely repressed, transformed into something harmless, indentured as chimneysweeps, or (if sufficiently threatening) burnt at the stake.[31]

6. The Joke and Joe Miller's Jests

THERE IS NO DOUBT that *Joe Miller's Jests* is *the* proverbial English jest-book. First published in 1739, it went through dozens of editions, each adding more jokes, until the original 247 grew by the next century to 1286. We now speak of a joke as a "Joe Miller," not as a "Pinkethman" or a "Peachum," although almost all the jokes in *Joe Miller* were taken from *Pinkethman's Jests* (1720) and *Polly Peachum's Jests* (1728). The reason, I suppose, is that *Joe Miller* chose from earlier jestbooks with the taste of the times and was subsequently able to absorb new jokes, winnowing and arranging a canon of "the English joke." The question is rather why the combined *Pinkethman-Peachum-Miller*, under the name "Miller," happened to produce the canon, why this happened in 1739, and how a "Miller" joke is typical of the mid-eighteenth century. It is, of course, hard to think of a joke being a "Pinkethman." Joe Miller was one of those names, simple but suggestive (like Tom Jones or Joseph Andrews), that was needed before the book could become canonical English. But this raises the further question of whether *Joe Miller's* success was due to timing. It appeared within a year of *Pamela* and three of *Joseph Andrews*, at the threshold of the great period of the English comic novel.

There were two basic forms of jestbook, by which I mean a book containing stories of a few hundred words or less that elicited or included (sometimes terminated in) a laugh.[1] One was the collection of amusing "tales" or moral fables arranged as an anatomy of society and the other was the loosely episodic adventures (or biography) of a practical joker. The earliest jestbooks in English, the *Hundred Merrie Tales* (1526) and *Tales and Quicke Answers* (c. 1535), are examples of the first type. The famous pudding joke (*Hundred Merrie Tales*,

64

no. 68) has a monk delivering a sermon on greed and a pudding falling out of his sleeve, followed by the congregation's uproar that forces him to step down from the pulpit in humiliation, and ends with a moral ("By this tale a man may see that. . ."), which generalizes the application of the hypocrite's discomfiture. The reason I defined a joke as including rather than necessarily terminating in a laugh is that the moment of laughter in the early jestbooks is usually followed by either a moral application or an explanation of the joke.

If a short "tale," a self-exposing gesture, is one kind of jest, a "quick answer" is another. The poet John Skelton, approached by a filthy beggar, exclaims:

> I praye the, gette the away fro me: for thou lokeste as though thou camest out of helle. The poure man, perceyuing he wolde gyue him no thynge, answerd: For soth, syr, ye say trouth, I came oute of helle. Why dyddest thou nat tary styl there, quod mayster Skelton? Mary, syr, quod the beggar, there is no roume for suche poure beggers as I am: all is kepte for suche gentyl men as ye be.[2]

The self-exposure of the greedy monk preaching upon greed has become the contest between the rich, comfortably-off man and the poor, filthy beggar in which the beggar's "quick answer" does the discomfiting. The jest is in this case an encounter between two people, and though it comes from *Tales and Quicke Answers*, it employs the basic structure of the jestbooks that are built around the personality of a single protagonist, usually a comic actor (occasionally a poet known for his humor). There were *Jests of Scoggin* (1563), of *Skelton* (1567), and *Tarlton* (1590), all before 1600. The definitive *Tarlton's Jests* (1611; ed. 1638) is a series of encounters between the actor Richard Tarlton and people representing the traditional areas of court, city, and country (the book is divided correspondingly). The world of *Tarlton's Jests* is hierarchical, progressive, and picaresque. One jest is called "Tarltons Quip for a Young Courtier":

> There was a young Gentleman in the Court, that had first lien with the Mother, and after with the Daughter, and having so done, asked Tarlton what it resembled: quoth he, As if you should first have eaten the Hen, and after the Chicken.

Tarlton is a kind of jester to whom respectable people come for wisdom, and his answers (the jests) are fables or metaphors reflecting folk wisdom. Which is not to say that (like Skelton the poet) he cannot himself be tested and bested when *he* asks a question:

> How Tarlton was deceived by his Wife in London.

> Tarlton, being merrily disposed, as his Wife & he sate together, he said unto her Kate, answer me to one question, without a lye, and take this crown of gold which she took on condition, that if she lost, to restore it back againe. Quoth Tarlton, am I a Cuckold or no, Kate? Whereas she answered not a word, but stood silent: notwithstanding he beged her many wayes. Tarlton feeling she would not speak, askt his gold againe: why, quoth she have I made any lye? no, says Tarlton: why then goodman foole, I have won the wager. Tarlton mad with anger, made this Rime,

>> As women in speech can revile a man;
>> So can they in silence beguile a man.

Even when bested, Tarlton has the last word, like the narrator of the pudding joke, uttering a moral that places or holds in check the energy of the witty wife. This is a joke structure of which we have not seen the last.

The watershed for English jestbooks, as for much else, was the Civil War. The old forms persisted in books like *Coffee-House Jests* (1688, 1733, etc.), whose title gives its historical nexus and organizing principle for a series of practical jokes and tales of filthy cooks and numbskull servants. By contrast, *The Tales and Jests of Mr. Hugh Peters* (1660) transforms the jestbook into a Stuart political tract, virtually a criminal biography, beginning with a narrative of the regicide's wicked life, followed by his jests at the expense of Charles I and other authority figures, and ending with his well-deserved execution at the return of Charles II. This is not far removed from the use of popular forms—almanacs, proposals, "advice to servants"—by Jonathan Swift and his friends. Another high-art phenomenon that intervened was, of course, the stage comedy of Etherege and Congreve with its verbal wit at the expense of every social pretension.

Joe Miller's Jests professes to be sophistications and updatings of the Skelton-type agon, containing (the title page tells us) "the most Brilliant Jests; the Politest Repartees; the most Elegant Bons Mots." Although of the actor-protagonist type, *Miller's* eponymous hero is merely a repository or witness of miscellaneous jokes. Except in three instances, the jests are not about (do not even refer to) Joe Miller. Their source, the title page tells us, is oral; they were "collected in the Company, and many of them transcribed from the Mouth of the facetious Gentleman," Joe Miller, though gathered and edited by one Elijah Jenkins. "Jenkins," however, was a pseudonymn for a hack dramatist named John Mottley, who actually gathered the jests with no help from the actor Joe Miller, who had died the year before.

The particular actor Joe Miller was perhaps relevant. It was part of the Miller myth that he "was, when living, himself a jest for dulness." Though a good impersonator of comic roles, in private life he was never known to laugh, and was famous for his "imperturbable gravity, whenever any risible saying was recounted."[3] Swift, we recall, is supposed to have laughed only twice in his lifetime, and Lord Chesterfield, who said of himself, "since I have had the full use of my reason, nobody has ever heard me laugh," advised his son "never [to be] heard to laugh while you live."[4] Joe Miller's name—or the reputation that was "found" for him—presumably indicated something about the manner in which jests were properly—that is, by gentlemen—or most amusingly told.[5]

The claim for an oral source for *Joe Miller's Jests* was, of course, quite unfounded. When the *Jests* had proved a success, Mottley admitted to its authorship and added that the collection was "made by him from other books, and a great part of it supplied by his memory from original stories collected in his former conversations."[6] What this shifty sentence does not quite admit is that virtually all the jokes were taken from printed sources, with very few exceptions from *Pinkethman's Jests* and *Polly Peachum's Jests*.[7] Mottley was a plagiarist or, at best, a compiler with no direct access to oral tradition.

His sources were, however, in large part modern and English. *Pinkethman* and *Peachum* were among the earliest surviving repositories of the new joke material that bubbled up after the Restoration. What distinguishes these jokes—even when they are modernizations of earlier ones, as is not infrequently the case—is the increasing concision of the combat, no longer either "tale" or fable and no longer moralized. The dependence on word play points to a native English stock of jests (there is a whole section on puns in *Pinkethman*).[8] And the topicality is insistent, and persistent, in a way it was not before. James Osborn formulated what he called "Joe Miller's Law," "that a good name (of a well-known personality, living or dead) tends to replace a less-known one." For example, the well-known story (no. 20) attributed to Colley Cibber as a retort to the duke of Wharton in the 1739 edition later is attributed to John Wilkes and the earl of Sandwich.[9] This is quite true, but the principle of reference throughout all the editions of *Miller* remains stable, linking a Cibber or Wilkes and a Wharton or Sandwich to Cromwell and Charles I. The Civil War is a topic that Miller–Mottley play down somewhat in the 1739 edition, but which returns in later editions and persists into the nineteenth century as a standard field of reference.

I have been unable to discover any principle of political censorship behind the omissions and rearrangements in the various editions of *Joe Miller*, even during the 1790s, except for the gradual expurgation of all sexual jokes by the 1836 edition.[10] On the other hand, there is no doubt that one of the basic, most prevalent jokes is based on the folk realization that under his dress and manners the great man is no different. The *Miller* jests—and this may be one reason for their survival—are sometimes safer, less witty versions of the jokes in *Peachum* and *Pinkethman*. *Miller*, no. 153 (omitted by the end of the century), has a gentleman say "of a young Wench, who constantly ply'd about the Temple, that if she had as much Law in her Head, as she had in her Tail, she would be one of the ablest Counsel in England." *Pinkethman* (p. 102) gives the unexpurgated version: "One seeing a kept whore, who made a very great figure, asked what Estate she had. Oh says an other, a very good Estate in TAIL." That is, her "estate" or fortune lies in her sexual equipment; and she has a life interest (through the gift of her lover) in an estate that will pass to its rightful heir when she is finished with it. Not the sexual but the political or social dimension of the joke is repressed in *Miller*.

The most subversive jokes in *Joe Miller* are attributed "backward," to a safe ancient, as Juvenal tells us he is forced to take the names of his objects of satire from the Roman graveyard. Many *Miller* jokes remain old and serviceable and (one of the reasons for their success) comfortable. No. 103 has a long history, is repeated in many later jestbooks, and ultimately was analyzed by Sigmund Freud:[11]

> The Emperor *Augustus*, being shewn a young *Grecian*, who very much resembled him, asked the young Man if his *Mother* had not been at *Rome*: No, Sir, answer'd the *Grecian*, but my *Father* has.

This joke is not attributed, as we might expect by "Joe Miller's Law," to George I, or even Charles II. When a king is mentioned in any subversive context, Charles or George becomes Alexander or Augustus. And when a contemporary king is mentioned and bested, the event is hedged by his generous response:

> George the First, on a Journey to Hanover, stopped at a village in Holland, and while the horses were getting ready, he asked for two or three eggs, which were brought him, and charged two hundred florins. How is this? said his majesty, eggs must be very scarce in this place. Pardon me, said the host, eggs are plenty enough, but kings are scarce. The king smiled, and ordered the money to be paid. [12]

The king always smiles and is a good sport. The structure remains a contest between unequal combatants, and the weak one wins by his riposte which exposes the weakness of the strong one. The ending covers the effect by allowing the king to absorb the subversion into a resolution of good feeling.

Freud used his version of the Augustus joke (he calls him Serenissimus) as an example of the "unification that lies at the bottom of jokes," a case of repartee, of "the defence going to meet the aggression, in 'turning the tables on someone' or 'paying someone back in his own coin'—that is, in establishing an unexpected unity between attack and counter-attack."[13] But, as he also notices (about the *Schadchen* or marriage-broker jokes): "Is it not rather the case that the jokes only put forward the marriage-brokers in order to strike at something more important? Is it not a case of saying one thing and meaning another?" (p. 105). The joke falls on the parents or on marriages contracted on such a basis, rather than on the broker who is ostensibly or centrally the subject—ultimately, Freud suggests, on the whole institution of marriage—or, in the joke about the royal personage (Augustus or Serenissimus), on the current king or on vested authority. Freud extricates from such jokes that have long been enshrined in jestbooks something of their original explosive nature, and of course he tries to reconstruct the original oral/aural situation. I am in the process of showing how the act of jestbook compilation serves to mystify, domesticate, and defuse jokes, but at the same time, by a kind of displacement or slippage that is in the very nature of jokes, leaves the reader uneasily aware of its true tendency.

Joke or jest, in other words, can be opposed to jestbook. What
the signboard is to the visual experience of an immediate environment, the joke is to the aural; and the situation in the eighteenth
century is one in which society suppresses by taking down signboards
and, with jokes, by making laughter a class response. As Chesterfield
explains to his son, laughter "is the manner in which the mob expresses their silly joy, at silly things." It is "the disagreeable noise"
and "the shocking distortion of the face" brought about by the response to a joke that Chesterfield associates with the lower orders (the
higher are "above" it). "True wit, or sense, never yet made any body
laugh; they are above it; they please the mind, and give a cheerful-
ness to the countenance."[14] A "Joe Miller" (or Mottley) then sets out
to raise a joke into verbal wit as it displaces the immediate presence
of the oral/aural action to the remote simulacrum of print in a book
that can be picked up or put down (or perhaps used as evidence in
court). It reduces them to a written canon and mixes or adulterates
them with the written tradition of *facetiae* and epigrams, of Restoration comedies and picaresque tales.[15]

As Chesterfield shows by opposing "wit" to "joke," the next
stage is for a critic to publish a book that imposes formulations on the
jokes to make them pass for wit. In 1744, five years (and four editions) after the publication of *Joe Miller's Jests*—and two years after
Joseph Andrews and four before Chesterfield's letter admonishing his
son not to laugh—there appeared a pamphlet by Corbyn Morris
called *An Essay towards Fixing the True Standards of Wit, Humour,
Raillery, Satire, and Ridicule.* Morris defines "wit" but his examples
are from jestbooks (all eventually appeared in *Miller*). The quality of
jestbook jokes to which he draws attention is their brevity, epigrammatic quality, and conversational polish. He tells us over and over:
Wit results "solely from the *quick Elucidation* of one Subject, by the
sudden *Arrangement*, and *Comparison* of it, with another Subject."
The essential is "to *enlighten* thereby the *original* subject." For, he
continues, "the only Foundation upon which the *new Subject* is
suddenly introduced, is the *Affinity*, and consequently the *Illustration*, it bears to the *first* Subject." "Humour," on the other hand,
depends on its being "in real life"—"*any* whimsical Oddity *or* Foible,
appearing in the Temper *or* Conduct *of a* Person *in real* Life"—
whereas "Wit appears in *Comparisons*, either between *Persons* in real

life, or between *other Subjects*."[16] As his examples will show, Morris cannot separate these two categories—one formal, the other referential—but he demonstrates that wit lies in something a jokester does to a situation, or sees lying in a situation. Parson Adams is humorous, but Henry Fielding is witty. Nature itself is probably humorous, but a witty intelligence—a Joe Miller or Henry Fielding or Corbyn Morris—can reveal how nature operates according to the laws of wit.

Morris' first three examples have in common the subject of a ruler who in each case makes an aggressive statement—like the emperor Augustus—and is put down. He clearly takes these to be typical jests:

> [1] *Henry* the IVth of *France*, intimating to the *Spanish* Ambassador the Rapidity, with which he was able to over-run *Italy*, told him, that *if once he mounted on Horseback, he should breakfast at* Milan *and dine at* Naples; to which the Ambassador added, *Since your Majesty travels at this rate, you may be at Vespers* in Sicily.[17]

The reference is to the Sicilian Vespers, when the French garrison was massacred by the natives—"a *similar* Occasion, when they formerly over-ran Sicily." "The sudden Introduction and *Arrangement* of this Catastrophe," says Morris, "with the Expedition then threaten'd, sets the Issue of such a Conquest in a new *Light*; And very happily exhibits and *elucidates* the Result of such vain and restless Adventures." And moreover, he adds, "there sits couched under the Wit, a very *severe Rebuke* upon the *French* Monarch."

(2) The second jest has Pope Alexander VI ask the Venetian ambassador "of whom his Masters held their Customs and Prerogatives of the Sea? To which the Ambassador readily answer'd; *If your* Holiness *will only please to examine your Charter of St.* Peter's *Patrimony, you will find upon the Back of it, the Grant made to the* Venetians *of the* Adriatic." The sudden illuminating juxtaposition is of the authority of Venetians and the pope, which the ambassador elucidates "to the *Pope*," and so "besides the Wit which shines forth," Morris tells us, "the *Pope* is severely expos'd to your *Raillery*, from the Scrape into which he has brought the *Charter* of *St. Peter's* Patrimony, by his Attack on the *Ambassador*." In other words, an aggressive act has elicited an appropriately severe one in return. But above all, he adds: "The *fictitious* Existence of both the *Charter* and

the *Grant* [is] being sarcastically pointed out, under this respectable
Air of *Authenticity.*"

(3) The poet Edmund Waller is the protagonist of the third jest.
He presents congratulatory verses to Charles II on his Restoration;
reading them, Charles responds peevishly: *"Mr.* Waller, *these are
very good, but not so fine as you made upon the* PROTECTOR.—To
which Mr. *Waller* return'd,—*Your Majesty will please to recollect,
that we Poets always write best upon* FICTIONS.*"

The original subject, Morris explains, is the superiority of
Waller's verses on Cromwell; "This he most happily excuses, by
starting at once, and *arranging* along with them, the Remark, that
Poets have always excell'd upon Fiction; whereby he unexpectedly
exhibits his *more excellent* Verses to *Cromwell,* as a plain *Elucidation*
of the *fictitious* Glory of the Protector; And intimates at the same
time, that the *Inferiority* of his present Performance was a natural
Illustration of his Majesty's *real* Glory."

But suppose, reading this joke parallel with the two that preceded it, as one must in Morris' ordering of them, that the original
subject is the restoration or authenticity of Charles II as ruler; then
the auxiliary subject, Cromwell's authenticity or lack of it, establishes
(to use Morris' words explaining the previous joke) "the *fictitious*
Existence of both." Even if the real versus fictitious character of
Charles's kingship is the point, the fiction of the one is going, in a
joke like this, to rub off on the other. Moreover, it is interesting to
note that Morris could have told the story of Waller/Charles as it
appears in *Joe Miller* (1836 ed., no. 364), where Waller replies,
"That may very well be, . . . for poets generally succeed better in
imaginary things, than in real ones"—where the idea of fictitious,
carried over from the pope's forged document, is avoided.

The final joke is quite different—about Leonidas' cheerful gallantry in the face of the Persian army at Thermopylae. This connects
with the end of the Waller joke as a compliment to Charles II, and it
suggests to me that Morris was not consciously arranging his jokes,
and himself saw no connection between the first two and the third. I
take it to mean rather that there is a subversive tendency in the joke
per se, which means that a primary meaning is subverted by a secondary one: first the king's or pope's, and second the apparent point of
the jester himself. Morris is formulating the very volatile matter of
the joke much as Pope and Fielding did the energy of the dunces,

without total success or (at least in his case) total awareness of the pattern that self-generates outside his conscious intention. His dedication of his essay to Sir Robert Walpole is only the most amusing evidence of his attempt to make intractable matter fit into formulations: here the formulation of a dedication, but in a book devoted to the subjects of irony and wit. [18]

He tries to keep a strong grip on the tendentious joke to prevent it from erupting in local English (as opposed to papal or French) irreverence. He neutralizes one jest by arguing that it is merely a pun, defined as a meaningless play on words, sound without matching sense. A pun, he says (vs. wit), shifts attention to an *un*related subject:

> A PEER coming out of the House of Lords, and wanting his Servant called out, *Where's my Fellow?* To which another PEER, who stood by him, returned, *Faith, my Lord, not in* England. [p. 12]

The wit, I suspect, lies in the intermediate term "peer" between the two senses of "fellow." The significant fact, which Morris avoids, is that the subject is a peer. [19] In short, this subversive form—representing *some* sub- or counterculture—is taken in off the stage or the street corner and covered up by being put in print, and even further by being explained by the eminently respectable critic Corbyn Morris in a treatise dedicated to the prime minister himself. But its origins in a subculture keep reasserting themselves.

Censorship seems to have been built into the very structure of jestbooks. *Pinkethman, Peachum,* and *Miller* all recall the common jestbook use of the actor-protagonist who undertakes joke making as he does role playing, and who is therefore not quite responsible for the role or the joke assigned him. It is worth remarking that 109 of the jokes in *Joe Miller* are taken from *Polly Peachum's Jests* (containing a total of 119), for this was a book launched on the tide of Gay's *Beggar's Opera,* with its subversive reputation, which led to Walpole's suppression of its sequel *Polly* in December 1728. Polly, in effect, bursts out instead in her jestbook: but "subsides" would be a more accurate word. *Miller* begins with a series of these *Peachum* jests, about performances of *The Beggar's Opera* and about playhouses. Gay's play is now only the occasion for an exchange between the duke of Argyll and Colley Cibber, at the expense of Cibber (the

actor). Corbyn Morris's statement about the danger of plays (justify-
ing Walpole's censorship in the Licensing Act of 1737) makes the
case for the power of the oral/visual tradition:

> For these profligate Attacks [on Walpole] made Impressions
> more deep and venomous than Writings; As they were not fairly
> addressed to the Judgment, but immediately to the Sight and
> the Passions [p. x].

The visual and the aural were naturally, for a variety of reasons,
modified and softened when reduced to the printed page. Despite the
fact that most of the jests in *Joe Miller* had been in print a decade
earlier, we might not be altogether wrong to see a parallel between
Mottley's playwright career coming to a stop in 1737 with Walpole's
Licensing Act and, two years later, publishing *Joe Miller's Jests*, and
Fielding's move, allegedly for the same reason, from playwrighting to
journalism in 1738 and to novel writing in the 1740s. Both Mottley
and Fielding were filling a public need that was no longer being
satisfied in the old way.

But how did Mottley satisfy it? That first sequence in *Miller*
moves from Argyll versus Cibber to a punning repartee of the actor
Robert Wilks to an account of how a commissioner of the Revenue
(N.B.: of Ireland, not England, and in a Dublin theater) is retorted to
by an orange girl he is handling: "Nay, Mr. Commissioner, said she,
you'll find no Goods there but what have been fairly entered." This is
followed by one of the three *Joe Miller* jokes, a pun on soles/souls,
and this by the repartee between the duke of Ormand and Lady
Dorchester concerning that lady's breaking wind in public.

The jokes stand out less as jokes than as a sequence that plays
upon transitions and juxtapositions, of the sort unconsciously employed by Morris. No. 64 is a joke by the court fool Tom Killigrew,
not on Charles II but on his subjects: he gives Charles a coat with
one large and one small pocket and tells him "one Pocket was for the
Addresses of his Majesty's Subjects, the other for the *Money* they
would give him"—a joke with perhaps some wry memories of the
king's father's experiences raising money from Parliament. No. 65,
however, is about "My Lord B——e":

> My Lord B——e, had married three Wives that were all his
> Servants, a Beggar-Woman meeting him one Day in the Street,
> made him a very low Curtsey, Ah, God Almighty bless your

Lordship, said she, and send you a long Life, if you do but live long enough, we shall be all *Ladies* in Time.

This sounds like a safe displacement of a joke about Charles II. As in Morris' "wit," the juxtaposition of these two jokes brings together one subject, Charles II, with another for purposes of elucidation. There are also jokes that link Thomas More and Algernon Sidney, men who refused to obey their kings and lost their heads, juxtaposed with jokes about kings who have lost or regained a throne.[20] No. 103, the anti-Augustus joke, is followed by 104, a pro-Cato joke. There are jokes on kings' favorites and other surrogates, and Charles I and Cromwell rub shoulders with Colley Cibber and Jack Ogle, the duke of Ormond with Joe Miller himself, kings and bishops with actors, beggars, and whores. The stronger but parallel formulations of this sort appear in *The Beggar's Opera* and Fielding's *Tom Thumb* and *Jonathan Wilde* (publ. 1730, 1743). But it was also the calendar festivals of these dead kings and their opponents, who could arouse by their names automatic political responses, that were the occasion for Tory and Whig clashes through the 1730s.

We all remember the joke teller's "That reminds me of a story. . ." In many jokes, and especially in jestbooks, the meaning is often not so much in the joke itself—whose meaning may be repressed—as in the transitions between jokes. Threat (or Freud's *tendenz*) has been displaced, in typical eighteenth-century fashion, from the center to the peripheral function of connection and relationship.

Let us take three nonpolitical jokes—*Miller*, nos. 106, 107, and 108, two of them about watches and the third about a pen.[21] In 107 a woman wears a watch that hangs *en chatelaine* over her pubis, and when a man asks her the time she tells him "her Watch stood" (i.e., has stopped). "I don't wonder at that, Madam, said he, when it is so near your ———." No. 106 is about a man having his watch stolen in church, a joke that elicits this wisdom from a bystander:

> He that a Watch will wear, this must he do,
> Pocket his Watch, and watch his Pocket too.

This formulation not only refers to watches stolen as another form of "stoppage," but contains a repressed version of the jokes (e.g., the Scotsman who cut the pockets out of his son's pants so he wouldn't have to buy him any toys) that equate hands in pockets with masturbation—which remains innocent until it is connected with no. 107, the next joke, where "watch stood" means an erection, but also, in terms of the watch itself stopping, the fear of impotence. This subject becomes explicit in 108, which is about the modest wife who, in order to show the court why she wants to divorce her husband, undertakes to write it:

> Whereupon she took the Pen without dipping it into the Ink, and made as if she would write; says the Clerk to her, Madam, there is no Ink in your Pen. *Truly, Sir, says she, that's just my Case, and therefore I need not explain myself any further.* [22]

The metaphor of the inkless pen that will not write supplies the common denominator of the other two jokes about stopped or stolen watches, and may suggest that the real subject is the fear of impotence. It also, of course, says that writing as a substitute for showing is itself capable of being a kind of showing; that one should look at as well as read the writing.

One conclusion we might draw at this point is that while the printing of jokes in jestbooks tends to be a conservative strategy, a pulling of their teeth, it appears ironically that the words and sentences in bald print actually reveal subversive implications which in some cases may not have been evident in the original version. Such slippages and fissures may be in the nature of printed language—of what has come to be called textuality—and the joke in a series of jokes merely offers the most alarming potentialities.

Another conclusion to draw from this particular sequence is that popular humor, in one aspect at least, is stoic rather than protesting. It is a way to come to terms with reality or to secure some sort of control over the hostile environment, along the line of gin drinking, gambling, and magic. "The folktale or joke therefore represents a protective mechanism whereby the seriousness, and even the physical *reality*, of the situation can be defined and made light of, by telling it . . . simply as a joke." [23] The joke then separates into central and peripheral, essential and accidental elements. The accidental includes not only the topical names inserted according to Osborn's Law but perhaps also the particular "punch line"—in the eighteenth century the verbal wit. The lasting, unchanging part of the joke, that which grips both teller and listener, is deep within the body of the joke—a basic situation of cuckoldry, seduction, impotence, castration, disease, and death, which are closely related, as common metaphorical equivalents, to political oppression and poverty. [24]

Go back to the example of the ancient pudding joke. Instead of a punch line, there was in those days the moral tag about the hypocrite's discomfiture. But the center of the joke was not so much the priest's hypocrisy as the pudding (a blood sausage), obtruding from under his robe to break the sexual repression which was at the heart of monasticism. Presumably, the scribe or printer added the moral; but various alternative explanations are possible. One is that the presentable moral is necessary for *any* joke that is subversive to one's own psyche as well as to society in general. Another is that the moral counsel or wisdom—the useful—is always the essential, nuclear element of the folk tale.[25] "Wisdom," however, in this case has to be divided into folk wisdom, which may be pretty subversive or terrifying in itself, and official wisdom which the scribe adds to return the sub- or counterculture wisdom to the fold and subordinate it to some useful social function.

It is the transmission of official wisdom which we have seen superimposed in one way or another on the actual fact of the agon or put-down, the challenge or at least explosion of feeling of a lower at a higher, a have-not at a have, an apprentice at a master. Jests about things done are transmuted into jests about things said, and thence into jests in which the epigrammatic quality turns upon itself. In the eighteenth century, with the authority of the Popean couplet and *The Spectator's* antitheses, the "quick answer" pushes toward maximum closure, a strong termination which focuses the content so sharply that it seems to have existed for nothing else. The closure returns the joke to the social fold, draws attention away from the problematic center, releases tension in a laugh, ultimately removes responsibility from society to a larger providential and generalizing pattern by way of the attached "moral." This kind of jest may also show an individual (a Tarlton or an Alexander Pope) coping with experiences or problems, giving moral formulations to others, putting in his last word. The latter can be subversive, but it can also be—as we saw in Tarlton's response to his wife—official wisdom, which domesticates the rebellious act. The husband–wife quarrel injects a subversion of the subverter, the comedy of which is partly Tarlton's attempt to absorb it, as he turns himself into the type he usually sees from the outside. The joke is about the joker's effort to come to terms with experience, perhaps only by turning facts into jokes or moral tags.

The process is visible at its most majestic in the ultimate jestbook (with some of the jestbook's audience still clinging to it), Boswell's *Life of Johnson* (1791). The basic structure is the Johnsonian exchange, where Johnson (like, for example, Tarlton) is asked a question ("Sir, what think you of . . . ?") and utters a strong answer, usually a put-down of the questioner or someone else present, often of the questioner-editor Boswell. The analogy, of course, extends to Boswell's role as compiler and author of the jests. When he puts them in print he cleans them up (as a comparison with his journals shows) and gives himself the last word in a way he never did, or could have done, in life. Ogilvie the Scotsman observes "that Scotland had a great many noble wild prospects." *Johnson*: "I believe, Sir, you have a great many. . . . But, sir, let me tell you, the noblest prospect which a Scotchman ever sees, is the high road that leads him to England!" (Johnson's joke is, of course, to play upon different senses of "prospect.") To this Boswell adds: "This unexpected and pointed sally produced a roar of applause. After all, however, those who admire the rude grandeur of Nature, cannot deny it to Caledonia."[26] Boswell demonstrates the power of the writer-editor-printer over the spoken and the experienced, while at the same time revealing—what we have noticed as well in the jestbooks—his discomfiture, for we see through him (as he probably meant us to) and he becomes himself part of the joke.

At a less majestic level, in *Wilkes' Jest Book; or the Merry Patriot* (1770) the energy and force of John Wilkes, the public hero-villain and Lord of Misrule, are transmogrified into anecdotes hinging on witty word play. The jests do not depict subversive actions such as making court officials toast "Wilkes and Liberty" but consist mainly of flattering personal stories that label him a subculture hero, without the deeds of a Jack Sheppard or Macheath. For example, a young man is recommended as a prospective suitor to a young lady: "Nothing could be found fault with except a cast in one of his eyes. 'O! said the lady, that's the *emblem of Liberty*, and therefore the *highest recommendation* he can possibly have" (p. 16). The number 45 (for *North Briton* No. 45) is played upon with such questions as just how many times would Wilkes have to be elected M.P. for Middlesex before being admitted to Parliament? (Answer: 45 times.) It is noted that the long beginning "'Tis Liberty alone that gives fresh beauty to the Sun," by Handel has forty-five bars, and that supporters should "sing to the praise and glory of *Wilkes and Liberty*" with Psalm 45 (pp. 190–200). The fact is recorded that no one has benefited so much by Wilkes "as tavern-keepers and publicans; for whenever any prosperous event happened to him, their customers got merry for *Joy*;—and when ever it happened otherwise, they have got drunk thro' *Vexation*" (pp. 6–7).

Wilkes's squint, the number 45, and inebriation (to celebrate or bemoan him) are contingencies or peripheralities that are used to symbolize a central concept, "Wilkes and Liberty"—or perhaps "Wilkes and Liberty" is also peripheral (for the same reason) to some unsaid central idea of antiroyal prerogative or antigovernment.[27] In any case, there is a self-censoring action, a displacement by Wilkes's supporters (or possibly by a publisher) from the dangerous to something ordinary and thinkable like Wilkes's squint.

Both society and the individual, by putting barriers of sophistication between themselves and an initial physical encounter (a joke), order what has come to be a disreputable drive in need of an outlet. But at the same time artists like Hogarth are trying to recapture and make use of the basic experiences of signboards and jokes as nuclear structures. When we find a Hogarth print based on a *Miller* joke, therefore, we should look closely to see what has happened. *The Second Stage of Cruelty* (fig. 9) is based on *Miller*, no. 8:

> An Hackney-Coachman, who was just set up, had heard that the Lawyers used to club their *Three-Pence* a-piece, four of them, to go to *Westminster*, and being call'd by a Lawyer at *Temple-Bar*, who, with two others in their Gowns, got into his Coach, he was bid to drive to *Westminster-Hall*; but the Coachman still holding his Door open, as if he waited for more Company; one of the Gentlemen asked him, why he did not shut the Door and go on, the Fellow, scratching his Head, cry'd you know, Master, my Fare's a Shilling, I can't go for *Nine-Pence*.

The joke balances the coachman's wit (or simplicity) against the stingy lawyers; Hogarth's print, in which the sign "Thavies Inn" indicates the farthest stage from Westminster for a one-shilling fare, exposes the dying horse, who has collapsed under the weight of the barristers and is being beaten to death by the coachman.[28] He has in effect deconstructed *Miller's* joke, laying open its repressed center. In other prints, the wit that appears to be decorative and peripheral serves to draw attention to the print's own hidden, repressed center. For Hogarth's prints have a *modus operandi* related to the joke, at least as Freud explained its basis in the pun with the joker "disregarding the meaning intended by the questioner and catching onto a subsidiary meaning."[29] But the subsidiary meaning is the core.

Hogarth is exceptional. In general, it was *Joe Miller's Jests*, and not the Hogarthian print, that proved paradigmatic. The verbal agon has itself become a formulation, and the joke has shifted from the real agon at the center of the joke to the appearance of one at the end. The joke has picked up too much literary baggage. With the punch line as formulation, it moves toward the even more literary status of comedy, of resolution and feasting which absorb all the alien forces into one happy family. (The jest of course shares with comedy the use of a slave or servant, a subculture figure, often a student or a youth—a young lover or an apprentice—who does the undermining, while the handsome young master gets the girl.) One hears the lines of Restoration comedy in these jests, which have become so well tailored that they may draw our attention to qualities at the center of society itself, of the polite culture.

By the end of Morris' *Essay* the sharp interchange, or "wit" (his refined way of referring to verbal mayhem), has become a way of seeing and coming to terms with the world, of "illuminating" subjects—and so we notice the kinds of subjects repeatedly illuminated by *Miller*. One of the three stories that introduce Joe Miller himself is no. 78, lifted from *Peachum* (no. 50), which goes as follows:

> Not much unlike this story is one I heard from a midshipman of his being in a violent storm, when everybody went to prayers but one man, whom they spoke to exhorting him to pray. Not I, said he, 'tis your business to take care of the ship. I am but a passenger.

Mottley uses almost the exact words, but he begins thus: "Not much unlike this Story is one told me by a Midshipman one Night, in Company with *Joe Miller* and myself, who said that. . ." Aside from the new concern with authority and *vraisemblance*, we note the progression from Tarlton the oracle, of whom people asked questions, to "Miller" the comedian, who listens to the story told by the midshipman, which, however, is actually told to "Elijah Jenkins" (pseudonymn of Mottley). Mottley is careful to establish and place his point of view. "I am but a passenger" would apply equally to himself, and to each of these people, maintaining his own narrow strip of responsibility.

If I had to pick one paradigmatic joke from *Joe Miller* it would be no. 118, which makes the same point:

A melting Sermon being preached in a country Church, all fell a weeping but one Man, who being asked, why he did not weep with the rest? O! said he, *I belong to another Parish.*

In this joke (taken from *Pinkethman*, p. 26) the pathos will later be increased by making it a country church*yard* with a burial service, and again, much later, a ladies' club in New Jersey where a guest speaker reviews a tear-jerker novel. Everyone weeps but one woman, and after the lecture the reviewer asks her why she was dry-eyed: "Oh, I'm not a member," she explains.[30]

This joke could illustrate equally Chesterfield's distancing of the body (by one who wants to feel superior to her surroundings) and Adam Smith's doctrine of the sympathies (she is too far from home); or it could serve as a parallel to Defoe's *Family Instructor* and other conduct books that aimed at showing apprentices, servants, and merchants how to make the proper moral/prudential choices that will keep them secure where they are; or to the new etiquette books, the germ of which was already in Defoe's and the apotheosis in *Pamela*, that taught the middle class how to rise, how to behave in unaccustomed social situations, how to write letters of condolence or invitation that will pass for educated and polite. *Miller* expresses precisely the tension between the two desires for security and mobility.

Both passenger and parishioner are caught up in the most limited social identities; we would seem to be dealing with a time when a person associates (or is thought to associate) himself with a series of discrete identities (say apprentice and then master) in society, in imagination, in love, or in war, and justifies his behavior—and is determined in his behavior—by this alone. The jokes indicate a nucleus of role consciousness comparable to Mottley's as collector and to the "imperturbable gravity" with which Joe Miller supposedly told or participated in these jokes as Miller the coffee-house habitué, distinct from Miller the actor in one of his famous stage roles. It is in this general sense that *Joe Miller's Jests* prepares us for the gravity with which Fielding tells us in *Joseph Andrews* about the passion of Lady Booby, which is itself related to the situation in which both she and Joseph fumble on the same bed, saying to each other, in effect, "I belong to another Parish" and "I am but a passenger." The re-

pressed center of *Miller's* jokes, as of Lady Booby's high-flown protestations of disinterest, is exposed to be the situation of the motherly
woman (the master's widow) and the handsome young apprentice on
a bed.

This deep anxiety about one's personal boundaries is behind the
need we have seen for the joke—the spoken or acted, the existential
gesture: Joseph and Lady Booby in a situation of sexual play; to be
surrounded, padded, muffled, or framed, as Fielding does with his
narration, or his characters' rhetoric, and even did with his scenes on
the stage, where he introduced "critics" and "producers" who tried to
interpret their words and actions, but in fact added encrustations of
their own—always as if afraid to let them stand by and for themselves.
Fielding dramatizes a self-censorship which is a self-irony and becomes the subject itself of comedy. The lead container must always be
included as well as the volatile substance; and this is the joke. In the
Fielding novel there is a nominal hero, but also an author on whom
everything in fact depends (for safety's sake), who establishes the complex interactions of different social identities. These identities take the
particular form of the respectable citizen versus the outrageous outsider, the guardian of the book versus those who act according to some
prior, some natural or animal principle. The censor is opposed to the
subversive young man with (apparent) lower-class origins who has to
make his peace with the censor within the novel and his author without (both of them lead containers trying to contain his volatility), and
does so through the parallel domestication earned by his social experiences and his sympathetic accompaniment of his creator, companion,
and mentor the author. For, as in the *Miller* joke, the movement
through time of the socially suspect hero is subordinated to the witty
consciousness that arranges the juxtapositions, the transitions, and the
"quick Elucidation of one Subject, by the sudden Arrangement, and
Comparison of it, with another Subject," which was Morris' definition
of the joke's experience.

As a jestbook, *Joe Miller* is refined into *Sir John Fielding's Jests*
(c. 1780)—not, note, Henry but his brother John, a magistrate, a
blind man who is never a participant in the ordinary sense but is a
keen "observer" or "spectator" from the legal bench and from the
tavern bench. Sir John is not a jester or court fool with partial license
nor an actor but an official who, though blind, comes into contact
with, or hears stories about, litigants, criminals, lawyers, politicans,

and courtiers. This is not a remote outsider but a man at the center of society—a figure created by John's brother, employed by him in his novels, but given a distinctly muffled quality now by his blindness, who acts as society's superego. (Samuel Johnson should, of course, like Sir John, have been the center of consciousness and authority in his jestbook. But it is the flighty, undependable Boswell, whose domestications are in every case his own and not society's.)[31]

There was one other tradition of the jestbook in the later eighteenth century. As *Joseph Andrews* was followed by Smollett's *Roderick Random* (1747), *Joe Miller's Jests* was followed by *retardataire* picaresque compilations like *Quin's Jests* (1766). The actor Quin opens with an introduction attacking the Joe Miller type of jestbook—"compilations from compilations"—and claims that this one is authentic, original, and true, drawn from Quin's own experiences. The result is Morris' "humour" rather than "wit," for the book consists of short (or not so short) narratives and anecdotes of Quin's adventures, practical jokes, and wisdom. The book ends with anecdotes about his dying, and with verses on his death and an epitaph, followed by a selection of his verses. Quin's jokes, which only occasionally qualify as *Miller* jokes, are closer to *Coffee-House Jests* (1688, 1733, etc.) in which there is no combat of higher/lower, no witty repartee, only misunderstandings based on the stupidity of one party. *Coffee-House Jests* was a collection which Mottley could have plagiarized as well as *Pinkethman* and *Peachum*, but he did not. Many of the stories (e.g., the filthy cook stories) could be joined with Quin's practical jokes to make a narrative roughly resembling *Roderick Random*. In the lineage of *Til Eulenspiegel's Pranks* (the English *Howleglas*, 1528?) and the picaresque jestbooks, often involving acts of physical violence, the novels of Smollett are probably truer survivals than any of the eighteenth-century jestbooks.[32]

*   *   *

The reader may wonder how Pope's *Dunciad* relates to these generalizations about jestbooks. *The Dunciad* is in a sense about a subculture, for hack writers certainly made up one.[33] These hacks, however, were characterized by their pretension toward high culture—toward the emulation of Virgil and Homer, toward the desire to supplant the high culture. Pope, who would have interpreted shop signs as the tradesman's attempt to raise himself to aristocratic status with his pseudo-escutcheon, shows the hacks trying to replace Virgil and Homer with their own "nameless somethings," their "jumbled race," of abortive inchoate uncreation. There is also a sense in which he is attacking the "Joe Millers" who gild and try to transform folk materials which are essentially oral and gestural, certainly preverbal (or even non-verbal), into printed matter, dressing them in the guise of Homer or Virgil, or simply of print itself. This commercialization of popular culture is seen by Pope as an attempt either to drag down the forms and contents of high culture or to trick out this preverbal matter in the forms of "literature." The horror Pope envisages, as did Dryden, is the mass of paper descending as snow, flooding the streets ("Loads of Sh—— almost chok'd the Way"). In practice, The Dunciad is the great example of high art trying to come to terms with subculture forms. It does so by attacking, absorbing, and transforming this material—not into something safe but into a tense, unstable amalgam of art and nature, of purity and impurity, which is a paradigm of the volatile relationship we are examining.

7. Card Games and Hoyle's Whist

THE EIGHTEENTH CENTURY'S CONTRIBUTION to card playing was the game of whist, another phenomenon thought of as English in origin. Writing in 1767 from Paris, Horace Walpole remarked that the French had adopted the two dullest things the English had—whist and Richardson's novels.[1] The nature of this game, and how it differs from earlier games (including the earlier forms of the game called whist), may therefore be as much a matter of interest as the nature of Richardson's novels.

The development of a "new" game of whist in England can be dated in the late 1730s, and following on its heels was one of the proverbial books in English, first published just three years after *Joe Miller's Jests*: Edmond Hoyle's *Short Treatise on the Game of Whist* (1742), popularly known as "Hoyle on Whist" and origin of the phrase "according to Hoyle." By 1769, when Hoyle died, it was in its fifteenth edition. As Robert Southey wrote, looking back from the early nineteenth century, "Few books in the language, or in any language, have been so frequently printed, still fewer so intently studied."[2] Hoyle's *Treatise* is a distillation of play into a series of verbal epitomes—rules and suggestions, together with a number of remarks on the laws of odds and probabilities. The book has its own structure, which organizes in ideal shapes the raw play of the game.

The nature of the game was supposed to be summed up in its name, which came "from the silence that is to be observed at it." *"Talking* is not allowed at *Whist,"* we read in *The Compleat Gamester* of 1734; "the very Word implies, Hold your Tongue."[3] As early as 1745, "Hoyle on Whist" had been absorbed as a sign into Hogarth's second plate of *Marriage à la Mode*, where, in the context of the errant husband returning from a mistress and the bored wife from a wild night of card playing and perhaps more, it signifies: Keep quiet about what has taken place here (or there).[4] As a floating signifier, the name served to reflect both the intellectual character assumed by the game in the eighteenth century (Keep quiet, I am thinking) and the rhetorical decorum of the period. Joe Miller, we recall, also dimly reflected the socio-literary mode of poker-faced, closed-mouth self-control that replaced for a while the direct statement and the hearty laugh. Whist stands somewhere on the road between irony and its sentimental equivalent, the silent nod or gesture that speaks far louder than words, succeeding at communication when words fail. The English game of whist was essentially a phenomenon of social and literary transition.

It appears that whist was an adaptation by men of fashion of a lower-class game. In the seventeenth century it "was chiefly played in low society, where cheats and sharpers assembled,"[5] and in Fielding's *Jonathan Wild* (1743) it is the game played in the sponging house where Count La Ruse is confined. *The Compleat Gamester's* 1734 edition shows that it was still considered "a tavern game" played by tavern habitués. It remained in part II, "City Gamester" (vs. part I, "Court Gamester"), up through the seventh edition. In the next edition, dated 1754, whist has been transferred to the "Court." What changed whist from a sharper's game to one of high society was the fact that it was taken up by gentlemen at the Crown Coffee House in Bedford Row and its principles both modified and formulated. The story attributes the discovery to the first Lord Folkestone and his circle, of which Hoyle may have been a part.[6]

For its importance to be understood, whist must be contrasted with the popular card games that preceded it and with its own "primitive form." On the one hand, card games (and the deck as we know it) have been traced back to India and the game of chess; if this origin explains something of the intellectual potential of the game, the other origin, in the tarot pack, in cartomancy or fortune-telling, emphasizes the other dimension of chance. One meaning of the word *tarocchi*, or "tarot," was "royal road of life" (*tar*, road, and *ro*, *ros*, or *rog*, meaning king or royal), which reminds us of the allegorical level never far from the surface of any card game. There was one tarot game called *triomphe forcée* in which "Death," if drawn, sweeps the board, and a form of this game, called trumps, was a precursor of whist.[7] In general, the card games that channel themselves into the eighteenth century have plots concerning an individual who pits himself against a number of other individual players and/or against the bank (or dealer or house) or some manifestation of chance or providence.

What sets off cards from dice and other games of chance is the images on the face cards which produce, with play, various sequences and arrangements of symbols which accompany (or signify) the kinds and degrees of victory or defeat. At the beginning of the eighteenth century the first card game we think of is Belinda's combat with the Baron, and we remember those images of kings and queens and warriors as the social equivalent—along with the cross Belinda wears around her neck which infidels may adore—of the heroic and religious ideals of a sterner age become mere social convention or ornament. We think of the ur–card game as one in which kings, queens, and their courtiers play with their own images. In fact, the four suits of cards originally (in Italy and Spain) corresponded to the four estates: cups (chalices) for king and church, swords for the military or nobility, money for the commercial class, and batons or clubs for the peasants. The designs were gradually simplified and modified as card manufacturing moved from Italy to Spain and Germany (where other suits were developed, symbolized by acorns, hawk bells, and leaves) to France, where the definitive structure evolved of hearts (for chalices) and diamonds (for coins), in addition to the continuing swords or spades and clubs or batons. Thence cards were imported into England by the fifteenth century—types of the Italian-Spanish as well as the French variety, with the chivalric names inherited from the French.

The main thing to notice about the development of the card designs between the sixteenth and eighteenth centuries is the need to humanize the deck, to search for analogies and familiar relationships such as those found by Pope and Belinda.[8] The French seem to have been responsible for the original naming of the cards, and the king of hearts has remained Charlemagne and his Queen Judith, presumably because hearts were the chief suit and Charlemagne was king of the pack. Judith was *dame de coeur*, as "heart" meant courage or alternatively the power of love, in either case referring to Judith as savior of Bethulia, conqueror and killer (in love and in war) of the besieging general Holofernes. The knave of hearts was called "La Hire," a youthful soldier of the Hundred Years' War and a friend of Jeanne d'Arc. A fifteenth-century French card maker of Lyons issued a set in which the king and queen of hearts are primitive, hairy versions of Adam and Eve. Moreover, in some French decks Judith is called Helen, and Paris is the knave; and the knave carries a torch, as a cupid setting hearts alight. All of this is involved with the fiction that the kings of France were descended from Priam (as the English were from Brute, grandson of Aeneas). But the potential of a romantic triangle in which the knave cuckolds the king (or at least dallies with the queen) is exploited, for example, by the way the sense of "knave" changed from "boy" to the rogue Samuel Rowlands celebrated in his satiric poems of the early seventeenth century in England. ("I would *all* Knaues who ere they bee," he has his knave of spades conclude, "Were knowne by sight as well as wee.")[9] Rowlands' point, and my own, is that a set of categories as well known as cards (whose own derivation is quite schematic) was used as a model for all sorts of references outward. As Pope saw, the game easily becomes a metaphor for—or indeed a representation of—courtship or some other activity of the great world.

During the Civil War, in a 1642 pamphlet, Charles I is illustrated by the image of the king of hearts;[10] and during the French Revolution, when the old card names were abolished (kings had their crowns cut out and were changed to sages or philosophers), Judith was transferred to the suit of swords and shown holding Holofernes' head and his falchion, above the motto *Ma force est dans mon bras* (My strength is in my arm). Jeanne d'Arc became queen of hearts with the motto *Rien ne m'arête* (Nothing stops me).[11] And we could follow the game of transformations to a Prussian deck of 1814 in which the king of spades, traditionally King David, a man of the sword, became the duke of Wellington (with Blücher hearts, Schwartzenberg diamonds, and Kutusov clubs), with England his queen (and theirs the queens of Prussia, Austria, and Russia) and a Scot in Highland dress his knave. In general, as Pope saw, in each age this heroic figure is related to his equivalent, whether Wellington or Belinda's Baron. The latter is only a mock-heroic anticipation of the bourgeois transformation in the nineteenth century, when the popular card games substituted for the king, queen, and knave the images of Mr. Bun the baker, Mrs. Bun the baker's wife, and Miss Bun the baker's daughter. Other suits are represented by Grits the grocer, Block the barber, Dose the doctor, Pots the painter, and Chip the carpenter. The game, called "happy

families," consists of face cards only, and has much the representational quality of Monopoly.[12]

But we must return to the situation of card games at the beginning of the eighteenth century. Lansquenet, the soldier's favorite card
game, ranged all the players against the dealer, in the manner of
vingt-un or faro or basset (or for that matter roulette). A card game
was clearly a symbolic action. For the courtier, the game was "la
prime" or "primero," in which the correct sequence of cards first
shown wins the game; or later basset, reckoned in the 1734 edition of
The Compleat Gamester "one of the most Polite Games on the Cards;
and only fit for Persons of the First-Rank to play at; by reason of such
great Losses, or Advantages, as may possibly fall on one Side or
other."[13] Gentlemen in the early part of the century played piquet, a
game for two. Hogarth has a lady in his painting *The Lady's Last
Stake* (1759) about to lose her honor to a man in this game: the
choices of a card game become the moral choices of real life.

Ladies played ombre, and Belinda faces "two advent'rous
Knights / At Ombre, singly to decide their doom." It was a game
played with three, four, or five people—most often three—and Pope
saw it as a sublimation of more overt physical acts of aggression, a
symbolic equivalent of society's conventions of courtship. *The Court
Gamester* tells us that "the natural Order of the Cards" is "their
several Degrees when they are not Trumps"—trumps being defined
as "a Corruption of the Word *Triumph*; for wherever they are, they
are attended with Conquest." And the point of the game is to declare
what is the trump suit. When Belinda gets the bid and assumes the
role of protagonist, her voice becomes that of God at the creation:
"Let Spades be Trumps! she said, and Trumps they were." The
protagonist is called the ombre, "the person who undertakes the
Game," that is, the one who declares trumps, pits him or herself (as
"ombre," the man) against the other players, and must make good
his/her boast or threat in the declaration of trumps or be bested.[14]

The old game of whist has been traced back to "triumph," corrupted to trumps, "and the essence of it was the predominance of one
particular suit, called the triumph, or trump-suit, over all the others."[15]
Bishop Latimer in the sixteenth century developed the metaphoric potential of trump cards in a "Sunday before Christmas" sermon:

> And where you are wont to celebrate Christmas in playing
> at cards, I intend, by God's grace, to deal unto you Christ's

> Cards, wherein you shall perceive Christ's Rule. The game that
> we play at shall be called the Triumph, which, if it be well
> played at, he that dealt shall win; the Players shall likewise win;
> and the standers and lookers upon shall do the same.

What, he asks, does Christ require of a Christian man? "Now turn
up your Trump, your Heart (Hearts is Trump, as I said before), and
cast your Trump, your Heart, on this card."[16]

The old game of whist was played for four, with thirteen cards
dealt to each player, and the last card turned up designated the trump
suit (and went to the dealer). The player to the left of the dealer then
played a card, to which the others in succession had to follow suit.
The object of the game was to win tricks, which was done either by
holding high cards in the suit led or by trumping. At the beginning of
the eighteenth century the game was played with partners, two
against two, and those rules that gave sway to the element of chance
were gradually modified. For example, one form of the old whist
employed a stock of unknown cards; this was abolished, enabling the
players to calculate more accurately the contents of each other's
hands. Another competing version of whist, called swabbers, had
introduced a disproportionate element of chance by creating four
privileged cards (ace of hearts, knave of clubs, ace and deuce of
trumps), called "swabbers" because they could sweep the board, enti-
tling them to take up a share of the stake whatever the actual result of
the game itself. (This was the form of whist played by Count La
Ruse.) There was even a three-handed whist, *The Compleat
Gamester* explains, in which "always two strive to suppress and keep
down the rising Man."[17] But the principle of whist that determined
its development and success was the playing of partners, two against
two, and all of the old versions lost out to the new game developed in
the Crown Coffee House and promulgated by Hoyle.

The object of the new game was the same: to win tricks; but the
modes of doing so changed radically. As opposed to the natural
playing from master or high cards or by trumping, Hoyle urged the
player to keep the master cards back for a time; because "trick-making
depended much more on the relative positions of the cards in the
four hands, than on the high cards in one hand alone." This was his
first point. His second was "that, if the results of the play of a hand
were carefully examined, it would be found that the majority of tricks
were made by means that could not be foreseen at the beginning by

any single player. Hence, he showed that by taking advantage of the *position* of the cards lying in the various hands, or by other skillful contrivances, tricks might be made by cards of lower value, even while higher cards of the suit were still in the opponent's possession."[18] Third, he showed the strategic advantage of a long suit of small cards over good suits held by one's adversaries.

Indirection was the chief principle of Hoyle's ironic game, and it was based on a social model quite different from the old one of lansquenet or *vingt-un*. Those features of the old game of whist which required a certain cooperation with the partner and a delicate balance of skill and chance were the ones markedly developed in the direction of the new game. The efforts of the player in the primitive game were determined only by the condition of his own hand, even when he was forced to be aware of his partner's hand. The new game required far more complex considerations of the other hands as well, and placed prime importance on watching "the fall of the cards." The tendency of this game over earlier ones, and over the primitive game of whist itself, was to make the player form a mental diagram or map of all four hands (as Hoyle apparently instructed his pupils by laying down, face up, the set of four hands, the pupil taking one of the four). The old baroque card games were seen only from the single, fixed point of view of one player. Whist forced the player to triangulate from the cards played the position of cards in all the other hands.

Because of the variety and chance in the distribution of the cards in the different hands, there was still a large emphasis on the aleatory. (Compared, for example, with the game of bridge that emerged a century later, where the element of chance is further reduced, and that of intellectual application increased, by the introduction of bidding, or stating apparently strong suits, and the invariable use of a dummy, with his cards visible, for the strong bidder's partner.) William Payne summarized the significance of Hoyle's game in the preface to his *Maxims* of whist (1770):

> The game of Whist is so happily compounded betwixt chance and skill, that it is generally esteemed the most curious and entertaining of the cards. . . . The great variety of hands and critical cases, arising from such a number of cards, renders the game so nice and difficult, that much time and practice has heretofore been necessary to the obtaining a tolerable degree of knowledge of it.

Payne draws attention to the balance between chance and skill, the basis of critical cases for an understanding of the game, and the difficulty of playing well, which has come to mean grasping the total situation (of all hands) and playing to win from low cards.

The change registered in the game is from a picaresque situation with a single protagonist to a complex interpersonal situation. In whist the odds and probabilities or hazards are considerably reduced, and the interpersonal relations complicated (without, however, the bluffing emphasis of poker), and the interactions no longer limited to the individual against every other player and the dealer. It is a game in which you are not playing against the house, with its killing percentage in its favor, but competing on your own merits. And it projects a situation of a man within society who sees himself in relation to a partner and also to his opponents, indeed acknowledges with the opponent a social solidarity against that "other," which is now Chance. It is a game in which you have to play out of your partner's and the other players' hands, hands you cannot see but have to infer from "the fall of the cards," from what *can* be seen—the small area of action that is visible.

These changes are, of course, reflected and magnified in the manuals on card games. *The Compleat Gamester* and *Lives of the Gamesters* are two titles that sum up the Restoration images connected with card games[19]: betting and gambling with large sums of money; cheating; and recording the life, perhaps the spiritual biography or only the admonitory example, of the sharper or, alternatively, of his unlucky dupe.

When Hoyle's little book appeared in 1742 it replaced Richard Seymour's *The Court Gamester* of 1719, which had replaced Charles Cotton's *Compleat Gamester* (1674), the dominant manual of the Restoration period. Seymour's fifth edition of 1734 (to which I have referred) was called *The Compleat Gamester*, and combined Seymour's own book with Cotton's.[20] Already the game of whist was "said to be the foundation of all the English games upon the cards," but the shadow of Cotton remains over the whole book in its emphasis not on how to play the game well but on how to cheat or avoid being cheated. We are treated to descriptions of "piping" and other gestural codes used by sharpers, which also establish by implication a certain kind of social situation, a certain world, characterized by conny-catching pamphlets and ruled by Hobbes's "law of the jungle," though held in check by a basic standard of hypocrisy which requires significant signs and gestures, and even a very un-Shandyean handling of a pipe or raising a finger to the nose: not merely to communicate with your brother but to deceive your opponent.

A prefatory letter to Hoyle's *Treatise* by "a gentleman at Bath" starts out in the same vein, but as the "gentleman" sets about "rescuing" players "from the Snares which they are too frequently caught in, by being over-matched in these sorts of Amusements," the answer he develops is superior skill. When he lost a large sum of money one night and yet could perceive no foul play, he had to conclude "I was beat by superior Skill." And so he inquires into the cause and comes upon Hoyle's manuscript treatise: "As soon as I perused it, I found I had heretofore been but a Bungler at this Game, and being thoroughly sensible of the Advantage which those that are possessed of this Book have over the innocent player," he urges Hoyle to publish the manuscript. Hoyle's title page sums up the aims of his little book and gives some idea of its place in the cultural history of the time: it contains "the laws of the game; and also some Rules whereby a Beginner may, with due attention to them, attain to the Playing it well."[21] It also contains "Calculations for those who will Bet the Odds on any Point of the score of the Game." The title goes on for several more lines, referring to "cases," "calculations" and "chance"—the significant words—along with words that emphasize skill as a partial hedge against chance.

The generous citation of cases is, of course, a sign of the empirical bent of the time. Hoyle is only one of many authors who talk about the doctrines of chance, from Abraham de Moivre, F.R.S., who dedicated his *The Doctrine of Chances; or, a Method of Calculating the Probability of Events in Play* (1718) to Newton, to Hartley, who assigns the association of ideas to combinations of accident and guile. Hoyle later summed up this aspect of his *Treatise* in *An Essay toward Making the Doctrine of Chances Easy to Those Who Understand Vulgar Arithmetic Only* (1754). All of these works reflect not only a sublimation of the gambling fever, seen at its most intense in the South Sea Bubble of 1721 (a case that remained in men's memories), but the concern with odds and probabilities rather than with directly causal or divine-providential relations, which we associate at the highest level with David Hume's *Treatise on Human Nature* (1739–40). The old card games were essentially lotteries (according to an act of 12 George II, the games of faro, basset, and hazard were declared lotteries and anyone setting up or maintaining a game was to forfeit £200 and all who played them £50),[22] and the only way to guard yourself was by cheating. The new game allowed you to guard yourself by intellection, by cooperating with a partner, and by projecting yourself into the hands held by your opponents. The individual was finding a way to be secure within a social situation.

Another consequence of the variety of chance in the distribution of the cards in the four hands is the impossibility Hoyle acknowledges of formulating general laws. Thus teaching the game was a matter of individual cases, preference of example over precept, of act over principle, and of face-to-face teaching by example over the written book itself. The book was nevertheless published, because, like Uncle Toby, Hoyle had found gesture insufficient and had written a few *aides memoires*, which other teachers were surreptitiously copying and using for themselves. In order to secure his copyright he published his book, which was itself notably unsystematic.[23] But once in print, the manual became *the* authority on whist, and in subsequent editions on other card games.[24] Soon its supporters were declaring the *Treatise* "the gospel of Whist-Players" and its author "a second Newton"; Horace Walpole claimed he was going to compose "a grammar" of "the noble game of bilboquet" (i.e., cup and ball) "in opposition to Mr. Hoyle's" of whist. Volumes by serious whist practitioners appeared to correct or modify Hoyle, but like *Joe Miller's Jests*, Hoyle's *Treatise* magisterially absorbed all these later treatises while retaining the canonical name Hoyle.[25]

Not everyone believed in the efficacy of Hoyle's method. In a satire called *The Humours of Whist* (1743) "Professor Whiston" (Hoyle) gives lessons in the game, and Sir Calculation Puzzle, an enthusiastic player, muddles his head with Hoyle's elaborate calculations and always loses, demonstrating that skill and calculation are of no avail against bad luck or premeditated fraud. On the other hand, a writer in *The Gentleman's Magazine* of February 1755 explains that "Hoyle tutored me in several games at cards, and under the name of guarding me from being cheated, insensibly gave me a taste for sharping."[26]

A scene in *Tom Jones* sums up the social function of Hoyle's game of whist. Sophia Western, playing whist with Lady Bellaston, Lord Fellamar, and Tom Edwards, is told by the latter (a practical joker) that Tom Jones has been killed in a duel. She resumes the deal "and having dealt three Cards to one, and seven to another, and ten to a third, at last dropt the rest from her Hand, and fell back in her Chair."[27] The "test" exposes Sophia's love of Tom to her rival Lady Bellaston (author of the scheme) and prepares the way for Fellamar's attempted rape of Sophia to get her out of Lady Bellaston's way. In short, it breaks through the socially agreed-upon rules of the whist game to reveal the real and disorderly world with which the game cannot in fact cope. But it is a world set up on the same principles, in which Lady Bellaston and Tom Edwards are playing out of each other's hands, and cleverly exploiting the "dummy" Fellamar, to defeat Sophia and win Tom Jones. Whist is a game which tries to guard us against a chance like the death of Tom Jones, but being only a game it leaves itself open to the other games like the one Tom Edwards and his partner engage in. Sophia at the moment is playing the wrong game with the wrong partner, triangulating the wrong hands, and therefore loses control of the situation.

In *Tom Jones* there is a great deal of talk about the possible and probable, which resolves itself into an emphasis on personal skill. Tom is the young man who must eventually learn the rules of play, how to judge the odds and probabilities, and how to be a Christian gentleman and a man of the world "according to Hoyle." It is, however, the narrator who demonstrates the mapping procedure required of the skillful player and represents the ideal whist player described by a later Hoyle. He should be endowed with "patience, charity, forgiveness and forbearance," vis-à-vis his partner and his opponents, and also have the more direct gifts of "promptitude, considerable readiness in emerging, fortitude under calamity, a clear faculty to calculate probabilities, an admirable memory, and a spirit at once self-reliant and trustful." "For the whist-player," writes another eulogist, "the gift which is above all necessary is that comprised in the single word *coolness*. He must be cool. If he becomes flurried and nervous, his faculties will slip from him."[28]

Hoyle in his *Treatise* is trying to compensate for—guard against—the old games of chance which represent the outer periphery where Tom Jones can lose all on the arbitrary turn of a lie (by Blifil or Tom Edwards). Hoyle, first in the reforms of the Crown Coffee House and then in his *Treatise*, is attempting to give order to something that is dangerously disordered—dangerously because of the money that changes hands, the gambling risks, the bluffs of such as Tom Edwards, but also because chance itself is terrifying in a world where divine providence, which can subsume apparent chance or fortune, no longer seems a very comforting answer.

Keith Thomas, writing of a somewhat earlier period, has pointed out that "the doctrine of providence was always less likely to appeal to those at the bottom of the social scale than the rival doctrine of luck." The doctrine of providence has been created for these poor folk but in fact is held to by its creators, the merchants and shopkeepers who were also most active to help themselves, combining "a faith in providence with an active reliance upon self-help, though the alliance was sometimes subject to strain." The laboring poor, by contrast, gambled, as they drank gin; and as Thomas concludes, gambling diverted their attention "from the possibilities of self-help and political activism, by holding out the prospect that a lucky person would be able to better himself despite the inequities of the social system."[29] This would seem to be yet another one of those cases where the bottom and top of the social scale find common cause against the middle—against those who see the individual's rebirth and earthly success as all important, his life a spiritual pilgrimage. It was precisely this class who most strenuously opposed card games, condemning poor Tom Idle for playing cards on a tombstone on Sunday—partly, perhaps, because card games so closely resembled a parody of their Calvinist belief in predestination.

But these same people found in whist a game they could play with impunity. Fielding, who in his *Enquiry* devotes a whole section to gambling with card games such as basset, which he calls mere "lotteries," makes no mention of whist.[30] For whist was not only an aristocratic game, to be emulated by would-be aristocrats, but also a summation of divine providence as self-help or a good compromise between chance and skill (or even cheating). In his *Treatise*, Hoyle (like Corbyn Morris with the jest) was out to make safe the popular anarchism of a disreputable game by raising it to a formulation of rules based on proper social behavior. The development he traces is from a transaction between the individual and God, based on sheer chance, to one that may not be called predestination but carries with it the skill of the elect; and the individual now plays in league with a partner (his helpmeet) against another couple, relying on his memory and skill and partner as well as on providence.

Roger Caillois in *Les Jeux et les Hommes* sums up the dimensions and implications of the metaphor of card playing. Besides *agon* (competition) and *alea* (chance), his terms are *mimicry* (or simulation) and *ilinx* (dizziness or vertigo).[31] While *agon* represents "the desire to win by one's own merit in regulated competition," *alea* is the "submission of one's will in favor of anxious and passive anticipation of where the wheel will stop." *Mimicry* involves "the desire to assume a strange personality," and *vertigo* a situation in which chaos is the norm, where "whirl is king."

> In agon, the player relies only upon himself and his utmost efforts; in alea, he counts on everything except himself, submitting to the powers that elude him; in mimicry, he imagines that he is someone else, and he invents an imaginary universe; in ilinx, he gratifies the desire to temporarily destroy his bodily equilibrium, escape the tyranny of his ordinary perception, and provide the abdication of conscience.

In the most general terms—perhaps as literary as social—Hoyle is substituting for superstition (counting "on everything except himself") role playing as a sense of one's position in society. This is the agon that Sophia Western (as her name suggests) is seeking in order to replace the response to chance which is the popular view of a passive reliance on a providence which is inscrutable. But since total control is impossible, the providential is a twig to which one clutches; and others are the assuming of roles, the large element of "as if" in any card game (as in the dealing of hands) which separates it from life, as if it were something else out in the macrocosm of business or politics or matrimony. The final alternative, vertigo, is both what is being avoided and what can, for some people and under some circumstances, be a satisfactory end in itself, a satisfactory escape from the aleatory into the whirlpool—say of gin or of the Wilkite crowd or enthusiastic religion.

The triangulation I have described of the content of partners' and opponents' hands from the overt playing of cards gives us an altogether new view of a protagonist and his role. To some extent, in playing whist one has sometimes a sense of foreseeing the outcome, of planning a strategy that involves several tricks ahead. But at bottom, whist is not the game of chess, where you foresee chains of moves, and alternative chains, and each new move unleashes its own several series of foreseeable alternatives leading to a checkmate. Whist asks for a bifocal view, one that can see only one move ahead but also strives to lay out the pattern of hands in order to allow for a successful prediction of what cards *can* turn up. It implies a progression based on taking tricks in a series leading to a victory which may, in the next deal, be overturned or compromised. The interest is both in the momentary surprise (or entertainment, enlightenment, or act of charity) and in the endeavor to predict, to project into the mind or hand of the partner, as well as into relationships of various sorts with the other couple. Though the desired end, this is only approximated in practice, with errors and misconceptions and lucky guesses. Not only Hoyle's *Treatise* but *Tom Jones* depends upon elaborate arguments concerning odds and probabilities. In Fielding's novel some of it is ironic, but all of it is urgent. Another literary analogy might be the letter form of Richardson's *Clarissa*, where we imaginatively project a true hand from the play of Clarissa and Lovelace, who always hold back crucial cards, while we are at the same time moving from letter to letter. I am, for that matter, reminded of Richardson himself as author, who tries to correct his own tendencies toward mimicry and ilinx by doing a Hoyle on his narrative in the second and subsequent editions, trying to turn it back into a spiritual pilgrimage or saint's life, depending on a single striking conversion and clear oppositions of good and evil.[32]

The final characteristic of Hoyle's whist to which I wish to draw attention is summed up better than I can in *Joe Miller*, no. 595 (1836 ed.):

> One day Charlotte Smith was walking along Piccadilly, when the tray of a butcher's boy came in sudden contact with her shoulder, and dirtied her dress. The deuce take the tray, exclaimed she, in a pet. Ah, but the deuce can't take the tray, replied young rump-steak with the greatest gravity.

As the card game that replaced in popularity *vingt-un* and other games in which cards are combined to reach a particular number, or are matched, whist was one of those games based on an unalterable and hierarchical sequence. Cotton, Seymour, Hoyle, Payne, and Mathews—all the authorities talk about the importance of the sequences of king, queen, knave; queen, knave, and ten; and so on.

"All cards are of value as they are superior one to another," we read in *The Compleat Gamester*—". . . if not trumps," for "the least trump will win the highest card of any other suit."[33] Hoyle revolutionized the use of trumps by introducing far subtler play: in many cases trumps could be used "to disarm the adversaries, and by that means to obtain secondary advantages in trick-making by other suits of less apparent power."[34] Besides trumping, the only way to break the hierarchical order was to finesse—to win a trick with a card that is lower than the card of the same suit held by your opponent. This too was one of Hoyle's most important points of instruction, part of the need to make a mental map of your opponents' hands.

We have seen how the concept of trumps could be allegorized by Bishop Latimer for Christian purposes. Something like trumping is also a principle on which the novels of Richardson and Fielding implicitly operate. There is a strict hierarchy, whether that of primogeniture or the "Great Chain of Being." But there is also the aleatory element in the fiction of the trump—a fiction in Tom's case because he is apparently a worthless foundling but in fact the illegitimate son of suitable parents. Hogarth's genuinely plebeian alter ego, his pug, was by no accident named Trump for the card that breaks rigid sequences, the suit that reverses priorities.

There was one other way to break the unalterable sequence of the suit signs, and it too was based on intellectual attainment and chance. A peculiarly English kind of card deck that was popular in the early eighteenth century printed (counter to the ordinary sequence) another sequence altogether which was based on history or geography, with its own temporal chronology or spatial order. Especially popular were card decks with the "counties of England," since there were fifty-two. John Lenthall's advertisement of around 1720 lists forty "entertaining Packs of Cards" of this sort "for the improvement of Gentlemen, Ladies, and others, in several Arts and Sciences, as well as [providing] the agreeable Diversion of CARD-PLAYING."[35] For "improvement" the cards contain signs of the "Arts and Sciences," and for "agreeable Diversion" the usual suit signs. For education there were historical series (naval victories of Queen Elizabeth's time or the reign of Queen Anne), sequences which build toward a triumphant conclusion, as a card game does toward a victory/defeat. Perhaps the real model, however, was the popular print series, for these were usually "historical" in a tendentious, nationalist, often partisan way, depicting political events: the Popish Plot, the Meal Tub Plot, the Rye House Plot, Monmouth's Rebellion, Marlborough's victories, the impeachment of Dr. Sacheverell, and the South Sea Bubble. All but the last of these retained historical chronology, though Marlborough's victories, for example, fit the political hero or villain to the card. In spades, the king is Louis XIV, stealing Spain; the queen is his mistress Mme. de Maintenon; and the knave a priest taking down the dying king of Spain's will (which left Spain to Louis XIV). Hearts have Prince George of Denmark as king and Anna Sophia of Hanover as queen; clubs have Charles III of Spain and Queen Anne; and Diamonds have Victor Amadeus of Savoy and the princess royal of Prussia in these roles. The knave in each suit is a profiteer or crooked politician exploiting the war. Wickedness in all the series tends to fall under the knave, or under the suit of spades.

The series called "All the Bubbles" is an arbitrarily ordered group of the crazy projects of 1720–22, whose only value signs are given by the suits. Other series—nonsatiric—follow only the roughly spatial arrangement of counties or cities. Others relate armorial bearings to the suit signs, or proverbs, aphorisms, and love mottoes. Carving and cooking cards use the suit of diamonds for foul, hearts for flesh, clubs for fish, and spades for baked meats or meat pies. The value of the card is indicated by a miniature card in one of the upper corners—which may or may not confer a similar value on the motto or historical event in relation to its fellows. A geographical series of 1678 assigns the hearts to Europe, the diamonds to Asia, spades to Africa, and clubs to America. The rough symbolism is obvious. For example, the association of clubs (of savages) and America leads to John IV of Portugal as king, with his card carrying a description of Brazil, and Queen Elizabeth presiding over the "English Plantations on or near the continent of America." The knave is a cannibal.

In all of these decks there are two parallel sequences, one rigid and hierarchical, producing a game of chance; the other "natural" in the sense of pertaining to something in the real world, with the intention of instructing in history or mythology or geography, or persuading to some political position such as support of Sacheverell. As I have said, these derive to some extent from the popular print series of current events, but they also draw upon the old prophetic use of card decks and the magic overtones of the tarot deck. They are in a sense a modern version of tarot superimposed on the conventional deck. But the point is that they express a way of thinking in the printing of a double series, both unalterable in their different ways but one relating (by accident or plan, by contradiction or support) to the value system of the other. By the 1760s and '70s the bifocal decks have begun to split into pure playing cards and the various games based on "Happy Families" or other natural or social sequences.[36]

The double sequence began, we can be sure, as a way of moralizing or making useful the questionable game of chance. Just as the game of whist transformed card games of chance into a predominantly intellectual contest built around socio-familial partnerships, the cards were being made educational and so respectable. Indeed, the rigid sequence of the cards has always been at odds with the aleatory quality of the games played with them. Now another sequence, less arbitrary and abstract, more natural and inevitable, tied to experience, was added, consisting either of the chronological events of history or of geographical facts that have a given spatial relationship to each other.

The bifocal card decks also represent a replacement of conventional iconography with topical images which on this humble level parallels the campaigns of Addison, Shaftesbury, and others, to replace obscure and hieroglyphic signs with reasonable ones. A kind of uneasy coexistence is a way of describing the phenomenon. A single-sequence deck of 1775 (Cary Collection, Yale) is intended to teach iconography, but while Justice still appears as a blindfolded woman in Roman dress, Fidelity is now a dog being tempted by a housebreaker with a bone, Wit is Sir John Falstaff, and a Parson is simply a country parson. The old Ripan system of correspondences is being interrupted, not only by biblical equations (Flattery or Deceit is Eve and the serpent) but by rational equations from contemporary experience, decidedly English in reference. Fortitude may still be Horatius Cockles, and Prudence still out of Ripa, but Crime is a robbery near a gallows in an English countryside, and a Gentleman and a Church are simply those contemporary entities. In these single sequences we see the same desire to modify rigid and ancient hierarchies, if only by placing them in relation to conflicting systems. While in the bifocal decks they appear parallel on a single card, in most places (as in the iconography deck I have described) they appear side by side in the same sequence.

To sum up, we can agree with the historians (and with Pope's

Dunciad) that we are describing a period of transition defined by a greatly enlarged reading public and a wider dissemination of subculture forms, as well as of aristocratic and tradesmen's assumptions, through printed books. The people who controlled the editing, printing, and distribution, whether of books or card games, I suppose we have to acknowledge to have been the tradesmen, though with many tell-tale traces of other interests and "classes." This fact may partly explain the transformation—determined though incomplete and unsuccessful—of both aristocratic and subculture values into what we shall call "polite" assumptions. "Polite" we are defining as a more uniform and standardized code which replaces magic (to use Keith Thomas' word) or providence as a way to control the environment with prudence, calculation, and regularity. Not only card games but also children's literature, the how-to-do-it manual, attempts at reform and the amelioration of the condition of the poor, voluntary associations (freemasons and friendly societies), and manners in general reflect an almost obsessive concern with the elimination of chance and the need to control the social environment in every rational way. What we see in the decade or so we are examining is that these generalizations have constantly to be qualified; that the subculture materials in important ways refuse to be transformed and inject an energy into certain of the "polite" or even "high" forms of art, where it is barely controlled; though at every stage we have to bear in mind the overdetermination of all phenomena and the general tendency (we have noticed) of textuality itself to deconstruct into secondary or latent meanings—into plots of desire that lie below the "meaning" imposed by the printers and booksellers.

II. Polite Metaphors, Models, and Paradigms

1. Bifocal Series

THE MOST RIGID SEQUENCE outside a card pack is the alphabet. The order of a child's alphabet book requires that A be followed by B. But in 1744 another era opened with the publication of John Newbery's *A Little Pretty Pocket Book*. The tiny book was well printed, competently illustrated, and priced 6d., and for an extra 2p. included a ball and pin cushion for the little boy and girl who would read it. There had been hornbooks for alphabet teaching before, but this was the first "children's book" that attempted to join instruction and delight: the first of many from Newbery's shop.[1] The principle of alphabet learning here is to add to the order requiring that A be followed by B another letter which is arbitrary and illustrative, placing spatially adjacent to the letter a word and, near that, a corresponding visual image. The variables increase with the need for novelty in each new alphabet (though such books were basically conservative, with the printers using the same illustrative blocks over and over again). But the possibilities were large: A could also be for the boy who *ate* the *apple* (or *ate* the pear), or even the boy who took *all* the pears or even took the *aged* pear. Here is a double sequence from *Tom Thumb's Play-Book* (1744?) that offers a narrative:

> A Apple pye
> B Bit it
> C Cut it
> D Divided it
> E Eat it . . .

By the time of George Cruikshank in the nineteenth century, the letters are merely a pretext like the rhyme scheme of a sonnet. A is *Alamode*, with a drawing of a huge cook and two men jamming food into their mouths. *C* is *Chimpanzee*, with a chimp swinging

105

from a tree in a zoo, reaching out his hand for the apish gentleman who is scrutinizing him. I am using these examples to show the direction in which sequences of the sort we saw in card decks were developing—toward new types of classification, toward the autonomy of the arbitrary sequence, and toward the proliferation of meaning in a visual image. But also toward excuses for drawing the funny pictures, one of which is to sweeten the lesson of the alphabetical order. And this is done by juxtaposing order with disorder, industrious with idle apprentice, in constant, though casual, tension.

On the much higher level of legicographical scholarship, Samuel Johnson's *Dictionary of the English Language* (1755) is, however, only a subtler version of the same relationship. The given sequence of the alphabet is qualified by the element of personal freedom and play Johnson allows himself in his definitions and examples. To the word and its meaning(s) Johnson adds the lexicographers' examples for each sense of the word, and both definitions and examples are interfused with the man Johnson's personal stamp, as if to demonstrate that the invariable alphabetical order is only part of the story.

> Ga'llicism. n.s. [*gallicisme*, French; from *gallicus*, Latin.] A mode of speech peculiar to the French language: such as, he *figured* in controversy; he *held* this conduct; he *held* the same language that another had *held* before with many other expressions to be found in the pages of *Bolingbroke*.
>
> In English I would have *Gallicisms* avoided, that we may keep to our own language, and not follow the French mode in our speech.

The forthright opinion is accompanied by the joke at Bolingbroke's expense. A subject like Bolingbroke becomes a running joke in the *Dictionary*: "irony" is "a mode of speech . . . *as Bolingbroke was a holy man.*" And so also with such favorite subjects as Scotland and the American savages, or with patriotism, which may go off into knavery, or patronage into exploitation. The quotations chosen as examples can also take one off in engaging ways into Milton, Dryden, and Pope; or Coke, Bacon, and Lyttelton.

The number of such divigations is not great. It is an exaggeration to say that the *Dictionary* was "more of an autobiography than a work of lexicography."[2] Of some 40,000 entries, perhaps 200 show signs of Johnson's strong personality. Besides a few jokes, one comes upon a dozen or so forthright opinions, twenty or thirty prejudicial definitions, a few references to Lichfield, and fifty quotations from Johnson's own works (many disguised as "anonymous," and almost a quarter of these removed on revision). But the point is precisely this: the ratio includes as much variety as is seemly within order. And the quotations, by themselves, introduce enough variety that we can see Johnson introducing them for purposes of pure pleasure as well as lexicographical context. They carry any word far beyond the dusty definition out into political and moral realms, and remind us of Freud's definition of a "system" as "best characterized by the fact that at least two reasons can be discovered for each of its products: a reason based upon *the premises of the system* (a reason, then, which may be delusional) and a *concealed* reason, which we must judge to be the truly operative and the real one."[3] Johnson is satisfied to develop the tension between the two premises of the system. We have seen, from Hogarth onward, more radical solutions which shatter all pretensions to unity, connection, and intelligibility of the system.

Johnson's whole process is the opposite of the one we traced in Hogarth. As he tells us in his *Plan of a Dictionary*, published in 1747 before he undertook the work, he hoped to "fix the English language." The metaphor he uses is of a journey of exploration: he hopes he will "at least discover the coast, civilize part of the inhabitants and make it easy for some other adventurer to proceed further, to reduce them wholly to subjection," he adds, changing the journey metaphor to one of conquest, "and settle them under laws." On the one hand he is an explorer whose intention is to reduce the reality to a map. On the other he is a Crusoe who does not finish until he has Christianized Friday and established an English colony. As Crusoe ordered and subordinated the elements he found into an obedient and consistent structure, Johnson intends to order the diverse elements of the language and subjugate all of us to the same system.

However, by the time he wrote the "Preface to the Dictionary" in 1755 he had changed his metaphor. Now he admits that he can no more identify and fix the elements of a living and changing language "than a grove in the agitation of a storm can be accurately delineated from its picture in the water." This is a metaphor the Romantic poets and painters were to pick up, turning their attention from the grove to its reflection. Johnson retains his concern with the accurate delineation of the grove itself, but he is aware of the doubleness of his enterprise. He knows that he has been forced to "sacrifice uniformity to custom," to map only the arbitrary order of an alphabet which conceals (or tries to conceal) chaos.

Of course, "chaos" is the wrong word; for what Johnson is in fact charting by the relationship between word, definitions, and examples is the manifestation of necessary change. The *Dictionary* shows him moving from the idea of words as definable objects to the practical experience of words as not determinate and complete meanings, but traces like Friday's footprint which mean different things at different times, and in the process tell us about ourselves in history.[4] Words proliferate into senses that are determined or influenced by structures of politics and economics. Johnson's enterprise is to chart as best he can a native English development, at the same time largely leaving the language to speak for itself rather than cutting or shaping it in the name of a fixed standard based on Latin or some other language. The Englishness of this dictionary is at least temporally related to Hogarth's signboard exhibition and his argument that Italian or French rules (conventions) of art do not apply to our native development in England. (Recall Johnson's joke about the French Academy's dictionary requiring forty scholars forty years to complete, which equals sixteen hundred—the "proportion" of an Englishman to a Frenchman.)[5]

The very qualities of difference and mutation that were to be overcome in the optimistic manifesto of the *Plan* have become in practice a basis for understanding the phenomenon of the English language. Starting with the metaphor of journey, quest, and exploration, Johnson ends with an organic metaphor, explaining the impossibility of accurately recording the language while "some words are budding, and some falling away." By this time he is looking forward to Coleridge's rejection of Hartley's idea of the association of ideas as a linear sequence, replacing it with his own of a stereoscopic effect of overlapping ideas. "Association depends in a much greater degree on the recurrence of resembling states of feeling than [as Hartley believes] on trains of ideas. . . . Ideas no more recall one another than the leaves in a tree, fluttering in a breeze, propagate their motion one to another."[6] This is a metaphor which does not quite serve Johnson's *Dictionary*, but it gives some idea of the formal innovation Johnson moves into. As Robert Langbaum has cogently put it, in Coleridge's view "partly we see the tree before us and partly we see all the trees we have ever seen," and when Wordsworth says in "Tintern Abbey" that "the picture of the mind revives again," he means that he is seeing the present landscape through his mental image of the landscape he saw five years before. "Because he discovers continuity in the disparate pictures through a principle of growth, he becomes aware of the pattern of his life."[7]

As a deck of geographical cards is less rigidly ordered than a historical deck (with chronology of the Popish Plot or the reign of Queen Anne), so a guidebook may be less ordered than a dictionary or an alphabet book, but the map of England nevertheless imposes an order of a sort, in effect, an itinerary on a journey. Defoe's *Tour thro' the Whole Island of Great Britain* (1728), the great English guidebook of the first half of the century (which continued to grow in revisions into the second half), begins by contrasting its own procedure with John Macky's, whose popular guide consisted of a series of entries for places quite unrelated geographically, except by the fact that they are all in Great Britain. As Pat Rogers has said, "It would scarcely matter if the putative geographical framework were demolished, and the work presented as an alphabetical sequence—Blackheath, Blandford, Blenheim, Bodmin, Boston, and so on."[8] Defoe criticizes Macky for being unable to follow the winding of a road. From York, Macky suddenly jumps "at once over the whole County . . . without taking notice of any Thing," and comes down "again sixty or seventy miles off, like an Apparition, without being seen by the way."[9]

It is absolutely characteristic of Defoe—the Defoe of *Robinson Crusoe* as well as of the *Tour*—that he believes that true knowledge of the country can only be obtained by moving through it along actual roads in a consecutive route. At the same time, however, he writes long, eloquent passages on the need for better roads, and complains of the limitation of being confined to the present ones. For the extant road systems, like the meanings that custom has built up for Johnson's words, have to serve him as his structure. He comes to accept them, but looks for ways around them that will solve his basic needs.

He wants to cover the *whole* countryside, whereas Macky went only into the larger towns and the seats of the gentry, reflecting the seventeenth-century view of England as a group of noblemen ruling, perhaps in tension, with a few merchants. Defoe's problem is to place these "highspots" in relation to all the other activities of Englishmen that were beneath Macky's concern. He had the further problem that he set out to describe a countryside and cities that were—again like Johnson's words—in a state of temporal transition. Earlier descriptions are for this reason unsatisfactory:

> No description of Great Britain can be, what we call, a finished account, as no cloaths can be made to fit a growing child; no picture carry the likeness of a living face; the size of one, and the countenance of the other always altering with time, so no account of a kingdom thus daily altering its countenances can be perfect.[10]

He also seeks a form that will convey both an economic survey of England and illustrations of the aesthetic values to be found in the places visited. This requires that he see each place from at least two different perspectives or vantage points, one within and the other at a distance, one *ambulando* or *en passant* and the other settled in the city, where he can talk to inhabitants and examine their records. Others, he recalls, have described Richmond Gardens in great detail:

> But I find none has spoken of what I call the distant glory of all these Buildings: There is a Beauty in these things at a Distance, taking them *en Passant* and in *Perspective*, which few people value, and fewer understand; and yet here they are more truly great, than in all their Beauties whatsoever; here they reflect Beauty, and Magnificence upon the whole Country, and give a kind of a Character to the Island of Great Britain in general. [I, 5]

The method requires backtracking but is based on the requirements of following unbroken linear progressions along roads; it requires giving "an Account of the whole Country" and doing so from different perspectives, economic and aesthetic, close and distant, in terms of the present and of change. He does not travel by spur shots—"for I shall not come back the same way I went"—but instead follows the structures of the circuit (I, 243). The first circuit, beginning and ending at London, is augmented by a second, somewhat different one which, however, allows him to see some of the same places at a later time from a different perspective, or even a different road of approach. Thus he travels by "circuits, in the plural," he writes, "because I do not pretend to have travelled it all in one journey, but in many, and some of them many times over; the better to inform myself of everything I could find worth taking notice of" (I,

5). The circuits offer him a way of capturing and representing change, as well as the different views of a single, relatively unchanging place.[11] He anticipates William Gilpin (whose travels in search of the "Picturesque" would change the nature of later editions of the *Tour* itself) by traveling with the eye of the aesthetician on the roads established for and used by merchants trading and peddling through the countryside.

Defoe's guidebook is, in short, for the tradesman who is also an artist, and for later Englishmen (as he shows he knew) who will be pleasure-seeking tourists. The structures are parallel and do not quite meet, although Defoe tries hard to make them do so, and Pat Rogers argues that he parallels his metaphor of the journey with the "journey" of writing it down. He superimposes on the itinerary the temporal structure of the letter, or series of letters, which also brings him into a fictively direct contact with his reader. Indeed, the letter form is most obtrusive when he blames it for the rigidity that prevents him from doing or seeing or telling all that he feels he ought.

In a number of ways Defoe's procedure also parallels that of the pictorial circuit in the English garden that was being developed from the late 1720s into the 1740s. He cannot have known of the revolution in garden design that was brewing, but he was a keen-eyed observer and would have seen the signs of the change and the nucleus of change itself in the Englishman's need to walk around his own property and to see more than one aspect of a landscape.[12] He is in effect employing the metaphor of England as a garden when he focuses upon his visual ordering of the English landscape. His *Tour* is a massive parallel to the guidebooks to Stowe that urged the visitor to follow in the author's steps, to be educated by him to the variety of prospects available to the enterprising and observant man. The most notable of the guides to Stowe, by none other than William Gilpin himself in 1748, is written as a dialogue between a speaker for the moralizing structure of the temples and statues and a speaker for the purely aesthetic experience of the landscape. In Defoe's *Tour* the prospects which expose the sources of raw materials and manufactured goods, the economic centers that are growing and decaying, will give the tradesman a model for creating his own "England," and if he is successful in this enterprise, he can hope to create his own personal "Elysium," like the one Henry Hoare the City banker designed at Stourhead.

Defoe's *Tour* gives some sense of the layered effect felt by a visitor to Stourhead. The circuit there is around the lake, looking in toward a few stable elements—the Pantheon, the Temple of Apollo, and grotto—which take on different appearances with each perspective and arrangement, in relation to each other as well as to their surroundings, the local village, and the neighboring fields. One was also made aware of change at Stourhead: the original structuring of classical temples and signs, with allusions to the *Aeneid*, was modified by the addition in the 1760s and later of references to England's own ancient heritage, with an Anglo-Saxon cross, King Alfred's Tower, and a Gothic cottage. The Anglo-Saxon reference transects the classical-Roman, acting as another perspective. The two coordinates on which all of these references are built are economic and national (Hoare's English bank) and aesthetic (his retirement to be a patron of the arts).

With these examples I have tried to tilt the balance from the point of view of the subculture to that of polite society. The norm is now a higher one, but often compromised by another less polite, and the compromises have taken the form of bifocal series and new classifications of series or progressions. (1) Bifocal series represent not only parallel sequences but two different readers reading what appears to be a single sign—reading it at different speeds and in different ways, arriving at different interpretations. Implicit are two kinds of order, as in the card decks both *utile* and *dulce*, high and low, the prescribed and the playful, business and pleasure, or industry and idleness. (2) The basic mechanical progressions—alphabetical, numerical, and so on—are complemented by what we might call organic progressions: the times of the day, the seasons, youth to maturity, son to father, or reign to reign; or even, over these, from confinement to freedom or from Eden to the fallen world. An order based on education, inheritance, and conversion may be qualified by another based on chance, vertigo, and self-absorption. Transitions tend to matter more than static entities or larger forms. Movement through a garden like that at Stourhead depends on the transition from one part—one temple or statue—to another, although the visitor may also try to divine a sense of the overall pattern. The fixed perspective point has been replaced by a roving one, extremely inferential, and requiring the materializing of relationships rather than a total plan.[13] The rest is subordinated to the immediate relationship between two places or experiences (or the contrast of two qualities or concepts), which is related to the binary structure so deeply implanted by, for example, the Plutarchian "Parallel Lives" and reflected even in the antithetical concepts of "dog" and the bifocal structure of some card decks. Charity as a religious ideal refers to a momentary action that may be at odds with the trajectory of a lifetime.

Even grammars printed a practical grammar in large type across the top of the page and in small type at the bottom the principles or theory of grammar. Charles Gildon's *Grammar of the English Tongue* (1711) urges "Children, Women, and the Ignorant of both Sexes" to read the top of the page, and "the reasonable Teacher" to study the notes at the bottom to get at the "Reason of Things." In 1735 John Collyer's *General Principles of Grammar* was using the same structure, but the notes now argued the fine points of practical usage. In general, these eighteenth-century grammars represented, as Murray Cohen has shown, the separation of practical from rational or theoretical grammar, of the language system from its explanation, and at length the general from the particular. By the second half of the century the process had divided—as in the card decks—into separate books of simple practical usage and of rational linguistics (as in Lowth's *Short Introduction to English Grammar* [1762] and James Harris' *Hermes* [1751]). [14]

As Cohen demonstrates, the grammar books of the early part of the century were a radical departure from those of the seventeenth in their turning away from theories involving correspondences between lexical and natural taxonomies—between words and things in nature—toward descriptions of the operations of the mind. They are always citing "the distinction between the arbitrariness of words and the universality of syntax." Words, as Locke argued, were so arbitrary and unreliable that little could be said about the relation between them and their referents, but much about their relationship with each other. One consequence of the Lockean view was that visual images were taken in some ways to be more reliable; but of course, as Hogarth for one realized, the visual image is another conventional sign, whether shop sign or iconographic image or mere "tree" or "house," and, like a word, can only have meaning in relation to other conventional images. So in both cases the real focus of attention becomes the relationship as such. Not the joke itself so much as its position in a series or, within it, the relation of things that is implied. Not a hand of cards so much as the relationship between this hand and succeeding hands from the concealed cards held by each player. Not so much a signboard as the relationship between the sign and the shop and its surroundings or other signs.

Thus in grammar books the emphasis is not on nouns but particles—on adverbs, prepositions, conjunctions, and interjections—and on verbs. As Hugh Jones says in his *Accidence of the English Tongue* (1724), it is "the proper Particles of Connection" that cement the "whole Discourse . . . together." For James Greenwood, particles are "the Names and Ligaments of all Discourse" since "the Mind is not always employ'd about single Objects only, but does likewise compare one thing with another, in order to express the Relation and Respect that things have to one another"—and this can take the form of "one continued Reasoning or Narration."[15]

The logic books demonstrate pretty much what the grammars do. Isaac Watts' *Logick* (1725; 8th ed. 1745) distinguishes the "order of nature," in which "the knowledge of things following depend[s] on the knowledge of the things which go before," from "arbitrary Method," which changes the "natural order" in order to "Persuade Mankind to any Practice in the religious or the civil Life; or to delight, amuse, or entertain the Mind." Both logic and rhetoric exist in terms of transitions, the "proper and decent Forms of Transitions" which Watts urges upon writers. He warns against "huge Chasms and Breaks which interrupt and deform the Scheme,"[16] but of course these are only another mode of transition. Watts is thinking of the aphoristic style of Bacon, but we could also recall Hogarth's series, where the transitions are necessarily "huge Chasms." In both cases the implicit transitions are at least as important as Watts' "proper and decent" ones. Bacon's defense of the aphoristic style argued that it eliminates the superficial and directs our attention to "the pith and heart" of the matter; and that it directs us "to action" rather than to "consent or belief," forces us to fill in the gaps ourselves, and prevents us from remaining in a passive relation to what we are reading. The omissions in fact draw attention to the relationships, one part illuminating another, which produce the bifocal series of double, coexisting, or mingled categories we have observed as the century approaches its midpoint.

2. Life as Pilgrimage and as Theater

My text is taken from The Spectator, that great mediator between cultures, or at least between the learned and the new reading public. In no. 219 (1711)[1] Addison says that according to one metaphor, from Scripture, men are "Strangers and Sojourners upon Earth, and Life is a Pilgrimage," but according to another, Epictetus' metaphor, the world is "a Theatre, where everyone has a Part allotted to him" and is judged by how well he plays his part.[2] Addison prefers the second, and I am going to show what his preference means in a few narratives of the 1720s to '40s. These are narratives in that they connect two or more points in time, but they are, to be more precise, a spiritual autobiography, a ballad opera, a graphic series called a "progress" and a "comic epic in prose." These are all works that in one way or another avoid being what the time would have considered "high art"; or if "avoid" is too strong a word, some of them ask us to redefine "high art" to include lower, more popular forms. In these narratives the metaphor of life as a journey, with its emphasis on sequential actions and a lone protagonist, begins to be augmented and radically altered by the metaphor of life as a stage, in which a role-playing protagonist has to interact with other actors; and this change is reflected in the major novels of the following decades.[3]

In the passage I have quoted, Addison uses the metaphors of pilgrimage and theater as alternative models of providential design. The pilgrimage stresses teleology: whether the Christian pilgrimage or the epic journey, whether the travels of Adam or Odysseus or Aeneas, it must have a destination. The aspects of divine providence Addison found in the theatrical metaphor were its apparent arbitrariness, inscrutability, and incalculable distance from our everyday concerns. This metaphor, he says, is "wonderfully proper to incline us to be satisfied with the Post in which Providence has placed us" (Epictetus himself, he reminds us, was a slave), for there may well be a discrepancy between the way the drama ends or the fate of the dramatis personae and the fate of the actors who played them. When the play is over and the roles relinquished, the actors are all equal; or, as Addison suggests, there may be new roles assigned in heaven commensurate with our performance in the assigned roles on earth.[4]

> The great Duty which lies upon a Man is to act his Part in Perfection. We may, indeed, say that our Part does not suit us, and that we could act another better. But this (says the Philosopher) is not our Business. All that we are concerned in is to excell in the Part which is given us. If it be an improper one the Fault is not in us, but in him who has cast our several Parts, and is the great Disposer of the Drama.

Whenever Addison discusses providential design he describes it in terms of a visual spectacle. Here in the present the pattern is seen as in a glass darkly; in heaven we will be able to look down, so to speak, and appreciate the pattern, which he describes as "an Entertainment" or "a Scene so large and various" offering "so delightful a Prospect" (no. 237).

But the example he gives is a grim one: Moses on Pisgah is shown by God a scene on a roadway, a spring where a soldier on his journey stops to drink and forgets his purse. When he has departed a child comes up, sees the purse he has dropped, and takes it; and then an old man arrives ("weary with Age and Travelling") and rests under the tree, the soldier returns to seek his purse, assumes the old man has taken it, and kills him. This scene causes Moses to fall on his face "with Horror and Amazement," but God explains that what he has seen is divine justice, for some years ago the old man had murdered the child's father. Addison is far from denying a providential pattern, but he distances it far beyond man's reach, portraying life as a journey interrupted by a scene in which three travelers come together in various roles, from the past as well as the present. To these people life *is* a journey; but to Moses, the human consciousness who observes them, it is a scene, and moreover one that has to be interpreted by the playwright himself.[5]

For Addison, the theatrical scene seems necessary to replace the determinedly teleological pilgrimage with a series of provisional structures, roles, and scenes, which are more appropriate to man's life in society. He can make use of both Plato's metaphor of "every living being as a puppet of the gods" and the idea that you "either learn to play it, laying by seriousness, or bear its pains," with its overtones of the immediate moment-to-moment functioning of the individual in society.[6] It is a metaphor quite different from the traditional one we associate with Jacques's speech in As You Like It that begins, "All the world's a stage." The emphasis now is on the willful adopting of roles (not the inevitable movement from one to the next, as from whining schoolboy to sighing lover) in order to control or conceal feelings in a polite society, to restrain natural instincts, and to distinguish social classes by tone of voice, gesture, and stance. For The Spectator creates a "Fraternity of Spectators," as Mr. Spectator tells us early on (no. 10)—"every one that considers the World as a Theatre, and desires to form a right Judgment of those who are actors on it." This is the theatrical situation, and these are the elements we find reflected in English novels from Pamela to Joseph Andrews onward—spectators, role players, frames and scenes, and a playwright. The journey does not disappear, but, no longer the steady forward flow of a Defoe novel, it is segmented: the lone hero does not vanish, but he becomes part of a configuration of characters, a group, often a family.

The situation is already implicit in the spiritual autobiography—a nonfictional narrative that becomes fictive or exemplary in the telling. Certainly in Robinson Crusoe (1719) the straight diachronic narrative of Crusoe's life is compromised by the fact that it is told by the aged, the converted, and so the new and different Crusoe. The pattern is seen by—written down by—the converted Crusoe, whose language makes it clear that the waves that bear the young Crusoe are the providence of God, to which he must entrust himself if he is to be safely borne to shore. The tradition of spiritual autobiography exploits the knowledge that people do not fully see the truth about themselves at the moment; the reason for writing such autobiographies is that the writer, in recording the information and later observing it, discovers some patterns that eluded him when the experience was new. Thus the convert can easily become the spectator of his own drama, or even the playwright, imposing providential roles upon those existential events.

At any given moment Crusoe is caught within typological or

legorical patterns relating him to Adam and the Prodigal Son, or to Jonah or merely to the spiritual pilgrim, but also to the selves projected in the alternative actions he contemplates as he moves along: what it would have been like had he never wandered, had he not been saved from the shipwreck, or had the ship sunk with all its provisions. His linear movement forward is structured by signs, suggesting another, a vertical system of analogues with an equally strong causal gravitation.

The important fact that connects Hogarth's "progresses" of a Harlot and a Rake (1732, 1735) with Defoe's narratives is that both center on the problem of the self and the process of an individual's defining and redefining himself in time. Hogarth, to the extent that he derives from the popular graphic tradition, emphasizes the left-to-right movement of causality from action to consequence and from crime to punishment, manifest in each plate and in the sequence of six or eight. But the story he has made of these elements is the spiritual pilgrimage, one concerning the search for a true identity. Brought up like Defoe on Nonconformist devotional literature, he shows an awareness that consciousness itself—and so the narrative flow—is not simply linear but layered. The distinction is between an allegorical world with allegorical figures and an allegorical world in which a Crusoe or a Harlot or a Rake moves about uneasily, trying on types or figures. Both Defoe and Hogarth produce spiritual allegories *manqué*. [7]

Hogarth, however, makes clear that his terms are theatrical. In the second plate of A *Harlot's Progress* (fig. 15) the mask, monkey, and mirror are straight out of Ripa's *Iconologia*, where the description of Imitation includes "a woman holding a bundle of brushes in her right hand, a mask in her left, with an ape at her feet." The ape is present, Ripa says (1709 translation), because of "its aptitude for imitating man with its gestures" (*ars simia naturae*), and the mask to suggest "the imitation, on and off the stage, of the appearance and bearing of various characters." Certainly "aping" and "masking," verbally and metaphorically, are present in the scene. On the level of story, the mask also alludes to a masquerade as the place where the Harlot has met her new lover: she has *worn* this mask, and so the metaphorical relationship is almost one of identity. The monkey too is a fashionable acquisition (like the black slave-boy) which has been made either by the Jewish merchant or by his mistress, and is itself an aping of fashion, which applies to both: she with her clothes and young lover, a "lady"; he with his old-master paintings and Christian mistress, a "gentleman." The monkey is shown trying on attire that resembles the Harlot's before a dressing table; and his expression of surprise at her kicking over the table (to divert her keeper from the retreat of her lover) is parallel to the Jew's.

In these terms, and in terms of those stage-set scenes through which she moves, we must say that the Harlot proceeds surrounded by alternative roles, indicated by the pictures (painted simulations from the brush of Imitation herself) which she and her keeper hang on their walls and by the poses, compositions, and iconography in which she places herself. These alternatives include, for example, the life patterns of the clergyman or the bawd, the ego ideal of a gentle-woman in keeping (which recalls Defoe's change from religious to social terms in *Moll Flanders*), and even the sentimental illusion of living the life of the Virgin/Magdalen and enjoying the successful criminal careers of Captain Macheath and Dr. Sacheverell. A nicely schematic example is the Rake (fig. 31), in the oblivion of a brothel, breaking the mirror, destroying his own identity, and cutting out the faces of all the portraits of Roman emperors on the wall with the single exception of Nero—who becomes thereby his new identity.

We should remember the Puritan doctrine that one must scrub away his own image from the mirror and replace it with Christ's. "We all with open face beholding, as in a glass, the glory of the Lord, are changed into the same image."[8] But the difference between the world of Hogarth and Defoe is that Hogarth, totally accepting the metaphor of roles, shows his protagonists, far from finding Christ, completely losing themselves. By implication there is something un-touched and pure—or at least authentic—about the original nature, back in the country, of the girl who *becomes* the Harlot. The reverse of the spiritual autobiography, his "progress" shows the closing off of awareness, as the Harlot's or Rake's models lead not to conversion but to self-annihilation. For Hogarth makes it clear that he has no doubts about the theatrical behavior of humans in the vacuum created by the inscrutability of unequal providence. The two ex-amples of divine justice, pictured above the Harlot's head on the wall of her Jewish keeper's room (or the one he has furnished for her), choose the moment when God has withdrawn and spared Nineveh and it is Jonah who is still cursing the wicked city; and in the story of

Uzzah touching the Ark of the Covenant, it is not God's thunderbolt but a human priest who stabs Uzzah in the back. The allegory has been humanized, and the providential structure removed, or rather displaced to human agents.

On the one hand, the order of divine providence has been reduced to the natural law of causality. It has been dismissed by the humans themselves insofar as they ordered the mutilated copies of the paintings.[9] But (except for one theatrical lightning bolt)[10] Hogarth never gives an indication of it either; and even his clergyman friend John Hoadly (son of the Latitudinarian bishop), who wrote the verses to accompany the *Rake's Progress*, refers only to the natural law of act and inevitable consequence.[11] While Hogarth demonstrates horizontal causality, however, he also shows the vestiges of vertical causality, which should be the divine pattern, but now consists only of humans imitating the models or the roles of the biblical stories and classical myths, and the vertical pull is that of puppet strings. When a priest stabs Uzzah and Jonah curses the sinners of Nineveh, beneath the picture the Jewish keeper prepares to curse the unfaithful Harlot and cast her into outer darkness.

The picture the Harlot hangs on her own wall (in imitation of her late keeper) above the portraits of Macheath and Sacheverell demonstrates the process by which spiritual autobiography becomes drama (fig. 16). This is a print of the angel staying the hand of Abraham about to sacrifice his son Isaac. The Harlot, who associates herself with Macheath and Sacheverell, criminals who were reprieved and lived happily ever after, sees the biblical scene as a comforting promise of mercy and reprieve for herself. The hand of the avenging father is stayed by divine intervention. But there is also the whore-hunting magistrate who has come to arrest her, and he associates himself not with Isaac but with Abraham. And the print is also, of course, an address to the audience, whose response is different from the Harlot's and perhaps parallel to the screaming admonitory choric face made by the knot in the Harlot's bed curtain: mercy, we tend to read, is better than rigorous Old Testament justice. My point is that once an object is interpreted in different ways by different characters, those characters have moved from the function of mere "others" (or objects) to subjects in their own right, with the capability of symbolizing their own "others." Defoe characters see the world outside as threat or providence, but for the Harlot and Rake the people around them are not only projections but real threats—cannibals who *do* devour Crusoe, as he fears they will. This is the other half of the Hogarth progress—the world in which the Harlot and the Rake find themselves, full of clergymen interested only in promotion or what's under young ladies' skirts, or magistrates who take too much pleasure in hunting down and punishing pretty young prostitutes.

It was not just any drama that picked up Addison's theatrical metaphor, but one which derived from the tradition of the rehearsal play, and so emphasized the elements of audience and playwright as well as the distinction between actors and roles in the drama on stage. Materializing precisely *The Spectator*'s metaphor, Gay's *Beggar's Opera* (1728) carried Hogarth from Defoe's portrayal of a subject encountering only objects to a dramatic model in which subjects encounter other subjects, who perhaps regard *them* as objects.

1728 saw the final flowering of the old Stuart world in Pope's *Dunciad*, which looks back and sees it all gone; but just a month earlier Gay's play had been produced, and within the year Hogarth executed his two major versions of *The Beggar's Opera* in oil, which set him on his course toward A *Harlot's Progress* and *Strolling Actresses Dressing in a Barn*. In the same year Fielding produced his first play, and by the end of the following year he had learned enough from *The Beggar's Opera* to write *The Author's Farce*. This conjunction of events represents, in its variety of visual and verbal forms, the transition from the literary world of the "Augustans," Dryden, Swift, and Pope, to that of Fielding, Richardson, Hogarth, and Johnson. Together, Gay and Hogarth showed Fielding how the Augustan elements of satire, irony, allusion, and analogy, from the protected position of a social and intellectual elite, could be modified into a more generous and wide-ranging—in some ways more sentimental but in others more questioning and skeptical, perhaps more "democratic"—mode. They showed, at the moment of political and social disillusionment, when it had become clear that the "Augustan Age" was a sham, the Stuarts gone for good, and the Age of Walpole (one of whose nicknames was "the Screen") there to stay—new ways in which cultural forms could continue to develop in England.

Gay's ballad opera and Hogarth's two main representations of it demonstrate the alternative solutions of a parody of high art and a viable substitute for it. The smaller version (fig. 27) shows large figures dominating the picture space and explores Gay's play as a popular, English version of opera—and of history painting. There is a small, intimate stage, subdued set, contemporary costumes, and a subject concerned with play acting. The larger version (fig. 28) puts a great deal more emphasis on the play as parody of high art, reducing the size of the players in their contemporary dress and playing up the operatic theatricality of the trappings that surround them. The effect is more clearly mock-heroic, reflecting Gay's intention to make thieves sound like opera singers playing gods and heroes.

One norm Gay and Hogarth have chosen is the bare, forked animal man—or the *tabula rasa* or even perhaps the Noble Savage. Then comes the criminal, who serves as another layer, a superimposition on the original, which if not good is authentic; and after that the courtier, politician, aristocrat, or merchant whose roles the criminal attempts to mimic. The second norm is the visual, the immediately seen and experienced. In both play and paintings the visual element relates back to Addison's emphasis on *seeing* as superior to what is *said*. "Every Passion gives a particular Cast to the Countenance," writes Mr. Spectator, "and is apt to discover itself in some Feature or other. I have seen an Eye curse for half an Hour together, and an Eyebrow call a Man Scoundrel" (no. 86). He concludes that he believes "we may be better known by Looks than by our Words; and that a Man's Speech is much more easily disguised than his Countenance." This is an emphasis on the visual to correct the verbal that derives from the stage and gives Hogarth many of his terms of reference.[12] Hereafter, as Fielding shows, we will have to watch the expression as we listen to the words; we will be participating in both a drama and a spiritual autobiography, observing an object while listening to a subject.

The dramatic scene is summed up by Mr. Spectator in an account of one of his participations in a spectacle (no. 19):

> Observing one Person behold another, who was an utter Stranger to him, with a Cast of his Eye, which, methought, expressed an Emotion of Heart very different from what could be raised by an Object so agreeable as the Gentleman he looked at, I began to consider, not without some secret Sorrow, the Condition of an Envious Man.

One man looks at another "with a Cast of his Eye"; Mr. Spectator sees "one Person behold[ing] another"; looking at the second, Mr.

Spectator sees an "agreeable" object (perhaps he knows his "character"), and, looking at the first responding to the second, he sees "a Cast of his Eye." He then raises these empirical observations to the status of generalization by concluding, but subjectively (and sentimentally), "not without some secret Sorrow," that the first is "an Envious Man." The interaction of spectator and scene, or of these three men, produces the general reflection on "the Condition of an Envious Man," but with no illusions on Mr. Spectator's part that this is more than a generalization raised by personal and perhaps idiosyncratic observation.

This scene will become eventually, in Mackenzie's *Man of Feeling* (1771), a situation in which the reader is a spectator to an editor, who responds to the author of the manuscript, who responds to the manuscript's protagonist Harley, who himself is responding to people and events he encounters (to understand which he sometimes needs an interpreter). In *The Beggar's Opera*, however, Addison's scene takes its definitive form as actors on a stage playing roles of criminals, who themselves play roles of "gentlemen," "merchants," and "ladies"; and these are observed by spectators in the audience who are no less part of the play because they are meant to read their own values into the models the criminals use as wish fulfillment, special pleading, and rationalization—and so include participants as well as spectators, some of whom talk among themselves and ignore the performance; and finally by the Beggar, who has written the play and revises it shamelessly in the light of the respectable audience's desires.

Hogarth's painting in its final version perfectly conveys this reading of the play, with the respectable spectators sitting on the stage, exchanging glances and roles with the actors themselves, and among them the lover of one of the actresses and both Rich the stage manager and Gay the playwright.[13] In the *Harlot's Progress*, then, the actor-spectator-playwright relationship remains in the clergymen and rakes and magistrates, who range from bored spectators to interested participants to models and authors of her "progress," which is (we have noted) a selection of roles. The first plate was already summed up by Mr. Spectator (no. 266), who plays the role himself of the clergyman who watches "the most artful Procuress in the Town, examining a most beautiful Country-Girl, who had come up in the same Waggon with my Things," but—and this is the point Hogarth makes—he does nothing more than remain a spectator. The causal pull of the Hogarthian plate slows down to comparison and contrast, or "this leads to that" becomes "this is like or unlike that," as within the scenes of a play. The structure of admonition or morality, which takes the form of crime leading to punishment, becomes one of definition of interpersonal relations.

Gay's *Beggar's Opera* was attacked as subversive because there were political references to Walpole, and because London lower-class types were said to be emulating the model of Macheath and falling into a life of crime. The second reason may have been an excuse for the first, but behind the Harlot's pin-up of Macheath was the fear, publicized in the newspapers, that people would imitate his charming, successful example.[14] In *The Beggar's Opera* the roles are no longer merely assigned by a stage manager, but chosen within the play by the individual himself, and so have become models.

The element of the theatrical metaphor given greatest emphasis by Addison is precisely this one, and the relation between a copy and an original:

> Instead of going out of our own complectional Nature into that of others, 'twere a better and more laudable Industry to improve our own, and instead of a miserable Copy become a good Original. [No. 238]

Quite different from Defoe's insistence on the need for rebirth or conversion into another role, Addison's assumption of an original nature that is good in the sense of authentic leads to the imminent danger of losing oneself, which I believe Gay and Hogarth describe. Epictetus' paradigm, in which roles are deterministic facts, has become *The Spectator's* primary awareness that there are human agencies which we *can* fathom behind actions: the fashions of gentlemen and ladies, the plays and novels, the social as well as the literary conventions, of the time. "Consider all the different pursuits and Employments of Men," says Mr. Spectator,

> and you will find half their Actions tend to nothing else but Disguise and Imposture; and all that is done which proceeds not from a Man's very self is the action of a Player. For this Reason it is that I make so frequent mention of the stage. [No. 370]

In *Strolling Actresses Dressing in a Barn* (1738), Hogarth shows the goddess Diana played by an actress who is caught backstage with her petticoats around her ankles, ignoring (fortunately, both he and Fielding would have agreed) her onstage role of Diana. Both aspects of the theatrical metaphor are implied: an actor plays the role, well or poorly, and we observe him behind the scenes, where we can clearly see the irreducible reality he is concealing in order to play the role.

Hogarth follows one way of playing *The Beggar's Opera*, in which there is only one system of roles/models, all bad. Fielding in his mature fiction plays it another way, as a misalliance of different model systems, one drawn from the Bible, another from the stage or fictional romance. In *Joseph Andrews* (1742) the comedy is generated when the innocent Christian models that govern Adams and Joseph come into contact with the models centered around affectation. Joseph sees himself as a male Pamela and as the biblical Joseph resisting Potiphar's wife—but in fact acts because (we learn later) love of Fanny Goodwill is in his heart. Lady Booby's models are something else again: "She held my hand," says Joseph, writing to his sister and model Pamela, "and talked exactly as a lady does to her sweetheart in a stage-play." She sees herself not as Potiphar's wife but as a Dido entangling a reluctant Aeneas—a tragic heroine who will end in self-immolation. The focus in the *Harlot's Progress* is on the relationship of the individual and his/her models; in the Joseph–Lady Booby scenes it is on the interpenetration of different model systems which never quite mesh. Joseph is unaware that Lady Booby is not Potiphar's wife, or a female version of Mr. B., and Lady Booby is unaware that Joseph is not a reluctant Aeneas.

Fielding comes fresh from rehearsal plays of his own in which the unit of narrative is the scene as observed by spectators, as well as by critics and by the author himself.[15] There is already a script, but in the rehearsal situation the author and his audience can collaborate and make changes even at this point, aware as they are of the characters as actors in their roles and out of them. The playwright's presence, nearby and ready to comment and explain, if not revise, is something with which Hogarth does not complicate his scene. For it is this amiable author who, like Gay's Beggar, feels responsible for pleasing as well as instructing his audience. The question of providential design in the structure of the narrative is therefore very differently solved by Fielding. The design is plainly present in *Joseph Andrews* and not explained away in terms of a convert looking back and seeing the divine pattern in existential events. The peddler *does* keep turning up at the right moment, and Adams or somebody else *does* appear just in time to save Fanny, who has called upon providence for aid. But this is also the story in which Slipslop, however grotesque, *is* just as she is described, because we recognize the literary conventions from which Fielding has constructed her. And the narrator is constantly explaining and demonstrating to the reader the literary artifice of the narrative he is writing. The providential structure is virtually congruent with the romance or comedy plot in this book which is being written to answer *Pamela*, a literary work that tries to conceal its literariness and pass as real as well as exemplary.

The graphic narrative is a very different tradition to be associated with than the tradition of romance or comedy. Herein lies the profound difference, despite so many similarities, between the worlds of Hogarth and his friend Fielding. In one, even in church *"Dieu"* is out of sight and only *"et mon droit"* remains in control (as in *The Sleeping Congregation*). In the other, human fates are still to a large extent governed by providence, a presiding comic Genius, or the author-historian who is creating the book. Whereas Hogarth imitates the *Beggar's Opera* structure in which the respectable criminals are present as spectators and models and are always pardoned, Fielding incorporates this structure within a larger romance plot with happy ending and rewards and punishments respectively for the good and evil. [16] The plot he follows is a spiritual pilgrimage, but he brings with him enough sense of the Beggar's forced ending or of the rehearsal play to hint that behind those happy endings can be either a sure knowledge of correspondence with providential pattern *or* a bitter awareness of the distance—of the conventional quality of a play's ending.

Tom Jones is Fielding's most complete manifestation of the theatrical metaphor. But by this time the density of reference to theaters and the theatrical model has become remarkable. We recall the jestbooks with their actor-personae (no longer court jesters) converging on the poker-faced Joe Miller and the theatrical game of roles and play projected by Hoyle, whose concern with the reading of significance in expressions and gestures of partners and opponents is as great as Addison's or as Fielding's in his "Essay on the Knowledge of the Characters of Men" (1743). Then there is Thomas Blackwell, who in his *Letters concerning Mythology* (1748) treats the metaphor of "the world's a stage" as of equal substance and significance as that of Prometheus' theft of the gods' fire or any other Greek "meta-phor."[17] Even David Hume describes the mind (in his *Treatise* [1739]) as "a kind of theatre, where several perceptions successively make their appearance; pass, repass, glide away, and mingle in an infinite variety of postures and situations"—and yet we have not "the most distant notion of the place where these scenes are represented, or of the materials of which it is composed."[18] In Hume's hands the metaphor lends itself to a radical skepticism about the possibility of rationally understanding reality itself, which was only faintly adumbrated in Addison's *Spectator*, no. 219.

The chapter in *Tom Jones* called "A Comparison between the World and the Stage" (bk. VII, chap. i) makes explicit the metaphor which permeates the novel. The journey—Tom's pilgrimage—is interrupted and broken into segments which are Tom's actions (climaxing in the bedroom farce at Upton in book IX), each involving an interaction with another person and the responses and observations of spectators inside the scene, various groups of spectators (readers) outside it, and the author himself. The climax is both Tom's arrival in London and his participation as spectator and actor in a puppet show, a performance of *Hamlet*, and a dangerously close rehearsal of *Oedipus*.[19]

The "Comparison between the World and the Stage," however, moves the emphasis from the stage (Fielding recalls Epictetus' analogy of men and actors)[20] to the audience, its divisions, different responses, and tendency to confuse actor and role. The audience becomes the most important part of the metaphor. Most of the characters in the novel, as well as its readers, fall into the category of audience, ranging from the credulous, the Partridges—who cannot tell the difference between Garrick and Hamlet and attribute human actions to divine providence (the audience to whom Fielding addressed himself exclusively in his "examples" of the *Interposition of Providence in the Detection and Punishment of Murder* [1752])—to the Blifils and Thwackums and Squares, who consciously misinterpret events, to the intelligent few who are expected to understand the ironies and, like some of the viewers of the rehearsal play, contribute to the construction of the fiction itself. These are the privileged members of the audience, like the author himself, who

admitted behind the scenes . . . can censure the action, without conceiving any absolute detestation of the person, whom perhaps Nature may not have designed to act an ill part in all her dramas; for in this instance life most exactly resembles the stage, since it is often the same person who represents the villain and the hero.

It appears that Epictetus' god, the playwright, has been replaced by Nature, or human nature, and the Passions "are the managers and directors of this theatre (for as to Reason, the patentee, he is known to be a very idle fellow and seldom to exert himself)"; and these managers "often force men upon parts without consulting their judgment, and sometimes without any regard to their talents." The author himself is merely a privileged spectator, whose only advantage over his reader is his ability to see behind the masks of the characters, whose role playing is self-determined and socially-determined.

He does emerge, however, as a "comic writer" who, by the conventions of poetic treatises, is entitled to use supernatural assistance for special occasions (XVII, i); and for a moment he is the "Creator" himself, though well aware of the discrepancy in his analogy (X, i). In *Tom Jones*, where peddlers only forward the plot when the hero has shown them a kindness, the outcome of the comic action is dependent on the freedom of characters like Tom, and the question is in what sense the "author" is governor of, and in what sense governed by, the unfolding pattern of events. The ambiguity lies, I believe, in the fact that while in the journey metaphor he is the *raconteur* of the tale, in relation to the theatrical metaphor he is only a privileged spectator (very like Addison's). He opens his last book (XVIII): "We are now, reader, arrived at the last stage of our long Journey," which is both Tom's journey along the road on foot and the journey of the author and reader alongside "like fellow-travellers in a stage-coach," with the author "an entertaining companion." ("Our pen," he writes earlier, ". . . shall imitate the expedition which it describes, and our history shall keep pace with the travellers who are its subject" [XI, 9].)

The activities of writing and living were, of course, in a sense parallel in the spiritual autobiography: Crusoe's act of writing was part of the incantation; his life was meaningless to him and to others until it was written down, materialized in words. The metaphor of journey, Fielding suggests in *Tom Jones*, remains as a means of explaining the process of living, writing, and reading the unfolding romance, with its clear-cut beginning, middle, and end; while the metaphor of theater must be resorted to in order to examine objectively and understand the problematic actions of both living and writing. The journey metaphor remains associated with the subject, who sees himself as a pilgrim (as both writer and protagonist), while the theatrical metaphor emerges when it is necessary to explain something about these figures in relation to the world—that is, in terms of custom, roles, and disguises. This is the metaphor they unconsciously live by.

Goldsmith was following Fielding's model in *The Vicar of Wakefield* (1766) when he had Dr. Primrose, his first-person narrator, tell us he sees life as a journey:

> Almost all men have been taught to call life a passage, and themselves the travellers. The similitude still may be improved when we observe that the good are joyful and serene, like travellers that are going towards home; the wicked but by intervals happy, like travellers that are going into exile.[21]

The Primrose family migrates to a new parish and begins to fragment as son George departs, daughter Olivia disappears, and Dr. Primrose sets out alone on the road to find her. The climax of his providential metaphor of life as a journey is reached, ironically, when his family is completely broken up and he is confined to prison (chap. XXIX, p. 163). In his sermon preached to the prisoners he asks them to take comfort, "for we shall soon be at our journey's end," and "the weary traveller" will "lay down the heavy burthen laid upon" him and find his heavenly (versus earthly) reward. The point is that reward is distanced into the afterlife from this point of immobility in the present. Earlier, when he sent George off into the world, Dr. Primrose had advised him to remember the 37th Psalm, "never saw I the righteous man forsaken, or his seed begging their bread" (v. 25, p. 26). The context of the quotation he chose is a journey: "The steps of a man are from the Lord, and he establishes him in whose way he delights" (or, "he holds him firm and watches over his path"); "though he fall, he shall not be cast headlong, for the Lord is the stay of his hand" (vv. 23–24). Though it appears that Dr. Primrose is intended to be in some sense educated, demonstrating a progress by his statement of the doctrine of unequal providence to the prisoners, the fact is that at the end of the novel a shower of earthly rewards vindicates his *first* interpretation (to George) of providence as justice on this earth. The fact that Primrose's progress is analogous to Job's may, as Battestin has suggested, help to explain why he too was returned his lost possessions.[22] But I suspect that the answer is involved in the other metaphor that informs Dr. Primrose's progress, and of which he is seemingly unaware.

On his travels in search of Olivia he encounters George, performing in a troupe of actors, and the progress George recounts takes the form of a journey, from the Primrose vicarage to London to Amsterdam to Louvain to Paris, and so on, each in a different profession: gentleman usher, writer, English teacher, Greek teacher, tutor, rhetor, and finally actor. "I was driven for some time from one character to another," George tells his father; and we recall that in each case he was given the idea of what profession to adopt by a friend. It becomes clear that Goldsmith has seen his journey as a series of roles adopted, and the metaphors of life as journey and theater have coalesced.

Once generated, however, by the recognition scenes with Arabella Wilmot and George and with George's performance in *The Fair Penitent*, the theater metaphor takes over: we are hurried into the grotesquely theatrical recognition of the lost Olivia and the revelation of her seduction (a fair penitent), the Vicar's arrival home with her just as his house bursts into flames, his imprisonment by the wicked seducer of his daughter, and so on to the final reversals, recognitions, and unmasking—a blaze of theatrical metaphor with which the providential resolution is expressed.

Only in the denouement of a play can the lowly find hope and the mighty beware (*Sperate miseri, cavete faelices*, according to the book's epigraph). The fairy tales and ballad romances, even the model of Primrose's life as Job's, are part of the system of analogies that becomes, with the appearance of George and his troupe of actors, specifically theatrical, with Dr. Primrose another actor. The members of the Primrose family are "all equally generous, credulous, simple, and inoffensive," and (like George) they pick up any role offered them. At the moment when Dr. Primrose is preaching life as a journey to an eternal reward, he is locked in a prison which soon turns into a set for *The Beggar's Opera*, with the Beggar himself virtually materialized to set things right. Even Job's story, parallel at many points to the Vicar's, is not a journey but a drama in which a puppet master takes away and restores possessions in a most theatrical way. Sir William Thornhill, like the duke in *Measure for Measure*, is merely the great Puppet Master's surrogate on earth.

The only scholar who has connected Dr. Primrose with the primrose *path* has cited *Macbeth* ("the primrose path to the everlasting bonfire").[23] The germ of the Vicar and his antagonist Squire Thornhill, however, as well as the novel's conjunction of metaphors, is in *Hamlet*—in Ophelia's speech to Laertes as he departs on *his* journey:

> But, good my brother,
> Do not, as some ungracious pastors do,
> Show me the steep and thorny way to heaven,
> Whiles, like a puff'd and reckless libertine,
> Himself the primrose path of dalliance treads,
> And recks not his own rede.
>
> [I, 3, 45–51]

Here is the pastor, the "thorny way to heaven" and the "primrose path of dalliance" in which the pastor does not heed his own counsel.[24] Here is the Vicar, the subject who needs to see his life as the hard journey of a Job with an inevitable reward for virtue, and the Vicar the object whose life is actually a theater with provisional roles and apparent rewards and punishments distributed at the denouement.

The *Vicar* sums up the various uses of the theatrical metaphor and serves as a retrospect on the period it closes. It shows us the two ways the theatrical metaphor was used by the contemporaries of Hogarth and Fielding. The patricians staged one form of theater for the lower orders, consisting of paternalistic gestures and costumes, and another for themselves, this one interposing masks between themselves and bodily contact with coarse realities (such as the lower orders). Both Squire Thornhill and Dr. Primrose (and his family) carry out these charades in their related ways. The Primroses imitate the Thornhills, as the hapless dwarf in the fable follows the giant into giant-battles.

The norms of self-control and protective masks to conceal the feelings reached to the satirists themselves. Swift and Pope, with their personae and ambiguous identities, eventuated in Goldsmith as "Primrose," who simultaneously criticizes the phenomenon and partakes of it. Addison saw role playing in society as essential (if not natural); the Augustan satirists largely echoed this—or rather Addison echoed them; and the earl of Chesterfield in his *Letters to His Son* merely overformulated Addison's formulation. But the generation of John Gay, Hogarth, and Fielding asks the question: When does the playing of roles become the imitating of models, which may not be provisional but prescriptive and self-enclosing? They attack role playing as pretense and as the loss of one's own identity in disguises. They share the belief that the original identity is probably better than the assumed ones (a notion Swift and Pope would have questioned). Goldsmith muddles these various positions and produces his magnificently ambiguous portrait of Dr. Primrose.

The case of the lower orders (if we recall our discussion of the crowd ritual) is analogous. For them the metaphor of life as theater— Epictetus' way of living with his slavery—was a form of effigy-making of themselves and thereby coming to terms with the harsh realities of their life. On the other hand, one of their few strategies for coming to terms with their rulers was to stage a series of theatrical threats for their benefit. Thus again one drama is staged for oneself and another for the "others." Or perhaps it is rather that the poor saw themselves within a normative theatrical metaphor of provisional identities and employed it to keep up a dialogue with the other group that mattered to them, the polite world. Perhaps they always took the roles less seriously than their betters did theirs.[25]

Imagine a country house picture gallery with portraits of Cicero, Sir Robert Walpole, and Jesus Christ. A Whig lord would see them as models for emulation—as would probably also a successful merchant or financier. A moralist would see such imitation as a loss of self, and a pious dissenter would agree, excepting the portrait of Jesus, which allows for an *imitatio Christi*. But Moll Flanders— someone below the level of official culture—would see such costume pictures as a means of personal transcendence or of escape. Her disguises, seen from above, are an obscuring or distorting of her true, absolute identity; but seen from below they are an opportunity for carnival, though outside the socially-acceptable forms of the calendar of crowd rituals. Even the moralist could not interpret Moll's desperately prudential costuming as social-climbing or an attempt to emulate her betters. The artist, on the other hand, could see his own adopting of personae as in some ways as desperate as Moll's.

For with the poor there was yet another dimension. The artists and writers—Gay, Hogarth, and Fielding—felt that they were themselves simultaneously living the metaphor and seeing through it, as part of a subculture of the artist in a hostile society they called the Age of Walpole. They therefore saw the subculture of the lower orders parodying the official acts of the official culture (as in *The Beggar's Opera*) and also regarded it as in some ways behaving itself *without* affectation, emitting vulgar laughter when it felt like it and not concealing its feelings by manners.

When Edward Young, in his *Conjectures on Original Composition* (1759), exclaims, "Born originals, how comes it to pass that we die *Copies?*" and refers to "that medling Ape Imitation" who "snatches the Pen, and blots out nature's mark of Separation, cancels her kind intention, destroys all mental Individuality," he is only materializing in Addison's metaphor the argument of his whole book:

> . . . illustrious Examples *engross*, *prejudice*, and *intimidate*. They *engross* our attention, and so prevent a due inspection of ourselves; they *prejudice* our Judgment in favour of their abilities, and so lessen the sense of our own; and they *intimidate* us with the splendour of their Renown, and thus under Diffidence bury our strength. [P. 17]

The concern with masking is only the obverse of a yearning for authenticity, which can be sought either in the high-art form of the retirement theme or Roman Republican virtue (another form of play acting), or in the low form of types who are outside the social structure altogether (or seem to be).

3. Instruction and the Family

JOSEPH ANDREWS' DESCRIPTION OF LADY BOOBY talking "exactly as a Lady does to her Sweetheart in a Stage-play" is followed by his conclusion: "But I am glad she turned me out of the Chamber as she did: for I had once almost forgotten every word *Parson Adams* had ever said to me" (I, x; pp. 46–47). He has changed the metaphor guiding his behavior from role playing to the related one of paternal instruction. He continues to adhere to educational precepts when, a little later, nearly dead of his wounds at the hands of robbers, he

> absolutely refused, miserable as he was, to enter [the coach], unless he was furnished with sufficient Covering, to prevent giving the least Offence to Decency. So perfectly modest was this young Man; such mighty Effects had the spotless Example of the amiable *Pamela*, and the excellent Sermons of Mr. *Adams* wrought upon him. [I, xii; p. 53]

Simple-minded chastity and nearly self-destructive modesty are the consequences of following literally the injunctions of Parson Adams and Joseph's sister Pamela. These are the educational models or mediators which Joseph learns to do without, aided, of course, by his *un*mediated love for Fanny Goodwill.

As a metaphor, the journey or pilgrimage becomes less a scene of conversion than of education. The two most popular foreign fictions-in-translation of the 1720s into the '40s, to judge by advertisements and references in the London newspapers, were Fénelon's *Télémaque* and Le Sage's *Diable boiteux*. The *Telemachus*, first translated in 1699, is a story of travel, education, and a son in search of his father.[1] The instructor is not, however, the father Ulysses, who is thought to be dead, but the wise tutor Mentor, whose body, moreover, has been taken over by Minerva or Wisdom herself. The plot of the *Telemachus* is not (like either the *Odyssey* or the *Aeneid*) about a hero trying to return home or trying to find a new home, or even (as we might expect in a romance plot) about the search for reunion with a lover, but about the son's search for his lost father—with, incidentally, his return home educated by his quest.

This prose epic begins with young Telemachus on Calypso's island, where his father had been earlier, telling her how he set out from Ithaca to find his lost father and save his mother from those importunate suitors. Both he and Mentor have by now concluded that Ulysses is dead, and he therefore needs to return home to his beleaguered mother. The knot here, as described by Andrew Ramsay in his "Discourse upon Epick Poetry" prefixed to the 1720 edition of the *Telemachus*, is "the Hatred of *Venus* against a young Prince, that despises Pleasure for the Sake of Virtue, and subdued his Passions by the Assistance of Wisdom."[2] Venus' surrogate Calypso detains him, having fallen in love with him as she did with his father.

Book VII points up, if we have not already noticed it, the parallel between the journeys of father and son, as well as the distanced version of Fénelon's popular fiction employed by Fielding in *Joseph Andrews*.[3] Prompted by Venus, Cupid naughtily makes Telemachus fall in love with a young nymph named Eucharis, and Calypso becomes insanely jealous in the fashion of Lady Booby:

> her Eyes darted forth Flashes of Fire, her unsteady Looks were thrown at Random round her, they had something gloomy and savage in them; black livid Spots distrain'd her trembling Cheeks, her Colour chang'd ev'ry Moment; a deadly Paleness did oft o'erspread her Face; her Tears did not flow so plentifully as before, Rage and Dispair having as it were dry'd up the Sources of them; her Voice was hoarse, broken, and trembling.[4]

She does a lot of such talking: "Where am I? O cruel *Venus*, what Course shall I take? O *Venus*, you have deceiv'd me. . . . O! that I could dye, to put an end to my Sorrows!" However, though Telemachus wants to stay on the island with Eucharis and Calypso wants to detain him, Mentor/Minerva forcibly removes him and they continue their quest. Taking the usual trip to the underworld and expecting to find his father there, Telemachus meets only his grandfather, who tells him that Ulysses is alive and will meet him back in Ithaca. There is a final victorious battle (among many), and he returns to find his father; but the meeting is offstage, after the epic's conclusion.

Joseph Andrews does not know that he has any father other than old Gaffer Andrews. When we first encounter him, as when we encounter Telemachus, he is not any longer searching for a father but only far away from home and (after being expelled from the Booby–Calypso house in London) trying to return home. When he gets home, however, he finds his real father. All the way from London he has been accompanied by his Mentor, or Wisdom disguised in the all-too-human attire of Parson Abraham Adams, who, when Joseph encounters the Antiope (Fanny) he loves instead of Calypso–Booby, keeps urging him to be patient and restrain his passion until they get home and can be married.[5] The narrative of Mr. Wilson serves structurally as the traditional epic descent into the underworld, where the voice from the past can be heard, and where (had Joseph not fallen asleep) he would have heard his father's story. But Joseph discovers his father, who has had his own odyssey, like Ulysses, and in both cases there is a father who has gone traveling and a son who, in some sense searching for his father, reenacts his odyssey, and achieves an education.[6]

Joseph's education is as stylized as Telemachus', beginning in book I with his confrontation by the prudential world of London and Lady Booby. He rejects both, though the second more emphatically than the first. After his expulsion by Lady Booby, he finds that the opposite, his pure simplicity and chastity, is vulnerable to the robbers and the coachload of respectable Lady Boobies. Next he encounters Parson Adams, who is at the other extreme of prudentiality from Lady Booby. But he learns in book II that pure simplicity is also folly: Mentor is discredited or at least subordinated. If Fielding opposes in a general way the old virtue/vices of Prudentia and Simplicitas in, respectively, books I and II, then in III Joseph begins to build his own structure out of their ruins: he begins to instruct Parson Adams.[7]

Telemachus emphasizes that an education is almost invariably the education of a son, and it implies a family from which he sets out and to which he returns prepared to assume his familial function. The individual is not a lone sojourner, as in picaresque fiction or spiritual biographies, but part of a family, of a group, as we saw in contemporary card games and in the metaphor of theater. Education was already defined in terms of the dissolution of a father–son relationship in *Robinson Crusoe*, and *The Family Instructor* and *The Apprentice's Vade Mecum* were only two of dozens of manuals that taught the "son" how to behave and advance in relation to a "father" and an extended family. But as in *Telemachus* and *Joseph Andrews*, the natural father missing, there is a substitute father, Mentor, and indeed while seeking his father, Telemachus enjoys a whole series of surrogate fathers, each offering a particular moral lesson. They extend from Hazael to Idomeneus to the aged Nestor himself, Ulysses' own preceptor and "father" of his mind.[8]

Moreover, one of the things Telemachus learns from his quest—from both friends and enemies of Ulysses—is that his father, while a great hero, was far from a perfect man. The lesson is that he must abandon the idealized image of his father. Then, when he learns that Idomeneus, the surrogate father he loves most, had years before in a momentary passion sacrificed his own son to the gods, Telemachus despairs of ever finding a perfect model of virtue among men. Minerva's advice introduces Telemachus to the subject which Fielding will call "mixed character" in *Tom Jones*, opposed to the theatrical "paragon":

> You ought not only to love, respect and imitate your father, notwithstanding his imperfections, but you ought very highly to esteem Idomeneus, notwithstanding such parts of his character and conduct which I have shown deserve censure.

But another implication of Telemachus' knowledge is that his father's absence has itself been a blessing in disguise, for without it he would never have been permitted to see beyond the illusion of human perfection (to which he would have been blinded at close quarters, at home) to the larger relationship of sons to a world full of "fathers" and tutors.[9]

These facts are more emphatic in the English translation because their context is Locke's immensely influential *Some Thoughts concerning Education* (1694), and behind that his *Treatise on Human Understanding* (1690) and the *tabula rasa*. Not only does the *tabula rasa* make education more important than before, but it raises the question, which Telemachus settles and about which Joseph and Parson Adams argue, of the relative advantages of being educated privately within the family and at a public school (III, v). Joseph takes the latter position, as does Fielding, siding with Locke, that "the only fence against the world is a thorough knowledge of it, into which a young gentleman should be entered by degrees, as he can bear it, and the earlier the better, so he be in safe and skillful hands to guide him."[10] And these skillful hands may denote the parent of one's disposition rather than the parent of one's being—just as the youth may seek the mate of love and compatibility rather than of a forced marriage. In *Telemachus* it is Mentor as Minerva as Divine Wisdom who functions as the ideal, transcendent paternal figure, who is actually a mother and so embodies both the disinterest and the feminine love absent in the real father. The irony of Fénelon's prose epic is that its hero has been journeying all along with his true or "greater father."

The other extremely popular foreign novel was Le Sage's *Devil on Two Sticks*, translated in 1708 and by 1729 in its sixth edition, when a much enlarged edition (based on Le Sage's revised edition of 1726) appeared and engendered many more editions. Le Sage's method is travesty, making his comic novel a perfect foil to Fénelon's sober *Telemachus*. Don Cleofas is a young scholar of the University of Alcala who frees the devil Asmodeo from a bottle and in return is educated by him: "I will learn you whatever you are desirous to know," says Asmodeo, "inform you of all things which happen in the World, and discover to you all the Faults of Mankind."[11] The practical education offered by Asmodeo is a very different one from Mentor's; indeed if Adams is a travesty Mentor in his ineptitudes, Asmodeo is another in his slant on education, though in fact he is a Lockean. Also a travesty Cupid, his figured cloak a parody of Achilles' shield, he educates Cleofas by removing the rooftops of Madrid to expose the hidden reality, demonstrating repeatedly that "the only fence against the world is a thorough knowledge of it." As Mentor showed Telemachus the positive way to behave in the situations of life, Asmodeo simply shows Cleofas life at its most deceptive and dangerous—the world that Fielding, as opposed to Adams, shows Joseph.

It should come as no surprise that the basic metaphor with which Asmodeo characterizes the journey around Madrid is that of a theater: ". . . for a Theatre is the truest Picture of Human Life," primarily because the great are not what they seem, and even *Lucrece* and *Tarquin* agree behind the Scenes."

> Such is the Force of Distance, and well managed Imposture, that the Pitch and Rosin that Fellow is mixing will appear to the Audience Lightning, and the rolling that Nine-pin Bowl makes him a Thunderer.[12]

This is precisely the world of Fielding's *Tumble-down Dick* (1736) and *Champion* (10 May 1740) and Hogarth's *Strolling Actresses* (1738): amid thunder machines and crowns and mitres being utilized by monkeys, the goddess of chastity is caught backstage with her petticoats down. *The Devil on Two Sticks* comes to an end after the tour when Asmodeo is swept back into his bottle and Cleofas is freed (from any demands Asmodeo might have made upon him) to put his learning into practice.

From 1736 onward Lord Chesterfield was writing his *Letters to His Son* (published in 1774 at his death, six years after the death of the son to whom the letters had been written). These letters perfectly reflect Locke's argument that education is not to secure the child's obedience, not to tyrannize, but to prepare him for an eventual emergence into the world—a moment of liberation. Chesterfield sums up the position when he writes to his son: "I think I offer you a very good bargain, when I promise you, upon my word, that if you do every thing that I would have you do, till you are eighteen, I will do every thing that you would have me do, ever afterwards."[13] The corollary is an emphasis on filial obedience *and* parental restraint for the purpose of obtaining greater obedience and therefore more perfect instruction. The image Chesterfield gives is of a man writing instructions to a son who is being handled by tutors and may, occasionally by appointment, meet his natural father. The letters are structured on a series of stages of maturation, which Chesterfield records in the changing styles of address: from "*Mon cher enfant*" to "Dear Boy," "Sir," and finally at eighteen, "My dear Friend." This progression is cut across by another: lessons of history, geography, and manners advance from entertaining stories to elaborate essays of practical advice. But the message is always to prepare for the moment of liberation:

> The more hours a day you travel, the sooner you will be at your journey's end. The sooner you are qualified for your liberty, the sooner you shall have it; and your manumission will entirely depend upon the manner in which you employ the intermediate time.[14]

In a curious way, this is a secularization of the old metaphor of life as a pilgrimage that ends in the release of death; the model is that of releasing a slave—or a colonial nation like the American colonies or any other oppressed group.[15] The father is the ultimate warden who deals with his prisoner through keepers. Though he never speaks of corporal punishment (which is left to the tutors), and holds open the future of freedom, he closes letters grimly:

> Adieu! and be persuaded that I shall love you extremely while you deserve it; but not one moment longer.
>
> I shall dissect and analyse you with a microscope, so that I shall discover the least spect or blemish. This is fair warning, therefore take your measures accordingly. Yours.
>
> I do not, therefore, so much as hint to you, how absolutely dependent you are upon me; that you neither have, nor can have, a shilling in the world but from me; and that, as I have no womanish weakness for your person, your merit must and will be the only measure of my kindness; I say, I do not hint these things to you, because I am convinced that you will act right, upon more noble and generous principles; I mean for the sake of doing right, and out of affection and gratitude to me.[16]

Even at his most urbane and ironic (or double-ironic), Chesterfield sounds distressingly like the Old Testament God. He puts a heavy emphasis on the necessity of copying, imitating, obeying, and remembering examples; on controlling and concealing the real, perhaps unruly feelings; and in particular on the essential avoidance of contaminating contact with low life in all its forms. Both he and Locke advocate the use of examples rather than precepts; and in practice this means that Chesterfield's own experiences are distilled into precepts, embodied in letters that hold the son at arm's length from any common experience. He is told that "the only fence against the world is a thorough knowledge of it," but is kept under wraps.

The position Locke and Chesterfield outline is one familiar to students of revolution: freedom is held out, chains are loosened, the student is urged to have experience of the great world; but the paternal demands become more shrill and pervasive as they become less easy to enforce. Chesterfield's letters, though in basic ways close to the assumptions of Fielding,[17] remain a manual and so precisely the antithesis of the form Fielding employed. The novel is in its very nature an anti-manual, hostile to all that is manual-like, and Fielding prefers to explore the implications of the pedagogic doctrines, which in practice means exposing their contradictions. He does this by speaking himself as a wiser, more generous Chesterfield, but including the point of view of the son. It is not only the son who demonstrates his maturity by introjecting the precepts of the father who believes that freedom is earned with age, but the father-author who introjects the son's (or apprentice's) common feeling that it should be *now*.

In the 1740s and '50s Fielding turns Mentor into a Parson Adams, and then into Partridge, who has the role but none of the substance. In 1759 the *Cyropoedia* and the Grand Tour—the materialization of the *Telemachus* pattern, the *sine qua non* of every young English gentleman—receive their ultimate parodies in Voltaire's Dr. Pangloss and Sterne's "Tristrapoedia." In the same year there is the Johnsonian Imlac, who, though characteristically wise, is no model for Rasselas. Only in *Tristram Shandy* is the Pangloss an actual father, with the parent of one's disposition, the ideal parent presumably to one side in Parson Yorick. Tutors, on the model of court ministers, become "false parents" who forfeit their educational responsibilities, or even false fathers who seduce their young female charges. To some extent the attacks can be attributed to the radicalization of empiricism and Addison's advice to but open your eyes and be struck by beauty; the mere sensation of seeing on the Grand Tour is hampered by a babbling moralist at your elbow. But as well as the built-in contradictions in the new official view of education, it is worth remembering that the apprentice's point of view was always popular with writers, especially comic ones, and a whole complex of cultural and social circumstances were producing a different attitude toward patriarchal structures in the family, to which Locke only offers a timid introduction.[18]

The process represented by the novel works, of course, in both directions. While Fielding was exploring the problems of pedagogy in relation to experience, other novelists were exploiting the social pressures to stress the moral and cultural significance of formal education by incorporating pedagogy into their stories. Moreover, publishers very shortly brought out volumes of the writings of Fielding, Richardson, and Sterne, "systemized and methodized" into undiluted didacticism with such titles as *Sentimental Beauties, Moral and Instructional Sentiments, Illuminations for Sentimentalists,* and *The Beauties of . . .* (for each of the novelists abovementioned), with selections arranged under the subject heads of "Parents' Duty to Children," "Children's Duty to Parents," "Gratitude," "Friendship," and "Power and Independence"—precisely those great moral subjects we have seen evolving in Fénelon, Locke, and Chesterfield.[19]

The Lockean argument was related to Shaftesbury's claim that the character of the ideal parent was identical with that of the True God—as opposed to the Old Testament God "who is considered only as powerful over his creature, and enforcing obedience to his absolute will by particular rewards and punishments."[20] And at the other end is Thomas Paine, declaring that "loving fatherhood" is what distinguishes his God and the God of the Old Testament.[21] The Fortunate Fall, which a number of scholars have seen as a fundamental structure of the novel as it emerged in the 1720s,[22] serves Locke as the myth underlying his doctrine of maturation. For God "allowed" Adam and Eve to fall so that after living in the world they could return at last to a more intimate relationship with their Father, one of greater love and understanding (along the lines of the story of Telemachus). Parents therefore should permit their children, at the proper moment, to leave the parental roof, so that they may return by a free choice earned by experience in society.

Many works of fiction in the period, ranging from *Robinson Crusoe* to *Rasselas*, and including *Clarissa*, send the protagonist out on his/her journey following a withdrawal from the patriarchal family, which is associated with the Garden of Eden. They may go of their own volition, as Crusoe and Clarissa and Rasselas do, denying their father or wanting to escape paradisal (parental) oppression or boredom; or they may be expelled, as Tom Jones is. The journey then becomes an attempt to re-create—with Crusoe, literally to reconstruct—that lost Eden out of available materials. But if Defoe's allusions end with God the Father and Adam, Richardson's and Fielding's extend back to Milton's Satan. Richardson attaches associations of Satan to Lovelace, who lures Clarissa out of her garden through lies and promises; and the Augustan satirists, of whose tradition Fielding's early work formed a part, evoked Milton's version of the Temptation as a paradigm of evil. Fielding is explicit after Tom is expelled from Paradise Hall: "*The World*, as *Milton* phrases it, *lay all before* him; and *Jones*, no more than *Adam*, had any Man to whom he might resort for Comfort or Assistance."[23] Blifil's name rhymes with the eighteenth-century pronunciation of Devil, and his lies help bring about Tom's expulsion; both Tom and the narrator later equate him with the source of evil, and at the end, after his own expulsion, he goes off, like the Devil, to live in the north.

Given his particular social and literary assumptions, Fielding was naturally more concerned than Defoe with the centrality of the society from which the individual is wrongly or rightly expelled. Looking therefore for an expansion of the expulsion story, as well as for explanations for its protagonist's actions, he pushes back his inquiry, like Milton's, from the fall of man to its antecedents and causes such as the fall of Satan. Bridget Allworthy and Mr. Summer, among other characters, have to fall before Tom can do so.

Fielding sets up a bewildering variety of families and heritages for the supposed bastard Tom, and to do so he begins the novel with the period before the hero actually makes his appearance and presents at great length the relatives and neighbors who are influences on his character. It takes two books (or twenty-three chapters) for Tom to make his appearance, during which time we get to know the Allworthys, the Blifils, the Partridges, and the gossipy Somersetshire community in general. Allworthy, despite a few half-hearted rumors as to Tom's paternity, is, in fact as well as practice, his uncle. Under his benevolent gaze move Tom's real mother, Bridget (his real father, the scholar Summer, is dead), and his stepfather Captain Blifil, who also soon dies; Benjamin Partridge, his putative father, and Mrs. Partridge, who suspects Partridge of the paternity, gets him expelled from the region, and herself dies; Jenny Jones, his putative mother, who is also expelled as a result of Mrs. Partridge's jealous accusations; and Tom's half-brother Blifil. So we have a real mother but only a very shadowy father, and a putative mother and father with whom Tom will have complex relations later in his history. In fact, Tom's history consists largely of his discovery of his true relationship to everyone else—to all those people in the first two books.

There is an interesting bifocality to these early books. Read chronologically, they leave Tom the "natural" child a blank among all these hypothetical genealogies, the point being that he is *without* the name, relatives, and fortune that would place him socially. One of the remarkable features of *Tom Jones*, however, is that Fielding deposits ambiguities along the way which have to be reconsidered by the reader when he finally sees the whole narrative in a true light. Scene after scene means one thing on first reading, and something different on second reading; the "sagacious reader," who is Fielding's equivalent of Hogarth's "reader of greater penetration," knows and does not know that Bridget is Tom's real mother and that Mrs. Waters is Jenny Jones, who is supposed to be Tom's mother but in fact is not. Knowing and not knowing, he experiences some very curious ironic effects in the scenes between Tom and his "mothers."[24] In book III, chapter 6, the narrator tells us of the stories being circulated about Bridget's "degree of intimacy" with Square, to which "we will give no credit, and therefore shall not blot our paper with them," which is usually Fielding's signal that where there is smoke we may expect fire. When the narrator then explains that upon Tom's growing up to be a handsome and gallant youth,

> at last she so evidently demonstrated her Affection to him to be much stronger than what she bore her own Son, that it was impossible to mistake her any longer. She was so desirous of often seeing him, and discovered such satisfaction and delight in his company, that before he was eighteen years old he was become a Rival to both *Square* and *Thwackum*; and what is worse, the whole County began to talk as loudly of her Inclination to *Tom* as they had before done of that which she had shown to *Square*. [Bk. III, chap. vi; I, 139–40]

Fielding gives this inclination as another motive for Square's dislike of Tom (as later in the parallel case of Square's and Tom's rivalry for Molly Seagrim). Yet it is hard to imagine why Fielding lumps together in just this conjunction what we suspect of Bridget's inclinations (and of Square's) with her affection for Tom. At the moment, we read this as sexual attraction; in retrospect, it refers to Bridget's motherly love; but does the former to some extent remain in the retrospect?

What such passages may mean is perhaps suggested by another irony, implicit in Mrs. Wilkins' remark that it would be better for such creatures as Tom "to die in a state of Innocence, than to grow up and imitate their Mothers; for nothing better can be expected of them" (I, iii; I, 41). Tom may be thought to have inherited his propensity for the other sex, or at least his acquiescence, from his mother, as Blifil presumably inherited his mother's *and* father's worst qualities of hypocrisy and gloomy ill nature. The mother–son relationship haunts Tom through the climactic books, in the figures of both true and false mothers, until the final revelation that his real mother had acknowledged him on her deathbed. Clamoring against the disasters at Upton and London is the less directly inherited blood of Squire Allworthy. The search into origins (though by the author, not by the protagonist himself) is a characteristic of *Tom Jones* in general, with its extraordinary emphasis on motives, causes, and explanations, especially as Tom approaches his crises with Molly in the bushes, with Mrs. Waters at Upton, and with Lady Bellaston in London. The family becomes one significant context which helps to explain Tom's character, conduct, and education.

Neither parental nor mythic figure (i.e., the typology of the Fortunate Fall) is altogether normative in *Tom Jones*. There is an irony at work when the narrator adds (after the passage about Tom's setting out in the world like a Miltonic Adam): "Men of great and good Characters should indeed by very cautious how they discard their Dependents; for the Consequence to the unhappy Sufferer is being discarded by all others" (VII, ii; I, 331). Allworthy, though the master of Paradise Hall, head of the family, and analogue to God, is nevertheless (like Telemachus' Ulysses) merely a human being. A more sympathetic version of Clarissa's father, he finds that he has driven out an angel and must himself seek forgiveness of Tom at the end. When the name "Paradise Hall" is first revealed, Allworthy is about to take his place on the "Chair of Justice" and wrongfully condemn and expel Partridge, as he later does Tom; and before this, Allworthy's house has been characterized as open "to all Men of Merit," "Men of genius and learning," who, however, turn out to be exclusively represented by Dr. and Captain Blifil, Thwackum, and Square. Allworthy is the man whose most significant actions, besides adopting Tom in the first place (a simple act of benevolence, which Bridget had prudently foreseen), are to condemn the wrong persons (Partridge, Jenny) and then the right person for the wrong reasons (Tom). Allworthy is the all-powerful patriarch, good but human, and therefore fallible enough to make misjudgments. One of the many examples in *Tom Jones* of absolute authority placed in a human being, he is the absolute head of a family. When Tom is in the family circle the problems are family problems, but when he is expelled into the world, the problems become larger— involving the threat of the Pretender, Jacobite "divine right," and absolute monarchy.

It is a suggestive fact that two years later Smollett's *Peregrine Pickle* (1751) follows *Tom Jones* by beginning with the period before the hero actually makes his appearance.[25] It takes eleven chapters to bring Peregrine on stage (whereas Roderick Random was in charge by chapter 2). I can think of no earlier English novels in which the appearance of the hero is so long delayed. It does not happen again until *Tristram Shandy*, where the idea of late entry is pursued with a vengeance, and Tristram does not emerge as an actor until the seventh volume.

The relationships and hereditary pressures that are only hinted at obliquely and ambiguously in *Tom Jones* are made explicit, indeed materialized, in *Peregrine Pickle*. At the outset of his history, Peregrine is not even in sight. Rather his uncle and father, representatives of the previous generation, appear. The weak but money-grubbing father, Gamaliel Pickle, already dominated by his sister Grizzle, marries Perry's mother, a far more demanding taskmaster. Once in charge of the household and pregnant with Perry, Mrs. Pickle sets about persecuting Grizzle until she drives her out. Grizzle then, looking around for a new kingdom to rule, hits upon the other household in the neighborhood, Commodore Trunnion's "garrison," a parody family which consists of himself, his first mate Hatchway, and Pipes, and has the advantage of lacking a female presence. She conquers poor Trunnion, who, like Pickle, is innocent of the wiles of women and their desire for domination.

The heading of chapter 11 tells us that Grizzle "Erects a Tyranny in the Garrison, while her Husband conceives an Affection for his Nephew Perry, who manifests a Peculiarity of Disposition even in his Tender Years." The chapter heading connects the two facts, intimating that the child is the new hope, the reaction against subjection and the affirmation of personal liberty. From his first appearance Perry demonstrates his independence and moral vigor; he is a chastiser of folly, a stripper-off of false appearances, in sharp contrast to the obsequious and dim Mr. Pickle and the subjugated commodore. Unlike his younger brother Gam (significantly, his father's namesake), he will not be curbed by his mother. But the danger in his self-expression and refusal to be curbed is evident in the fact that if he does not resemble his father, he does, in a remarkable way, resemble his mother.[26]

The satiric yet painful jokes she plays during her pregnancy on poor Grizzle remain in the reader's memory when he encounters Perry's jokes, which amount to his most pronounced characteristic, and suggest a similarity in disposition. Mrs. Pickle's pranks are calculated as part of her plan for driving out Grizzle and subjugating the household, and yet, like Peregrine's, each practical joke reveals something true about a foible of the victim as well as the perpetrator. To get Grizzle out of the house, she exploits that woman's folly concerning her family pride, sending Grizzle all over the countryside to satisfy Mrs. Pickle's pregnant cravings and ensure a good birth. She satirizes not only Grizzle's fixation on a family heir but Trunnion's pose as Hannibal Tough (she exposes his cowardice by craving three black hairs from his beard). But the jestbook aspect is always absorbed in the larger matter of Mrs. Pickle's character, for she is not merely demonstrating folly but tampering with other people's lives, using their follies for her own ends, producing painful effects, and revealing her basic desire for dominance.

Practical jokes, like those of Mrs. Pickle and Peregrine, were always ambiguous symbolic acts to Smollett, both the satirist's devices for exposing and punishing affectation and a cruel imposition of oneself on others: the jestbook as a popular source of energy in an overly sophisticated world, and as seen by a civilized eighteenth-century Englishman. As a novelist, Smollett tries to use its energy while absorbing both aspects into the subject of his fiction. He is writing *about* the Eulenspiegel/Howleglas figure as a denizen of eighteenth-century England, one aspect in Mrs. Pickle, another in Perry. He reminds us of her through his "Peculiarity of Disposition"—"a certain oddity of disposition," and "the caprice of his disposition."[27] The equally apparent caprice of her disowning Perry is the logical conclusion of their incompatibility. They are so alike that neither will allow himself to be subdued by the other. She is appalled to discover that, having found a perfectly subservient husband, she has produced a son who is a chip off her own block. She needs another son who resembles the father, and so she banishes Perry and sets about producing other children who will be more to her liking.

Her dismissal of and refusal to acknowledge Peregrine as her son also point up the difference between mother and son: he is proud and arrogant, but generous and somehow lovable—loved by the Trunnion clan, and in particular by Hatchway, who can hardly tear himself away from Perry when the latter goes off to school. He never loses his generosity and kindness, and his evil tendency is merely the reverse side of his good characteristics, which are his moral independence and his indignation at the folly of his superiors. Carried far

enough, however, his indocility can become a servility to social status, to sophistication and luxury, very like that of Grizzle and Mrs.
Pickle. The point is underlined when Perry, at his lowest ebb, ends
as a dependent not unlike Mr. Pickle and Trunnion.

But these are the consequences that fill out the novel up to his
final redemption. We are concerned with his relationship to his
parents. Like Tom Jones, he has a bad real mother who repudiates
him and a shadowy cipher of a father. All that he inherits from his
parents comes from his mother; he has none of his father's mercantile
obsession, let alone his stolidity—his brother Gam inherits these.
Dispossessed by the mother, Perry goes to live with his uncle and
aunt, the Trunnions, where to Grizzle he becomes increasingly "the
very image of her papa" (p. 88). To her he is a projection of her
inordinate pride in family and desire to have another generation to
carry it on; if he inherits anything from her side, it must be more
pride. But Perry's protector is his uncle Commodore Trunnion, as
Tom's, once his mother has denied him, is his Uncle Allworthy; the
pranks of both Tom and Perry affect their uncles. Both boys also have
younger brothers who are as cold and unfeeling as the heroes are
outgoing and generous.[28] There are also wicked schoolmasters who
side for prudential reasons with the worse brother, and a girlfriend
who is brought into conjunction with the families. And so on.

Although specific borrowings may not be out of the question, I
wish to stress only the parallel emphases on the relationships within a
family as dominant, replacing the shifting relationships of chance
encounters on a road. The effect is perhaps more striking in Smollett,
for this is the part of *Peregrine Pickle* that coheres, that has a kind of
unity and imaginative interest that is lacking except in isolated scenes
in the rest of the novel; nor would Smollett write as well again until
he undertook *Humphry Clinker* (1771) and developed the idea further
with the Bramble family group. Though known as a picaresque novelist, Smollett always becomes a tighter, more intense, more interesting writer when he gets to a small hierarchical group. The best part
of *Roderick Random* is the naval episode where Roderick is placed
under the control of a captain and a ship's doctor, both oppressive
and evil, and turns to a good first mate for help. The family-like
structure of a ship's crew remains in Trunnion's garrison, which is
converted by his marriage into a real family.

There had always been coincidental reencounters in the picaresque with figures like Ginès de Pasamonte, and Don Quixote had his Sancho for most of his journey. Joseph Andrews soon picked up with his Adams, and he had not seen the last of Lady Booby; Roderick had his Strap and continued to meet Squire Gawky and other unsavory characters. In England, picaresque structures of satiric exposition, as they grew increasingly more complex, tended to become intense knots of these chance relationships. But there is no real precedent in the picaresque tradition for Fielding's opening of *Tom Jones*. It reminds us that the relationship that most interested English writers was that between Don Quixote and Sancho, but Fielding goes much further in the direction of replacing coincidence of recurrence with causality by choosing the family as his locus.

It is possible that Richardson's example may have suggested the virtue of using the family as a center of relationships. By replacing the servant–master relationship in *Pamela* with the family in *Clarissa*, Richardson was able to correct some of the misunderstandings that arose from Mr. B.'s being both Pamela's master and the man she wanted to marry. In the patriarchal Harlowe family the father *does* exact complete obedience, and there are also grandfathers, uncles, and siblings who exert their various pressures on the daughter-heroine; the lover, a tempting symbol of freedom, is therefore outside looking in.[29] Clarissa disobeys an inexplicable and patently unjust demand of her father and is (therefore?) seduced from his garden by the serpent-like Lovelace. A family is Richardson's meaningful unit of relationship; and the effect of this patriarchal structure is almost wholly prescriptive, opposed implicitly to the love match that would result from the daughter's choosing her own husband and leaving the family stronghold.

The significant facts would appear to be, first, that the fall in *Tom Jones*—perhaps as a further testing of Richardson's limited definition of virtue as chastity—is sexual, though the evil is not in the sexual act so much as in the betrayal of Sophia; and secondly, that the true sin is thus contrasted with the sin Allworthy *thinks* Tom perpetrates, which is disobedience of, or disrespect for, the father. Tom is not guilty of Adam's and Crusoe's sin, nor can he, under the circumstances, be guilty of Clarissa's (it is Sophia who successfully weathers that storm). But he is made to appear to be in the opinion of the world—which is, I take it, the function of the Miltonic echoes.

Smollett makes no meaningful allusions to the Christian myth of the fall that lies behind Perry's "expulsion," but his treatment of the plot reveals its shadow. Once away from the family, the process of his dehumanization moves apace. As long as he was near people like Trunnion, Hatchway, and Pipes, or Jennings the schoolmaster, his egoism was directed into a desire to excel at laudatory pursuits. Off on his own, with only fools like Hornbeck, Pallet, and the doctor for company, he rises toward the eminence of hubris, from which he is eventually able to contemplate raping his beloved Emilia.

Perry's attempt upon Emilia might be compared with Tom's fall, a similarly sexual encounter in which, however, he succumbs to a second girl, with whom he was *not* in love.[30] Moreover, Perry's fall does not involve alleged disobedience of a father. He could not be expelled by the father-uncle Trunnion; but as if Smollett considered this possibility and discarded it, some chapters earlier Trunnion comes close to breaking with Perry over the latter's disobedience in his single-minded pursuit of Emilia, but the commodore capitulates and apologizes.[31] He is not an Allworthy. However, as if he were unable to abandon the idea completely, Smollett has Trunnion die in the proximity of the attempt to rape Emilia, and Perry's expulsion from his loved one coincides with his being cut off from his uncle and the garrison. Perry returns there momentarily at the end of this part, but all Smollett gives us is the epitaph on Trunnion's monument; the dismissive letter from Emilia's mother and Trunnion's epitaph, both in chapter lxxxv, close off the past for Perry, and he sets out into the world, a Crusoe or Tom Jones. It is as if both Smollett and Fielding felt that the expulsion had to involve loss of the father as well as loss of the loved one.

Peregrine Pickle has run over half its rambling course, and the next large part is not Perry's story at all but the Lady of Quality's. Only then does Perry set out with a new surrogate father, Cadwallader Crabtree, and chapters lxxxix to the end are interrupted only by a return to the garrison in chapter xciv to "perform the last Offices to his Aunt." This part, corresponding to a pilgrimage, documents his decline in fortune but ascent in awareness, and ends with his return to his real father's deathbed and his reconciliation with Emilia. On his return, we are told, "Peregrine, instead of alighting at the garrison, rode straightway to his father's house" (p. 262). His father, all passivity, has been able to use his passivity to one active end: by failing to write a will, he assures Perry of succession and thwarts his wife. Thus Perry does in fact resume his real father's estate at the end, something that Tom cannot do.

Looking back, we are reminded that Perry's life was in fact a series of expulsions. As Tom's first expulsion was his mother's renunciation of him to save her reputation, Perry's was also from the house of his real father and mother, for sinisterly obscure reasons. He had done nothing, his mother irrationally expelled him (though, as with Bridget, we divine her motives), and the uxorious Mr. Pickle acquiesced. There is not even a feigned disobedience of the parents, only a basic discontinuity between the generations. But the precise Adam and Eve situation has been transformed into one in which their sin leads not to their expulsion (Eve has deceived the patriarchal figure of Paradise Hall) but to the expulsion of their offspring. After his expulsion, Perry goes to his second father and mother, his uncle and aunt, and builds himself a more satisfactory life. When he leaves to tour the Continent it is his own doing, as conscious an act as Crusoe's and as disastrous, but without the explicit disobedience. The second explicit fall is his own but parallel to his mother's; his rape attempt as effectually drives away Emilia as her fury did him. It is the complication of this pattern, perhaps inherited from *Tom Jones*, that makes the first half of *Peregrine Pickle*, even when it is not admirable, interesting. Adam and Eve betray us and send us out naked into the world, but we betray God ourselves every time we sin, re-creating our parents' sin. "In Adam's fall / We sinned all."

In *Tom Jones* and *Peregrine Pickle* the fiction appears in its clearest, least concealed form, and this is a story distinct from Richardson's in which the father is a strong and cruel tyrant, the mother weak and acquiescent. The son has a real mother and father who are wicked and shadowy respectively; the one repudiates or expels the son, the other is dead or so uxorious as to offer no opposition. The blame was clearly placed by Defoe on the son, but here the father, as God the Father, is replaced by an Adam and Eve couple who quite literally visit the sins of the fathers on the son. The son, having inherited his original sin (unlike Crusoe, who created it himself), reenacts the parents' fall; Tom does so quite literally, but in both cases the fall comes through a sexual lapse, followed by repudiation by the girl they love. Their pilgrimages are directed toward salvaging this love and building a new life, not toward reconciliation with the parent. In somewhat different terms, perhaps we can say that one solution to the problem of the patriarchal family is the displacement of the distrust to fear of a wicked mother, who can at length be replaced by an idealized wife. Another solution is to displace the distrust to a surrogate father, who may well become as comic as a Parson Adams or Commodore Trunnion.

Smollett's earlier novel, *Roderick Random*, may be helpful in this regard. The actual mother dies as a result of the grandfather's cruelty and the actual father disappears; the grandfather then replaces the dispossessed parents, and the good uncle, Bowling, is required to save Roderick. Smollett conceals his myth here by displacing the guilt from the parents to a grandfather, pushing it back one genera- tion and then dropping the parents completely (the father reappears only at the end). Even here, however, it is the mother who is in some sense to blame; she was the outsider the grandfather refused to accept. The ship's crew offers another example of displacement: the captain is bad but a relatively passive figure, like Smollett's uxorious fathers, while the ship's doctor, who, Eve-like, influences the cap- tain, is Roderick's implacable enemy. The mate (who reminds one of Uncle Bowling, another mate) is Roderick's protector.

In *Tom Jones* and *Peregrine Pickle* the uncle has come to the center and adopted the repudiated son, but as soon as he becomes a substitute father, and not merely a rescuer, he takes on some of the father's authoritarian aura, and the second fall is away from him. The reenactment of the parents' sin causes Tom to be expelled from Paradise Hall by his uncle, and Smollett almost does the same with Perry and Trunnion, but the commodore simply lacks the authority for such a role. Trunnion is, after all, a comic parent, reminding us that in *Tom Jones* the structure is further complicated by a set of putative parents, Jenny Jones and Partridge, who give Tom love of a sort denied him by his mother and dead father, although that love happens to be the love of a mistress and of a scheming servant.[32] As a pair of parents, Perry's second set, the Trunnions, are as comically and as obviously surrogates.

There was, of course, in *Joseph Andrews* not only a good uncle (or father substitute), Parson Adams, but also a bad sibling, Joseph's putative sister Pamela. Here, where the family situation is most con- cealed and conventional, are the putative mother and father who exist only so that Fielding can use their daughter Pamela as Joseph's bad adviser and later repudiate her by revealing that she is not really his sister. The putative parents as well as the true father Wilson are minor figures in the background. Adams is in his way as human a paragon as Tom's uncle: as Allworthy is associated with God, Abraham Adams carries echoes of the biblical Abraham, at least partly to suggest the loose fit that results when placed on a human being.[33] Adams himself sets up the test equation when he says, "Had Abraham so loved his son Isaac as to refuse the Sacrifice required, is there any of us who would not condemn him?" (p. 308). Immediately following are the news that his own young son has drowned and his very human reaction. Adams' assumption that "Knowledge of Men is only to be learnt from Books" (p. 176), his reliance on the authority of the church Fathers, the Stoic philosophers, and his own sermons (such as the one on vanity) lead to folly and misjudgments not unlike Allworthy's, though on the level of unpaid inn bills; and Joseph's problem is to learn to act without hindrance from the two authorities that have formerly guided his life: Adams' "excellent Sermons and Advice, together with [his sister Pamela's] letters" (p. 46). Adams is both a good parental figure as uncle and a representative of the folly of following authority for authority's sake.[34] We must conclude that Fielding, while not wishing to repudiate the father and mother as such (and so making them only particular fallen persons), attempts to question the whole matter of the father's absolute authority. And so he includes an uncle who is the patriarch, the effective father, and proves that the whole patriarchal structure is, because embodied in humans, oppressive.

In the prominence they give to the family, *Tom Jones*, *Peregrine Pickle*, and Fielding's other novel, *Amelia*, are the harbingers. The last is almost wholly concerned with the family, focused on the husband and wife, though the parent figures remain. From these we look ahead to *Tristram Shandy*, where time is pushed back until the family, heredity, and environment of the hero, rather than the hero himself, make the novel's subject; the emphasis has been shifted completely from the pilgrimage back to the cause of expulsion (the Fall being another way of describing what Tristram is trying so desperately to explain with his typography and marbled pages). The pilgrimage is never undertaken; only an epitome is vouchsafed in Tristram's tour of France in volume VII. We never move beyond the family.

Tristram Shandy always makes clear what is obscure in other eighteenth-century novels. The tight, close interrelations of the family, which of course are nothing of the sort, become a symbol of unrelatedness, the more unrelated because among people who should be close. While in one sense this is turning the family structure on its head, in another it is merely detecting the broken relations inherent in Fielding's, Smollett's, and Richardson's families as well. Once again Tristram follows his uncle rather than his father and mother; and the uncle, though lovable, is hardly an ideal example or an ideal tutor to set before him. While the mother, compared to the rest of the family, is characterless, she is also the wife who at a crucial moment reminds her husband to wind the clock and stops his ardor with a cold, cold eye, and reminds us that the eighteenth-century novel is largely male oriented—subliminally so, as with the signboard of "The Silent Woman." The relations between the father and mother and uncle tend to define Tristram, who himself appears as a character only fleetingly.[35]

As a writer, Tristram describes the process as a journey, to be followed by the reader, another traveler; and for one volume life and writing are in fact parallel in a journey. But the question of how he got to be as he is (the question of his being), which he is trying to explain and understand, has to be presented as a series of theatrical scenes, largely about other people whom he can describe objectively or at least with detachment, and with no sign of providence anywhere among the natural laws of gravity and association of ideas. In short, in this novel, in which the pilgrimage of a lone individual turns into a kind of family, there is also a figure who sees life as a journey and at the same time sees it as a series of theatrical scenes in which actions are determined by roles called hobby-horses.

In his last novel, *Humphry Clinker*, Smollett brings the family and the pilgrimage together by taking the family group on a tour of Great Britain—a kind of journey through life, but punctuated by impersonations (Dennison disguised as Wilson disguised as an actor), which reminds us that there is a displaced romance plot. But it is for Bramble, the guiding force behind the itinerary from Wales to London to Scotland, that life is a journey; his view is teleological (morally and geographically) and he is himself on a spiritual pilgrimage back to his origins, which come to include baptism, rebirth, and self-discovery. His letters are panoramas and diatribes, speeches and satires describing the stages of his journey. His nephew Jery Melford, on the other hand, sees the journey as a series of comic scenes, which he presents for the "amusement" of his correspondent; he refers to conversations and characters by which he has been "much diverted," complains at Bath that the "same dull scenes perpetually revolve without variation," and describes his pleasure in viewing incidents which "are truly ridiculous in their own nature, and serve to heighten the humour in the farce of life."[36] But more important than his words is the fact that he does not take an active part in the scenes. He and Bramble run along at counterpoint, the one isolating and regarding individual scenes with detached omniscience, the other journeying on, a pilgrim in pursuit of health, virtue, and identity.

But the object of the pilgrimage is the rediscovery of a family. The loose-knit family of the beginning becomes a reconstituted and unified one at the end. Bramble starts as Humphry's protector, fulfilling the uncle's function, including his comically ambiguous wielding of authority; but at the end Bramble, the good uncle, turns out also to be the true father, who abandoned Humphry long ago, and the comically unrelated letter writers have become, as Win Jenkins says, a "family of love."[37]

By this time Goldsmith had published *The Vicar of Wakefield* (1766), in which the family is the social unit: the father the protagonist, the problem that of disposing of sons and daughters, and the pilgrimage the father's attempt to retrieve a lost daughter. He is still, however, a weak husband with a wife who dominates him (as indeed Tabitha Bramble dominates Bramble until Humphry's arrival) and has her unfortunate way with the children.

Perhaps with the *Vicar*, which relies so interestingly on the metaphors of journey and theater, we should notice what the various metaphors share: they have become provisional structures, of language or of mind, employed by the writer to express the difficulty—perhaps the danger—of representing any kind of firm normative paradigm. The journey now describes the fabrications of a raconteur, or the rationalizations of a clergyman, rather than the divine plan of God. The family is now loose and fragmented, and education is compromised by tyranny and rebellion. God's plan offered the model, but the novelist lets his readers know that he is taking them somewhat closer to existential experience than did the theologian or pedagogue—without, of course, reaching it. Unlike the theologian, he lets his readers know that he writes with metaphors or fictions, as society itself lives by the mediation of manners.

The theological term we have been skirting is *typology*, a term which describes Defoe's allusions in *Robinson Crusoe* to Adam and the Prodigal Son, as well as Fielding's way of writing in *Joseph Andrews*. Either Crusoe acts according to (or fulfills his) type or the old Crusoe, who writes the story of the young one, makes certain that the typology is clear to the reader and rewrites young Crusoe's life to conform to its pattern. The discrepancy in times and points of view is for a moment explicit when we read the different versions of Crusoe's landing on the island: in his journal, written some weeks later, he stops to thank God for his preservation; as he lives it, however, he can only run about the shore crying out against his hard fate. His memoirs mark the moment as a failure on the way to a successful conversion.

Typology in a first-person narrative like *Robinson Crusoe* creates character not as essence but as a triangulation of external forces. The resulting coordinates are what Paine would have called "the authority of the dead over the rights and freedom of the living,"[38] for typology offers an overpowering precedent (in the legal sense), which is in the past. It is a special type of allegory in that Crusoe, in the present, must make his life conform to the type in the past, as the allegorical figure must conform to the demon in him that signifies relentlessly "Prodigal Son" or "Spiritual Pilgrim."[39] As in allegory, we are dealing with an artificial world invented in order to talk about the real world of behavior; there is no insistence on the reality of the invented world, which indeed tends to be prescriptive, a representation of how one ought to act rather than (or in juxtaposition to) how he does act.

Typology therefore has two aspects: genealogy as well as precedent. Christ and Crusoe are determined by genealogy in that Christ has to fulfill all those prophecies of a Messiah, and Crusoe backslides because Adam, his ultimate ancestor, made his own slip; but the pressure of the model forces one by custom to live the *imitatio Christi* (or of a Prodigal or a Pamela). This, another statement of the theatrical metaphor, is the *modus operandi* of the novel as it begins to emerge in eighteenth-century England, and it defies any deterministic analysis, whether Marxist or providential-Christian, which is reductive applied to fictions that are *about* human freedom in relation to closed social and literary forms.

4. The Good Samaritan

THE LAST TWO CHAPTERS may have provoked some question of the relationship in terms of value or privilege between the models, systems, and maxims which trap the characters in the novel and the author's own models for writing the novel. These are very closely, but not exactly, congruent.[1]

The essential part of the myth developed by Defoe, it has always been apparent, is less man's isolation after the "fall" (from a father's good wishes or from a socially viable position) than his attempt to bring order out of the unfamiliar and minimal materials—which he proceeds to do in terms of the already known (his father's and society's assumptions). The desire for redemption or for gentility is the conscious or unconscious end that raises the endeavor above mere survival; but what gave Defoe the extraordinarily large public he enjoyed then and has enjoyed ever since, and also his existential (rather than allegorical) plot, was the how-to-do-it of building a house with minimal materials on a remote island or getting money in the metropolis if you are a female and no longer young or attractive. There is even a kind of admiration attached to the *ad hoc* construction of an identity out of what is minimally available, which may explain the ambivalence Hogarth shows in his treatment of the Harlot and Rake. Hogarth's model is the Adam cast out of his Eden, who, for Defoe, is someone who tries to rebuild his lost world— whether it is his gentlemanliness or his middle-class business—even if the former was only imagined—out of the limited materials at hand. And this reconstruction is analogous to the process of the writer, the Crusoe who is the providence-oriented allegorizer of the narrative. The narrative itself is a demonstration, following from the function of the Puritan diary and spiritual autobiography, first to the narrator himself and then to his reader.

157

In Fielding's case there were, in his rehearsal plays, not only actors and their roles but the playwright, who assigned the roles and passed judgment on the actors. Like the rehearsal plays, his novels have a strong sense of the writing *being done*—of the working at the writing itself as spectacle or as instrument, which is the centerpiece of these fictions. In the introductory essay to book XI of *Tom Jones*, Fielding makes explicit the relationship that is everywhere else implicit between his flawed but benevolent hero and his book, between Tom's attempts to rebuild his life and the author's own, of which Tom is a part. Once cast out of Paradise Hall amid echoes of Adam's expulsion of Eden, Tom sets about reconstructing a simulacrum of his own, which in his case means a world in which he can earn Sophia on his own terms. He must save his soul by regaining a place in society, and so he rebuilds his lost world out of kindness to the beggar, to the Merry Andrew, the Andersons, and the Millers, even to Mrs. Waters—a structure that will eventually buoy him up in time of crisis, because it is based on substantial values and a loyal few, strong materials, compared to Blifil's shoddy structure of lies, depending on such weak straws as Dowling. In the case of the author, he is trying to construct a moral fable out of recalcitrant materials— farces, epics, histories, contemporary novels, current events—and tells us so.

Crusoe's wandering comes to a stop when he builds—and though he tries to continue his wandering, it is clear that he must stay in one place and build his own home and his little society, which is a reconstruction of what he left behind him in England. So both narrator and protagonist of *Tom Jones* must, in a world where paragons no longer exist (and absolute monarchs are not to be trusted), construct a provisional world of mixed character and mixed government and of imperfect but suitably exploratory writing. Fielding shows his awareness that this book is, like Tom's life, a creation at a distance from—by no means the same as—the one before the fall. In the introductory chapter to book X, Fielding calls his work "a great Creation of our own," but labels his words "Allusion and Metaphor" which "we must acknowledge to be infinitely too great for our Occasion."

My test case, however, is *Joseph Andrews*, which begins with a chapter on "examples," by which Fielding means the literary models of Richardson's Pamela and Colley Cibber's "Colley Cibber"—both as characters and as written narratives that allegorize existential experience—and ends with Joseph's refusal to make himself into a literary model like these, declaring that he will never "be prevailed upon by any Booksellers, or their Authors, to make his Appearance [as Pamela did] in *High-Life*" (p. 344). In between, Fielding shows Parson Adams trying to live according to books alone, and in moments of great feeling throwing his book into the fire. There is a point at which a literary creation (Fielding never denies that either Joseph or Adams is this) can become mere fiction, by which he seems to mean mere model, as the book itself runs the same risk.

If, however, literary models are in general bad for the characters to follow—and the novel is about Joseph's breaking away from them and creating an identity of his own—for the author himself, one or two are, if not normative, at least paradigmatic. The parable of the Good Samaritan stands firmly behind the episode of Joseph, the robbers, and the coachload of Pharisees and Levites with its one Good Samaritan (the postilion), and its memory remains as a kind of armature supporting behavior patterns in the rest of the journey to Booby Hall. The allusion to the Good Samaritan shows the reader how he is to take each encounter when there may not be a postilion present but only a chambermaid named Betty. Without this precedent, we the readers might read some of the subsequent episodes with a wrong emphasis. Put another way, structures like the parable of the Good Samaritan offer signposts in a new form of writing in which (or so Fielding would have us believe) there are as yet no conventions, only the rejected fragments of Pamelian and Cibberian apologies.

In 1742 the Good Samaritan, illustrating the importance of charity over faith, was a natural paradigm for Fielding to employ. One of Bishop Hoadly's favorite (and most repeated) sermons was on the subject, and one passage hits Fielding's particular emphasis vis-à-vis that Pharisee Richardson–Pamela:

> We must be . . . certain, That an honest *Heathen* is much more acceptable to [God], than a dishonest and deceitful *Christian*; and that a charitable and good-natured *Pagan* has a better Title to his Favour, than a cruel and barbarous Christian; let him be never so orthodox in his Faith.[2]

In Fielding's version, Parson Adams tells us that "a virtuous and good *Turk*, or Heathen, are more acceptable in the sight of their Creator than a vicious and wicked Christian, though his Faith was as perfectly Orthodox as St. *Paul's* himself" (I, 17, 82). This parable, described by Hoadly as inculcating "the great Duty of universal Charity, and a most comprehensive Compassion," implicitly comments on those who are "never so orthodox in their faith."

Besides the sanction of Hoadly's sermon, the parable had a far more visible and public one after 1737 in the paintings by Fielding's friend Hogarth for the great staircase of St. Bartholomew's Hospital (figs. 29, 30). Hogarth executed two larger-than-life scenes, *The Good Samaritan* and *The Pool of Bethesda*, one illustrating human charity and the other divine; his pictures carry precisely the emphasis of Hoadly's sermon and of Fielding's scene a few years later in *Joseph Andrews*. When they were finished and in place, a newspaper report noted that they were "esteem'd the fairest in England" and, to judge by the testimony of Mrs. Pendarves and others, they became a tourist attraction, one of the places to see on a day in London, along with Faulkner's lapidary shop, the Holbein *Henry VIII* in Surgeons' Hall, the Tower of London, and the Mint. In other words, these pictures were seen, were part of the London landscape and the popular consciousness.[3]

A few facts about these paintings are relevant. For one, the act of painting them is as much their subject as is the act of writing in Fielding's novel.[4] The place was St. Bartholomew's Hospital, a hospital for the poor, and so the topos was charity, and the pictures themselves were a charity—Hogarth's own gift to the hospital. But he also painted them to demonstrate something about his artistic aims, and more generally about those of any English painter trying to express himself in a time dominated by Continental rules and standards; this was his first hopeful attempt to come to terms with high art, the last being the sardonic Sign Painters' Exhibition of 1762. When many years later he recalled the fact which was for him most memorable, that the figures were "7 foot high,"[5] he was contrasting them with the small figures in his conversation pictures and "modern moral subjects," or, as Fielding called them in *Joseph Andrews*, "comic-history paintings" (he had just published A *Rake's Progress*, before he undertook these sublime history paintings), and telling us that these panels—rather more than was expected of him—were painted in order to show the connoisseurs that he could also paint in the grand style and how such painting is to be carried out in England in the 1730s. What he painted, therefore, were the diseased and crippled patients of St. Bartholomew's Hospital, in order to represent the diseases cured by Christ *in terms of* those treated at this particular hospital in this particular time. He brought the Bible story up to date, and so created something which was a history painting but related to the "modern moral subjects."

The subject was appropriate to the hospital; but it also shows how central charity was in the religious assumptions of the time. Popular (that is to say Latitudinarian) theology taught that an active charity was at once the condition of salvation for the individual soul and the keystone for the practical betterment of society. Hoadly was Hogarth's friend (whose portrait he painted at least twice), and he was probably thinking of his sermon on the Good Samaritan, though there were many others who made the same points. He chose to represent in both canvases the wounded or sick, a ministering figure of charity, and some Levites and Pharisees who, in the Good Samaritan parable, as Hoadly explained, are "in the Service of God, and devoted to the external Offices of their *Religion*."[6] The verses in the story of the Pool of Bethesda that connect the two stories are these (John 5:10, 16): "The Jews therefore said unto him that was cured, It is the sabbath day: it is not lawful for thee to carry thy bed"; "And therefore did the Jews persecute Jesus, and sought to slay him, because he had done these things on the sabbath day." The point is that the miracle takes place on the Sabbath, and both Christ and the lame man carrying his mat toward the curative waters of the pool are violating the Old Testament law. The story of the Good Samaritan (Luke 10) is Christ's reply to the lawyer's question "What shall I do to inherit eternal life?" The law forbade the Levite and Pharisee from touching bloody or possibly dead bodies, which would make them ritually unclean, whereas the Samaritan was already unclean. And so, as Christ makes clear to the lawyer, an act of charity transcends faith, the law, or orthodoxy.

Hogarth and Fielding shared a preference for New Testament subjects, whereas the Old Testament story of Potiphar's wife is obviously an inappropriate model for Joseph facing Lady Booby, as the role of Abraham leads Parson Adams to defend the prophet's sacrifice of his son Isaac, though a few moments later he has broken through the role and is lamenting the announced death of his own son. The Old Testament God was precisely what religion, love, and charity were not about. The paradigmatic story was Abraham's sacrifice of Isaac, summing up the patriarchal family, filial obedience, and arbitrary justice of a sort that could easily be associated with classical (especially Ovidian) mythology. Whereas the New Testament is the story of Christ's attempt to bring man back to the undefiled source of religion in love, in the face of the opposition of the scribes and Pharisees—those who repeat by rote, who go by the written, the inscribed law, and who associate Christ with publicans, sinners, and harlots—the stories Hogarth chose were precisely those where the New Testament ethos of Christ comes into conflict with the Pharasaic law.

In Hogarth's case I suspect that references to legality make a comment on the rules of high art as well as those of society and religion. He is saying something in favor of the artist-Samaritan who refuses to follow blindly the rules of the art treatises or those of patrons. One rule is that a painter of drolls does not attempt the highest genre, history painting. After he had finished the two large panels, Hogarth added three small reddish monochrome panels beneath telling the story of Rahere, the founder of St. Bartholomew's Hospital, thus connecting divine charity with an even more human and outcast Samaritan. For Rahere was a *jongleur* or public entertainer who recounted tales of comic heroes, sang, tumbled, and led dancing bears. But he rose from humble origins and little education to be the favorite entertainer of King Henry II, and with his wealth he endowed the church and hospital. Hogarth, whose childhood was spent in the shadow of the hospital, and who by 1737 was a successful engraver and a governor of the hospital, suggests a parallel to his own career of painting comic histories, which has now ascended to this large gift of charity in the form of the highest genre.[7]

And yet the celebration of charity, couched in terms of history painting, is a biblical retelling with variations—a special case of travesty—of his comic-history paintings. In the foreground of *The Good Samaritan* is the wounded man and his helper; in the background, the Levite walks past without pausing, his head buried in a book of the law, and the priest mounts the hill looking to heaven and accepting the homage of an admirer. In *The Pool of Bethesda* the lame man is in the foreground, and behind him is a little group that is not in the biblical text. It is added by Hogarth to explain why the lame man cannot get into the pool: like the woman and her ailing child, he has been pushed aside by a burly attendant who accepts money to assist a more prosperous, indeed more "respectable" group, consisting of a rich man and his attractive mistress. One of Hogarth's implications is that the disease of the young woman, who resembles a Titian Venus, is a disease of love, a perversion of the love which is charity. The most radical case of this structure in Hogarth's comic-histories is the *Harlot's Progress*, where the only "charity" the Harlot receives is venereal disease; but in all the progresses the protagonist, however guilty, is essentially the poor robbed man, ignored by all the Pharisees and hypocrites who pass by, pushed aside by the "great men" and their mistresses. The exception in each case is a single Good Samaritan: with the Harlot, a poor noseless servant woman (again suffering from venereal disease); with the Rake, a fallen young woman named Sarah Young. The difference is between a satiric and a heroic mode: in one the Samaritan is peripheral, in the other central.

It is a question with Hogarth, however, whether we can say that *eros* is a perversion of *caritas* or whether *caritas* is a sublimation of *eros*. Sarah Young is the Rake's cast-off mistress, whose love—once thwarted—takes the form of charity: in plate 4 (fig. 32) she saves him from the bailiffs with her "widow's mite" in a gesture which resembles Christ's in *The Pool of Bethesda*, and she is last seen (fig. 33) administering to him (now himself burned out by syphilis, the end of *eros*) in Bedlam in a pose which recalls both pietàs and Hogarth's own *Good Samaritan*. In short, the meaning of his Christ and Good Samaritan is less the sum of a series of resemblances to works of art in the great tradition of European art than to his own recent engravings of *A Rake's Progress*.[8]

Five years after its unveiling, *The Good Samaritan* was used by Fielding as the moral paradigm of *Joseph Andrews*. Hogarth's version of charity was, as I have suggested, part of the London landscape, but it was also the work of a friend, whom Fielding acknowledges in his preface as the "comic-history painter" whose graphic work is most like his own, and to whom he alludes more than once in the course of the novel. When Joseph encounters the robbers on the highway, we recall the Good Samaritan because the story and setting are similar, but also because before Joseph leaves London analogies have already connected him and the biblical Joseph, Parson Adams, and the biblical

Abraham. The encounter on the road is then followed by one with the Tow-wouse family in the inn where Joseph is taken for treatment; the Good Samaritan is in this case a servant girl named Betty, who is later discharged for going to bed with her master, Mr. Tow-wouse. There are other occasions, such as the unpaid inn reckoning, when the Levite Parson Trulliber refuses to help his fellow clergyman Adams, and a poor peddler gives his mite. Fielding too stresses the Samaritan's uncleanness: the postilion is later transported for robbing a hen roost, as Betty is discharged for her sexual transgression.

I am arguing that though Hogarth and Fielding share the assumption of charity's preeminence, the Good Samaritan is based by Fielding on an existing image by Hogarth, and the context of that image determines in various ways his use of it. For one thing, there is something distinctly odd about Betty the chambermaid. We are told that she is charitable because she is sexually attracted to Joseph; details are given of her passing on to him an ex-lover's shirt and (less pleasantly) to other lovers her ex-lover's disease. Her ex-lover has deserted her, and she may be reacting to Joseph as another surrogate. Certainly, when he will have none of her, she gives in to Mr. Tow-wouse's entreaties and goes to bed with him—an act of charity analogous, we might think, to her care of the wounded Joseph. She is, of course, like the postilion, an anti-Pamela whose transgression in Pamela's strict world would cast her into outer darkness. But she is also related to the charity of Hogarth's Christ figure, which finds its parallel in the strange Sarah Young of A Rake's Progress; both are mediators, but Sarah is a person whose *caritas* is a development out of a frustrated *eros*. This suggestion of an etiology for charity (perhaps already overdetermined by the precedent of Pamela) derives from the conflation of the St. Bartholomew's pictures and the Rake's Progress, and it suggests that for Fielding, as for Hogarth, the context of the St. Bartholomew's images includes the Rake's Progress.

Fielding's use of The Good Samaritan also shows awareness of its context as part of a pair with The Pool of Bethesda, human as against divine charity. When Fanny Goodwill, carried off by the henchmen of a brutal squire to be ravished, calls for help, she first cries out for assistance to the henchmen and to the countryside around her, "but finding none, she lifted her Eyes to Heaven, and supplicated the Divine Assistance to preserve her Innocence" (III, xii, 268). And at just that moment "a Horseman now appeared in the

Road" and asks what is the matter. But when he is told that she is an adulterous wife being returned to her husband, he (a husband himself) rides on. Then a second pair of horsemen pass, one of whom wishes he were the "Adulterer," while the other (a servant of Peter Pounce) recognizes Fanny and saves her.

Again, when Parson Adams' son is drowning, there just happen to be two passersby, one of whom runs to tell the family the news of their son's death, and the other (the same poor peddler who helped Adams with his inn reckoning) dives in and, at the risk of his own life, saves the boy.

A divine providence, which answers Fanny's plea and puts two passersby near the pond where Jacky is drowning, is introduced by Fielding to offer an opportunity for human charity to show itself. It was characteristic of Hogarth to keep the divine and the human acts of charity separate, two alternatives in two different worlds. It is equally characteristic of Fielding to conflate the divine and the human, but for a particular purpose: by repeating the situation (as well as the peddler) he introduces the divine pattern in order to allow a deeper analysis and a more probing conclusion about the possibility of assessing human charity. The contrast emerges as less between Levite and Samaritan than between interested and disinterested responses. For only the poor postilion and peddler are, perhaps *can* be, genuinely disinterested. Other Samaritans act only because they happen to be acquainted with the victim: Fanny is saved from her abduction only by the servant who knows her. In another scene, following another cry of Fanny's for divine assistance from a would-be rapist, she and Adams, among Levites who are convicting them and freeing the rapist, are saved by a gentleman who happens to recognize Adams and can identify him.

These are situations in which divine providence serves as a test of human charity, with as many degrees (and qualifications) of the Samaritan image as of the Levite. Only, moreover, by a gross manipulation of things can God or the author (in Fielding's terms, a surrogate creator) at just the right moment bring just the person who recognizes Fanny and Adams into the picture. Fielding seems to be introducing the hand of divine providence largely to demonstrate the problem of human choice at the heart of charity, which puts in question the parable of the Good Samaritan itself.

Hoadly's sermon on the Good Samaritan had taken pains to

remind its auditors of the crucial consideration from *their* point of view:

> That this universal Charity is not designed to break in upon those *Duties* which we owe to *Ourselves*, our *Parents*, our *Children*, our *Friends*, nay, and our *Acquaintances*. It is not in the Power of Any Man to assist every One in distress: and Nature directs Him to prefer *These* before *Strangers*, when they come in Competition, and are in the same Degree of Want, or Distress.[9]

This, he explains, is why Christ takes the case of a person in the most dire need. And yet, had the Levite and the priest been on their way to succor some near friend or relation, their conduct would not have been as blameworthy. The "doctrine" which the parable teaches, according to Hoadly, is "that Whoever of the human Race stands in need of our Assistance; whom we can relieve without Injury to *Ourselves*; or without neglecting *Others*, in the same Condition, whom we much more ought to relieve; has a Title to our Benevolence and Kindness."

I do not mean to suggest that Hoadly's sermon, from being a positive model, has become a negative one; Richardson's *Pamela* intervenes, and, more directly related to Hoadly's sermon, Richardson's *Apprentice's Vade Mecum* of 1734:

> But after all, there may be *some Cases* that may be very critical, and in which a worthy Friend may appear to be so plung'd, as that it may, without *great* Risques, be in your Power to save him from impending Ruin: In such an arduous Case, it may not be unworthy of your Prudence to step something out of the Way to rescue such a one: But then even in *this* Case, let a *young* Man do nothing rashly, nor of his own Head, but consult his Friends before he makes a hasty Step, lest the Consequences of his Kindness should prove fatal to him.[10]

From the spectrum of prudence in the coachful of respectable people who attend Joseph, naked in the ditch, to the cases of Betty and the later passersby, Fielding indicates how prevalent in this world are the demands of self, and how they can serve both good and evil ends.

The model of the Good Samaritan, then, does not—cannot— precisely fit a given situation; at least not as it is interpreted by a contemporary divine in a published sermon. It operates, I believe, rather like the Choice of Hercules in Hogarth's *Beggar's Opera* or the first plate of *A Harlot's Progress*: it is a model for the action, but one that is part of a structure of divine providence in which Levites and priests are *not* rushing to their mothers' bedsides and there are no conflicting loyalties, and therefore it shows the deviations rather than the congruences.[11] Any structure that is identifiable and redolent of the past is going to be inappropriate to a situation here and now. But, as I have tried to show, this is truer of the Old Testament than of the New, truer of the Biblical parable than of the Hogarthian painting in the middle of London, which already retells the parable as Fielding thinks it should be retold, in terms of his own time.

The paradigmatic plot of *Joseph Andrews*, as is well known, is an epic one, which draws attention away from contingencies and ambiguities to what Fielding wishes the reader to see as essential. Joseph's travels have suggestive affinities with Ulysses' and Aeneas', and Lady Booby and Joseph may recall Dido and Aeneas (at least in Lady Booby's interpretation). A more precise model, however, is Fénelon's *Telemachus*, which, I have argued in an earlier chapter, shifts the emphasis from the search for reunion with Fanny onto the son's search for his father.[12] Adams is of course a travesty Mentor and Joseph, when he falls asleep during Wilson's story, a travesty Telemachus; but even Adams is more than this; he is a contemporary parson whose function in the plot is clarified by the parallel with Telemachus' adviser. Joseph's journey, as the overlay of the *Telemachus* tells us, is an education, another version of a *Cyropoedia*. Andrew Ramsay, who himself produced a *Travels of Cyrus* (tr. 1727), in his "Discourse upon Epick Poetry" appended to the *Telemachus* distinguishes between the model for a character and for an action, arguing that the characters of Homer's gods, who do not act properly, are below those of Fénelon's heroes. A writer therefore should not use characters uncritically as models for his own, but he can imitate the epic actions of Homer and Virgil and draw upon their undeniable strengths.[13] Telemachus himself is above the heroes of Homer precisely because he is not *supposed* to be a perfect hero: Fénelon "stirs up our Emulation, by setting before our Eyes an Example of a young Man, who, with the same Imperfections that every one finds in himself, performs the most noble and virtuous actions" (p. xl). Telemachus—or Joseph—is intended to rub against, jostle with, the ideal models, like Pamela in her way, the biblical Joseph in his, and Adams in his, and come out ("with the same Imperfections that every one finds in himself") as winner.

The *Telemachus* remains a prescriptive narrative structure: it is the prototype of education manuals, and it says that Joseph *ought* to act as a son in search of his father and education. But Joseph himself, not knowing that he lacks a father, *cannot,* and so is quite different from the character who imposes on his experience or on the natural objects or people around him *his own* interpretations. Fielding's narrator is like Robinson Crusoe in that he imposes value-centered models of his own, separate from the self-images or ego ideals of his characters. His characters' readings are symbolic ones, but his own reading is allegorical.

Insofar as the literary quality of any character's experience is stereotypical, so is the narrator's with his Good Samaritan and Telemachus; and Fielding is aware of this, balancing a biblical analogue against a classical analogue and carefully deviating from both. In the same way, he leaves no doubt that divine providence is a structure closely allied to his own artifice as author. But distinctions can be made and degrees measured. It is noticeable that the examples in the first part of *Joseph Andrews* are predominantly from literature—Pamela, Cibber, Abraham, and Joseph, and even the stories of the Good Samaritan and Telemachus. Then, with the sharp contrast of the totally literary tale of "Leonora the Jilt" (going back to Le Sage's model in *The Devil on Two Sticks*), followed by the experiential tale of Mr. Wilson, the examples begin to be less literary and more from life. Pamela, for instance, appears in the first part of the novel as a literary model—in Richardson's novel and in her own letters to Joseph—and in the second part as a character in the "real" world of the novel's Booby Hall, behaving both as sister and as one shaped by Richardson's and her own strictures.

With the introduction to book III, which follows upon the Leonora story, and is about the imitation of "life," Fielding begins to introduce living people, contemporaries, as models—the earl of Chesterfield and Ralph Allen; and he follows these in the next chapter by introducing Mr. Wilson, who is neither Levite nor Samaritan but simply a life lived in the 1730s. To emphasize the nonliterary quality of his narrative, Fielding precedes it by Adams' pedantic harangue on epic actions; and follows it by Joseph's sermon in which more live examples (the Man of Ross and Alexander Pope) are introduced, including Hogarth himself.

Wilson's narrative is itself a "rake's progress" that nicely complements the models of *The Good Samaritan* and *Pool of Bethesda*. The materials are far less stylized than in the story of Joseph and Adams, let alone in the models behind and around them. The spiritual pilgrimage and the Hogarthian progress are forms which Fielding apparently regards as different and more closely related to life, perhaps because they do not carry a specific title or name like *Pamela* or *Telemachus* or *Samaritan*, or a generic name like "classical epic" or "biblical parable." I would suggest that Fielding probably uses "progress" for Wilson because Hogarth's *Harlot's* and *Rake's Progress* were visual and so not "literary," and this may tell something about the distinction between visual and written fictions in the 1740s—of the privileged status accorded the visual and gestural over the written by writers as different as Fielding and Richardson.[14] Hogarth's "progresses" were also about the poor and criminals, people beneath the regard of "literary" forms, and yet people like Wilson who try on the masks of gentleman, rake, lover, and the rest. The only structure of the narrative itself is the catalogue and the downward slope, which were a non-"literary" structure. The effect is of a real life which Wilson allows to be ordered (and so distorted) by imitation of social models into the life of a rake: precisely Hogarth's image of what life *was* in the 1730s.

Then emerging from Wilson's story, Fielding gives us the first simile which replaces gods with "Miss (whatever the Reader pleases)" (III, iv, 225), and this leads on to the simile of Joseph himself in the battle with the squire's hounds. No simile, no figure from literature, says Fielding, is "adequate to our Purpose":

> For indeed, what Instance could we bring to set before our Reader's Eyes at once the Idea of Friendship, Courage, Youth, Beauty, Strength, and Swiftness; all which blazed in the Person of *Joseph Andrews*. Let those therefore that describe Lions and Tigers, and Heroes fiercer than both, raise their Poems or Plays with the Simile of *Joseph Andrews*, who is himself above the reach of any Simile. [III, vi, 241]

This is perhaps only another way of saying what Hogarth said of the contemporary artist's model: "Who but a bigot, even to the antiques, will say that he has not seen faces and necks, hands and arms in living women, that even the Grecian Venus doth but coarsely imitate?"[15] The falsity of the classical analogue is emphasized to set off the superior reality of the "human" Joseph. Real people are not only not Cibbers and Pamelas, biblical Josephs or Abrahams, but not exactly Samaritans either. When at the end Joseph refuses to be made a literary model in a bookseller's continuation, Fielding is demonstrating that his perception of the complexity of the real world would be only an exercise in bad faith if Joseph were to end as a new incarnation of hero, engendering yet another set of maxims. Instead, he brings his story to a close by sending Joseph to bed with Fanny, an experience and not a demonstration.

Three years later (in 1745), in the first print of Joseph Highmore's *Pamela* illustrations, the heroine is shown sitting at a table writing her letter to her parents describing the death of Lady B., her mistress and protector, while approaching her is the son, Mr. B., about to make his first advance.[16] On the wall hangs an approximate copy of Hogarth's *Good Samaritan*, apparently representing the ideal which Mr. B. should but does not live up to in relation to his new charge. The interesting point is that Highmore has done (for him) an uncharacteristic thing by including this picture-on-the-wall; he does it only this once in the twelve scenes. But he has also imported into Richardson's *Pamela* a situation from *Joseph Andrews*, where the Good Samaritan is an anti-Pamela paradigm.

But it also is a Pamela paradigm. For Pamela is herself, from one point of view (her own), the Good Samaritan in relation to Mr. B.: the *true* Good Samaritan, and at the center of the novel as at the center of Hogarth's painting. (There is in fact one sequence in which Pamela herself seeks help among neighbors and *no* Samaritan emerges.) The female–Christ intercessor, whose love turns to charity, or vice versa, connects Hogarth and Richardson. What they share is the symbol of woman as victim and redeemer. In Hogarth's crowd scenes she replaces the squinting Wilkes figure, who might otherwise be its source of energy. In the *Rake's Progress* she is both love and charity, but a failed Pamela, another Clarissa, who however refuses to die because she holds too firmly to the ideal of charity melted down from sexual passion. Around her in Richardson's novels is the family and all organized society, levitical and pharasaical, ranked against this isolated figure of the woman as both savior and lame man, Samaritan and robbed man. Perhaps we can say that Fielding takes the Good Samaritan–Christ at the level of models and paradigms, mixing Christ and Sarah Young in order to show the difficulty of true charity—or of understanding *any* human action. Richardson, like Hogarth, takes it at a much deeper level, expressing a basic ambivalence toward the victim–savior woman as toward sexual love in relation to charity.

5. The Iatrohydraulic System

Two books published in 1748 were Dr. William Cadogan's *Essay upon Nursing and the Management of Children* and Fielding's *Tom Jones*. Cadogan's *Essay* went through twenty editions in fifty years and was the book that registered or brought about (it is always hard to say which) a transformation in child rearing parallel to the transformation wrought by Capability Brown in landscape gardening. Both men removed obstructions and advocated open structures, but there the resemblance ends. For Cadogan in effect takes the position of the apprentice who would push back the freeing of the child from maturity to childhood, reversing the educational assumptions of Locke and the manuals of Fénelon and Chesterfield.

Cadogan begins with the observation that the children of the poor are healthier than those of the rich because they are breast-fed by their mothers and not kept shut up in stuffy rooms, wound about with swaddling bands, and filled with rich food. Cadogan, in effect, makes the lower orders the model for the higher. For his proof he turns to the Foundling Hospital, addressing himself to one of its governors. Poor foundlings taken in by the hospital have proved healthier and live longer, he argues, because they are "bred in a very plain, simple Manner: They will therefore infallibly have the more Health, Beauty, Strength, and Spirits; I might add Understanding too, as all the Faculties of the Mind are well known to depend upon the Organs of the Body."[1] These children "are under the immediate Nursing of unerring Nature, and they thrive accordingly":

> Health and Posterity are the Portion of the Poor, I mean the laborious: The Want of Superfluity confines them more within the Limits of Nature: . . . The Mother who has only a few Rags to cover her Child loosely, and little more than her own Breast to feed it, sees it healthy and strong, and very soon

172

able to shift for itself; while the puny Insect, the Heir and Hope of a rich Family lies languishing under a Load of Finery, that overpowers his Limbs, abhorring and rejecting the Dainties he is crammed with, till he dies a Victim to the mistaken Care and Tenderness of his fond Mother. [p. 7]

The symbol to which Cadogan attaches his indignation is the swaddling clothes with which babies were wrapped to keep them safe, immobile, and under control.[2] He urges parents to lay aside "all those Swathes, Bandages, Stays, and Contrivances, that are most ridiculously used to close and keep the Head in its Place, and support the Body" (p. 11). The general principle he expounds is to let the child alone, free him from the start to develop according to "Nature, exact Nature." Cadogan's physiological model emerges from his description of the swaddling bands' effect on the body:

Besides the Mischief arising from the Weight and Heat of these Swaddling-cloaths, they are put on so tight, and the Child is so cramp'd by them, that its Bowels have no room, nor the Limbs any Liberty, to act and exert themselves in the free easy Manner they ought. . . . The Circulation restrained by the Compression of any one Part, must produce unnatural Swellings in some other; especially as the Fibres of Infants are so easily distended. To which doubtless are owing the many Distortions and Deformities we meet with every where. [p. 10]

Cadogan's argument for mothers' nursing their own babies (vs. the custom of putting them out to a wetnurse or surrogate mother) is based not only on the benefit this will have for the infant in love and tenderness, but for the mother herself. The argument is based on the idea of the cause of all diseases as

too great a Fulness and Redundancy of Humours; good at first, but being more than the Body can employ or consume, the whole Mass becomes corrupt, and produces many Diseases. This is confirmed by the general Practice of Physicians, who make holes in the Skin, perpetual Blisters, Issues &c. to let out the Superfluity. I would therefore leave it to be consider'd, whether the throwing back such a Load of Humour, as a Woman's first Milk, be most likely to mend her Constitution, or make her Complaints irremediable. [p. 15]

The "forcing back" of the mother's milk, "which most young women must have in great abundance, may be of fatal Consequence: Sometimes it endangers Life, and often lays the Foundation of many incurable Diseases" (p. 14). A mother's milk is naturally "poured forth from an exuberant, over-flowing urn, by a bountiful Hand, that never provides sparingly. The Call of Nature should be waited for to feed it" (p. 15).

In Cadogan's case, the object of the writing was to correct a pattern of behavior found in the well-to-do with a pattern derived from, supposedly found naturally in, the poor.[3] Cadogan also used personal experience, both negative (he had seen babies die) and positive (his own practice as a physician). By the 1780s the doctrine had reached the continent and foreign observers were noticing that English children were no longer swaddled—and were talking about this as another English innovation. "Swaddling was condemned in England since it was seen as an assault on human liberty, and its early disappearance there and in America" were connected by foreign commentators with the talk of English "Beef and Liberty" from earlier in the century.[4]

The "Foundling" Tom Jones sets out on a warm June night, drunk and ebullient because Allworthy is recovering from what appeared to be a fatal illness. He walks through an erotically stimulating landscape thinking "on his dear *Sophia*," from whom fortune has irrevocably separated him. But when Molly Seagrim passes he promptly disappears into the bushes with her—because (among other reasons) he "probably thought one Woman better than none" (V, x, 256).

The scene is linked by emphatic parallels to the other main scene of book V, which begins with an essay on contrast (intended to "open a new View of Knowledge") and is constructed on the two "contrasting" exposures of Molly's liaison with Square and Tom's with Molly. Both are introduced with protestations of undying fidelity to the beloved, which are immediately followed by, respectively, the falling rug, which reveals Square, and the accidental rendezvous with Molly. And yet Tom *does* mean what he says about his love for Sophia, and Molly in some sense believes what she says about her fidelity to Tom. Fielding's explanation for Molly's affair with Square, for whom she had no great fondness, is "the Absence of *Jones* during his Confinement" with a broken arm (p. 231).

I find it interesting that almost precisely the same situation in which Tom finds himself takes place a few years later in *Amelia*: Billy Booth is in Newgate; he meets Miss Matthews, an old flame who is still in love with him, although he has married Amelia, the only woman he really loves. Miss Matthews feeds him rack punch, gets him to talk about and think about his absent Amelia, and at length he goes to bed with her. In both cases the narrator is at pains to explain the hero's seeming infidelity, including many reasons clustered around the physiological center I have described.

Joseph Andrews of course does not behave in this way, but we can detect the first signs of the paradigm when he rebuffs Betty the chambermaid, who has fallen in love with him and, shortly after Joseph's rebuff, gives herself to Mr. Tow-wouse when he makes an advance, although she is not attracted to him and has until now consistently fended off his embraces. We are told that her "Passions were already raised, and . . . were not so whimsically capricious that one Man only could lay them, though perhaps, she would have rather preferred that one" (I, xviii, 88). And of Tow-wouse himself: "for as the Violence of his Passion had considerably abated to Mrs. *Tow-wouse*; so like Water, which is stopt from its usual Current in one Place, it naturally sought a vent in another" (p. 87).[5]

The repetition of this situation—A loves B, but in his/her absence makes love to an inferior surrogate, C—calls for some examination. In *Tom Jones* the physical explanation of the general phenomenon precedes the particular case of Tom–Molly. In fact, it is initially applied to Sophia earlier in the same book V. She has fallen in love with Tom but she restrains herself from any show of her feelings:

> Notwithstanding the nicest Guard which *Sophia* endeavoured to set on her Behaviour, she could not avoid letting some Appearances now and then slip forth: For Love may again be likened to a Disease in this, that when it is denied a Vent in one Part, it will certainly break out in another. [V, ii, 218–19]

And so Sophia blushes and turns alternatively hot and cold: symptoms exactly paralleled in Tom when he realizes he has fallen in love with her, which elicit the question concerning the play of art against nature—

> whether the Art which he used to conceal his Passion, or the Means which honest Nature employed to reveal it, betrayed

> him most: For while Art made him more than ever reserved to *Sophia*, and forbade him to address any of his Discourse to her; nay, to avoid meeting her Eyes, with the utmost Caution; Nature was no less busy in counterplotting him [vi, 236].

The metaphor related to Sophia's love is of a disease, but when this is called Nature versus Art (disease vs. doctor's ministrations), Fielding produces a larger, more normative model along the lines of fluid mechanics. And when Tom ascertains the truth about Molly and Square, "His Heart was now, if I may use the Metaphor, entirely evacuated, and *Sophia* took absolute Possession of it" (p. 235).

A page before the account of Sophia's "disease," Square is shown in Tom's sickroom arguing with Thwackum. He gets so excited that he bites his tongue, which gives Thwackum the opportunity of carrying the argument, and leaves Square furious: "as he was disabled from venting his Wrath at his Lips, he had possibly found a more violent Method of revenging himself," had the discussion not been brought to an end (ii, 217). It is following the frustrations of argument and repression of emotion in Tom's sickroom, we learn three chapters later, that Square vents himself in his affair with Molly; he is explained as the philosopher whose search for the Idea, "however sublimated and refined the Theory," is liable to "a little practical Frailty" (V, 230). In a somewhat wider perspective, we might also speculate that his thwarted passion for Bridget Allworthy (or her money) has been diverted to Molly.

Square, I think we can see, is related in a general way to those philosopher–enthusiasts in Swift's *Tale of a Tub* who gaze at the stars but are seduced by their lower parts into falling into a ditch. The model that explains all of these enthusiasts, however, is in the "Digression on Madness," where, for example, (A) Henry IV of France lusts after (B) a pretty girl but cannot obtain her, and so the semen generated, having lost its normal outlet, mounts to his brain and makes him mad, leading to (C) war, unless evacuated by (D) a "state-Surgeon's [the assassin Ravaillac's] Knife." "Nature shut out at one passage," as Swift puts it in *The Mechanical Operation of the Spirit*, "was forc'd to seek another."

The medical model behind both Swift and Fielding is explained by Burton in *The Anatomy of Melancholy*: if there is no evacuation of the sexual vapors, melancholy and madness will follow.[6] Melancholy is implicitly what is avoided by Tom—by Booth and Betty, and in their different ways by Molly and Square, when they open another vent. These are lusty characters: as the doctor notes of Tom after his wounding by Northerton, "the Pulse was exuberant and indicated [i.e., called for] much Phlebotomy" (p. 381).

We could go into the contemporary medical controversy over fluid mechanics, as propounded by the "iatro-hydro-dynamicists" who saw the body as a complex of canals through which fluids pass; the ease or difficulty with which the fluids moved caused the various symptoms associated with diseases.[7] We have already seen Cadogan's use of the model, which is close to Fielding's. But to see how Fielding relates to Cadogan, we need to put, alongside babies and swaddling bands, the toilet training of the earl of Rochester. Rochester told his tutor that he sometimes went months at a time without a bowel movement, and that this distemper

> was a very great occasion of that warmth and heat he always expressed, his Brain being heated by the Fumes and Humours that ascended and evacuated themselves that way.[8]

His costiveness implicitly led to melancholy, which was relieved by the release of either sexual energy or satire. The subject is treated most explicitly in "The Imperfect Enjoyment" and "A Ramble in St. James' Park," but it is also implicit in "The Scepter Lampoon" and many of his other poems. When for both men and women the spiritual vent (of the Ideal or of the beloved) is stopped up, all that remains is a substitute evacuation—into a whore or one's hand, in a curse (on the loved one or the sexual organ), or in some other restless and aimless activity, not unlike the wars of Henry IV. Rochester's ultimate image for male satisfaction is breaking into whores' houses and beating up the watch; for a female, Signor Dildoe.[9]

Of course, we are talking about an ancestor of the Victorian husband who put his wife on a pedestal and could only have satisfactory sexual relations with the maid or a prostitute (a situation described by Rochester in "Fragment of a Satire on Man").[10] In the eighteenth century the syndrome is anticipated in the problem of Marlow in *She Stoops to Conquer*, who cannot face or court a woman of his own social class, and uses barmaids as his sexual outlet. There is no indication in Tom, however, that he suffers any constraints with his Sophia; it is only that without her he must evacuate into other available women—and that this does not altogether disprove his love of her. (There is no indication that he visualizes or thinks of her when he takes the surrogate.) What in Rochester is a pessimistic view of man, suffering from "soe great a disproportion 'twixt our desires and what is ordained to content them,"[11] in Fielding becomes a statement of how physiological nature operates, especially when constrained by some form of "art," and perhaps also a self-defense for human frailty of a certain sort.

But from our reading of Cadogan's *Essay*, we can state the case in another way. The problem embodied in the upper-class rake who can only have sex with a lower-class woman, because he is impotent with his true love, is quite a different thing from young Tom's need for a "release valve for the letting off of psychological steam." The phrase is Lawrence Stone's, applied by him to the poor.[12] Although the common factor remains an ideal which is unattainable, with Jones the ideal is merely beyond reach, a loss which he can compensate for only by this outlet, just as the poor escape poverty by drinking gin. It is the lower-class model which Fielding is using, which (rightly or wrongly) he associates with the freedom from inhibitions.

There is, after all, the well-known version in Fielding's own life (mentioned by Horace Walpole and other contemporaries)[13] at just the time he was writing *Tom Jones*. His marriage with his housekeeper, in order to legitimize the child she was carrying by him, had followed upon the crushing death of his wife Charlotte, whom he equates more than once with Sophia. The literary structure had only been indicated in *Joseph Andrews* in the case of Betty the chambermaid, and not repeated in Joseph or any of the other characters; but it applies to almost everyone in *Tom Jones*, and Booth was to play it out again in the last novel, in a further attempt at exorcism.

Allworthy may be thought of as a positive projection of this aspect of Fielding himself—how he would have *liked* to act. Allworthy, a lusty man in youth who married for sex as well as "love" (in the sense of the opening chapter to book V), has lost his beloved wife and sublimates the loss by his faith in an anticipated meeting in the afterlife and by service and charity in this life.

The point to emphasize is that the syndrome also explains Tom's immediate responses (his charity) to the beggar, the highwayman, Mrs. Miller, Nancy Miller, and the rest. Perhaps we have to go back to the melancholic model and those who do *not* respond as Tom does, those who do *not* find a vent. Fielding's version seems to accept the assumption that evil people are those who repress and therefore allow (or direct) their sexual urges toward perverted intellectualized ends. One of the orthodox explanations of melancholy was that the "humour" originated in Adam's body as the result of the fall; it was "born in the first fruit of Adam's seed out of the breath of the serpent (*de flatu serpentis*) when Adam followed its advice (*suggestione diaboli*) by devouring the apple." At the moment when Adam took the apple, melancholy "curdled in his blood": "as when a lamp is quenched, the smouldering and smoking wick remains reeking behind."[14] Swift used this model but believed that the humour might be controlled; the more optimistic Fielding believed in release—in laughter or in innocent sexual play (though not always so innocent in its consequences, as he acknowledges).

Even Bridget and Square eventually find vents; only Blifil and Thwackum remain relentlessly costive. Blifil is the prime example of those who retain or control their vapors, which then are diverted into plotting and sedition, like the vapors of the Aeolists and Achitophel (as opposed to the fecund and prolific King David). Blifil—whose father the captain was a melancholiac—has "not the least Tincture" of true love in his composition, and his sexual appetite is "so moderate, that he was able by Philosophy or by Study, or by some other Method, easily to subdue [it]." While "some other Method," in Fielding's language, may refer to masturbation as well as sublimation, what he means is that Blifil was "altogether as well furnished with some other Passions," namely "Avarice and Ambition." Sexual attraction for Sophia is translated into lust for the power and fortune to be gained by possessing her (VI, iv, 284).

Sophia herself illustrates what can happen when she is tempted to give in to her father's demands. She begins to feel the old religious emotions celebrated in "The Digression on Madness" and "The Mechanical Operation of the Spirit."

> Lastly, when she reflected how much she herself was to suffer, being indeed to become little less than a Sacrifice, or a Martyr, to filial Love and Duty, she felt an agreeable Tickling in a certain little Passion, which tho' it bears no immediate Affinity either to Religion or Virtue, is often so kind as to lend great Assistance in executing the Purposes of both. [VII, ix, 360]

The cherished muff, which Tom has kissed, gives her the release she needs into natural instinct, and she breaks out of the house, pursuing

Tom. In the next chapter, in fact, the Quaker gives Tom an account of his daughter, who is in love with a poor youth like himself whom she has known since infancy; the Quaker has "preached to her against Love" and locked her up—"and yet, at last, [she] broke out at a Window" (x, 364).

Another version, perhaps the fullest expression, appears when Squire Western is hunting Sophia, has lost her trail, and the sound of hunting horns reaches his ear: he is off after the pack, and we are told that "if we shut Nature out at the Door, she will come in at the Window," for Fielding insists again that "we are not to arraign the Squire of any Want of Love for his Daughter: For in reality he had a great deal; we are only to consider that he was a Squire and a Sportsman" (XII, ii, 623). Western really loves Sophia, but this spiritual object is not present (is not alone in his temperament: avarice or the thought of status has forced it out of place), and the stimulus to his animal nature—his instinct—sends him off after the hounds. And, as the last quotation suggests, he is to be related to Black George, who does love Tom (who is departing the country in disgrace and so is a lost cause for George) and yet steals his money.

To the extent that this model is a physical system, involving a distinction between a spiritual and a physical need—a blockage of the former leading to an evacuation of the latter—it is supported in *Tom Jones* by the more inclusive metaphor of appetite, which distinguishes from true love the need to feed one's body with food and sex. Fielding opens his novel with a "Bill of Fare to the Feast" and shows that in gustatory terms human nature, including love, is no simple, single thing.[15] In book VII (i) he distinguishes true love from "the Desire of satisfying a voracious Appetite with a certain Quantity of delicate white human Flesh," and this is to explain Tom's defection with Molly that follows in that book, another part of the explanation that includes Tom's hydraulic system. (Allworthy's sublimation, referred to above, is embodied in his adjustment from a lusty husband to a widower who "hungers after Goodness"—a meal which thoroughly satisfies him and affords him more repose than that "occasioned by any other hearty Meal" [I, ii].) Blifil's desires, such as they are, tend toward appetite alone—in Sophia he experiences only "the same Desires which an Ortolan inspires into the Soul of an Epicure" (VII, vi).

The metaphor of appetite is fulfilled at Upton: only when Tom finishes filling his stomach can he evacuate into Mrs. Waters; which might be read to say that the love and frustration concerning Sophia find vent in a hearty meal, but when this outlet is not sufficient there remains enough to be exploited by Mrs. Waters, another (parallel) natural outlet. It is interesting to compare Tony Richardson's film version of *Tom Jones*, where the food *led to* sexual appetite and was the means of seduction employed by Mrs. Waters. In the novel, eating and sex are linked as two forms of appetite, with hunger being the stronger, and sex following (despite Mrs. Waters' attempts at seduction) only after Tom has satisfied the first.

Perhaps all we are dealing with is a distinction between the physical and the somewhat more spiritual. But is this merely a physiological fact which Fielding finds unavoidable or part of a moral structure that can subsume it? Even Sophia, near the end, once victory is in sight, lets us see in her own realistic but discrete way what might have happened if she had been forced into marriage with Blifil. She says to Allworthy:

> to lead our Lives with one to whom we are indifferent, must be a State of Wretchedness.——Perhaps that Wretchedness would be even increased by a Sense of the Merits of an Object to whom we cannot give our Affections [i.e., Tom]. If I had married Mr. *Blifil*——

She does not finish her sentence, but given the physical structure presupposed throughout *Tom Jones*, we can imagine the sequel.[16]

In Jones's case, however, something does apparently happen. When he is preparing to go to the masquerade in London, where he hopes to meet Sophia, he must nevertheless eat. The metaphor of appetite is reactivated: love offers "delicious Repasts" to some senses, but "it can afford none to others"; it can offer Tom such "delicacies" as "the Hopes of seeing Sophia" but he nevertheless begins "to languish for some Food of a grosser Kind" (XIII, vi, 710–11). Appetite has apparently reduced itself to the purely gastronomic, and its sexual counterpart is left to express Tom's real love for Sophia. His sexual release is presumably no longer the equivalent of "the abundant Gratification of every sensual Appetite" of modern epicures (p. 783). The two final examples of the Upton temptation are triumphal vindications of Tom's new balance of humours. In his moment of deepest despair about the possibility of a physical reconciliation with Sophia, he nevertheless turns down the alternative of Arabella Hunt: there is the usual list of reasons for accepting her, parallel to those he had for accepting Molly Seagrim, but they no longer overbalance his love for Sophia (XV, xi, 827); and it is natural instinct that forces him to refuse. Finally, he refuses Mrs. Fitzpatrick's suggestion that he woo Mrs. Western in order to get at Sophia (to "make sham Addresses to the older Lady, in order to procure an easy Access to the Younger" [p. 867]), which is precisely parallel in a perverse way to the earlier situations with Molly and Mrs. Waters, and his refusal stimulates Mrs. Fitzpatrick's passion. But "his whole Thoughts were now so confined to his *Sophia*, that I believe no Woman on Earth could have now drawn him into an Act of Inconstancy" (p. 871). It may be that the muff has become a Sophia substitute to replace the morsel of flesh (Mrs. Waters). He finds it on the bed on which he had Mrs. Waters, sleeps with it on his journey to London, and it is with him when he finally rejects Arabella Hunt's proposal (he kisses it).

But while something of a solution seems to have been worked out by Tom, we cannot dismiss the presence of the structure we have been discussing as a governing principle, a kind of spring at the center of that great complex clock which is *Tom Jones*. The moral of both macrocosm and microcosm (the Rebellion of '45 and Tom– Sophia) is summed up in the simile:

> As a conquered Rebellion strengthens a Government, or as Health is more perfectly established by Recovery from some Diseases; so Anger, when removed, often gives new Life to Affection. [p. 933]

Fielding applies this simile to Allworthy's regard for Blifil after his first suspicions, and it represents the false calm before the storm: the rebellion is going to destroy, not strengthen, Blifil's government. But the simile is a peripheral sign which describes the central, unre- pressed characters for whom rebellion conquered may indeed strengthen the government; a disease cured may strengthen health; and anger removed may strengthen affection. Here are other possible formulations:

With the fear of detection, the vent of showing attention to the one you love is closed, and so you blush.

Sometimes attention overflows at B because it is stopped at A.

When a censor is present, you do B but mean (wish it were, or think about) A, as in irony when you say or do this in place of that, what you do not mean in place of what you do mean, in order to circumvent a third party.

"Whether . . . or . . . , I will not venture to determine," but the truth (unstated) is obvious.

You say the unimportant, leave the important thing unsaid.

Satirists say the times are lewd, but they are quite wrong: "Our present Women have been taught by their Mothers to fix their Thoughts only on Ambition and Vanity, and to despise the Pleasures of Love as unworthy their Regard" (p. 743).

You are accused of an unimportant charge but guilty of an important one (to you at least). You are accused of disrespect but guilty of unfaithfulness to the one you love.

If that is the ironic aspect, another is the understanding of the peripheral sign and how it can be used. Lady Bellaston, "contented with the Possession of that of which another Woman [Sophia] had the Reversion" (p. 748), recalls the *Pinkethman* jest about the whore who has "a very good Estate in TAIL." Fielding may be playing upon the structure of the joke itself, at least as formulated by Corbyn Morris, whose *Essay toward Fixing the True Standards of Wit* appeared between the publication of *Joseph Andrews* and *Tom Jones*. Morris' definition of wit is "*the* Lustre *resulting from the* quick Elucidation *of one Subject, by a* just *and* unexpected Arrangement *of it with another Subject*."[17] The object of pure wit is "*to enlighten* thereby the *original* Subject," and this is done by the "Introduction of another similar, or opposite Subject." First there is Sophia, or Tom's love for her, and this is "illustrated" or "complimented" by comparison with another different, indeed low and vulgar, essentially physical subject: "whereby, upon their Arrangement together, the original Subject may be set off, and more clearly enlighten'd, by their obvious Comparison." Somewhat later in Allison's version of associationism, a strong emotion may be aroused by some intermediate object, of no importance itself, which acts symbolically—one with which the real source of emotion is connected subconsciously by some train of association.[18]

As Allison's formulation suggests, Fielding's structure has more in common with the Freudian joke than with Morris' wit. When the object of desire (Sophia) makes herself, or becomes, inaccessible to the first person, he takes his revenge by making her the object of an obscenity. Thus the absence of the desired woman results in the transformation of an erotic into an aggressive impulse toward her, though of course one carried out on an effigy. The third party (Molly or Jenny) is required to make the joke, replacing the second as object of the first: "So that gradually, in place of the woman, the onlooker, now listener, becomes the person to whom the smut is addressed." Clearly "it is not the person who makes the joke who laughs at it and who therefore enjoys its pleasurable effect, but the inactive listener"—this other one being a Molly or Jenny who is quite happy with a displaced enjoyment.[19] (Compare, for example, the process for lending and borrowing money in Fielding's time: You lend your money to the borrower, but if he does not pay you back you throw not him but his co-signer, the man who stands surety for him, into prison.)

The transformation of erotic into aggressive impulses (as in Henry IV in "The Digression of Madness") recalls the little boy in *Beyond the Pleasure Principle* who deals with his absent mother by "throwing her away" and retrieving her. He is concerned not with objects but with signifiers, and he punishes her in surrogate, as Tom does the ideal and absent Sophia. Sophia's muff is only the ostensible signifier; the other woman is the real signifier for Tom's love of Sophia—until he reaches the point where he is willing to accept the muff instead. The procedure Tom carries out is, of course, the same we saw employed by the plebeian crowd with its patrician masters.

The puppet show which Tom visits (XII, v–viii) has suppressed its Punch and Joan, the raucous couple (Punch ends by beating Joan to death, as he does everyone else he encounters) who are the plebeians' ultimate comic effigies of themselves in relation to the "other." Tom's visit follows directly upon his demonstration of good appetite despite despair about the loss of Sophia (p. 637). Punch and Joan are an outlet for a part of the audience that needs expression; but here, where only "the fine and serious Part" of the play has been retained, "without any low Wit or Humour, or Jests," or "any thing which could provoke a Laugh," the outlet for the Merry Andrew and the maid (ironically named Grace) is diverted into unmediated sex. As Tom says, "so far from improving, I think, by leaving out [Punch] and his merry wife *Joan*, you have spoiled your Puppet-show," and here he brings together the whole negative aspect of Fielding's concept of "mixed character": indecency, bawdry, obscene jokes, farce, buffoonery—and impure matter—which, once censored, leaves only repression, hypocrisy, and melancholy.[20] In the same way, Fielding's book of *Tom Jones* requires its Punch and Joan, and the low-comic strain of the novel finds its equivalent in Tom's sexual energy, both of which could be summed up as the material of the subculture.

This turn of Fielding's fictional consciousness may show a deep-seated sympathy with the subculture world which was not overtly expressible in his *Enquiry*, perhaps not even in the novels. Fielding is looking at Tom, as he looked at Bosavern Penlez or the Penlez riots or at gin drinking, as "a release valve for the letting off of psychological steam," which is the object of most subculture customs and activities. The difference between Penlez and Tom is that Fielding was on his defensive, caught off balance in the Penlez case; Tom is his own version of Hogarth's Tom Idle, the aspect of himself he had to make understandable or endurable, if only as a "joking" fiction. The association between Tom, "young dog," and the hydraulic model of antirepression conveys much more positive connotations than did Tom Idle. Jones is, however, a figure who teeters between aristocrat and plebeian, both of whom react against the sexually inhibited, property-owning middle class. He avoids aristocratic debauchery, the *je m'en fiche* pose of the court wits, and also the model of the genteel poor, those younger sons and unpensioned Opposition poets sympathized with in the *Champion* (16 Feb. 1739/40). His vigor draws upon the desperate poor "to whom virginity was not important, and foresight, prudence and planning were irrelevant to their dismal economic future."[21] By which I mean that his ambiguous actions with Molly and Jenny Waters are committed in a state of plebeian hopelessness. Tom is distinguished only in degree from the Merry Andrew who naturally rolls in the hay, and from the myth of the vigorous lower-class lover, unhampered by the neuroses of his betters, who later appears as Corporal Trim (with Bridget) in relation to the family of impotent Shandys.

The iatrohydraulic system may be a particular case of the whole subculture phenomenon as seen from the upper-class perspective. But in itself it carries no fixed significance. We find it in *both* the radical rhetoric of Paine, with his talk of removing barriers, tollgates, and outmoded laws, and in the *laissez-faire* system of Adam Smith's *Wealth of Nations* of 1776 (in fact, probably one of Paine's sources), which preaches the advantages for everyone—artisan as well as merchant—to be freed from the smothering bands of customs, regulations, and status.[22] The image is of natural rights and freedoms, covered by these conventions and only waiting to be released. But the poor's model was both more timid and more stoic, based on the mercantilist controls they were losing in the onslaught of *laissez-faire* practices on prices. The poor would have seen personal freedom as in fact a threat, and desired a return to the protectionist code of the past; as they would also have repudiated the image of themselves as a class "to whom virginity was not important."

Revolution, when it came in France, was made to follow from the *laissez-faire* position in terms of the need of the individual of talent to break out of the existing social order, with its hierarchy based on primogeniture; and from the return to the protectionist position in terms of hunger and starvation. In the 1790s the one represented Liberty, the other Equality. It would be a mistake to say that Fielding in *Tom Jones*, Cadogan in his *Essay*, or even Paine in some of his basic images in *Rights of Man* was assuming the point of view of the subculture of the poor, whatever precisely that might have been at the moment. The poor were simply a malleable mass which could be fitted into a number of paradigms (aristocratic or middle class, Tory or Whig) *by* those various groups, and only in a general way characterizable as antiauthoritarian. The subculture, then, was any one of several separate, "Opposition" sets of mores, only more radical than the Opposition, who in fact shared the assumptions of the court party but employed a contrary rhetoric so long as they were in opposition. A phenomenon like John Wilkes, and then the Gordon riots and the French Revolution, was necessary to reveal the different senses of "Liberty" as it proceeded from the mouths of Whigs to Jacobins—from "Liberty and Property" of the Whig Opposition to Walpole, who called themselves Patriots, to "Wilkes and Liberty" and the French *Liberté*.

Nevertheless, the cluster of books published around 1748—*Clarissa, Tom Jones, Fanny Hill*, Cadogan's *Essay*, Hogarth's *Industry and Idleness*, Smollett's *Roderick Random*—all deal with different forms of freedom and restraint. They also represent, in their different ways, uses of sub- or counterculture materials as a source of renewing and revivifying energy for life and for high art. The aspect of youth is becoming more interesting and central—more serious, more analyzed—than it had been in the genre of comedy *per se*, and also more significantly related to the low and popular. In Fielding's plot, love of the ideal is displaced to an inferior object, and this serves only to strengthen the ideal—though it has to be followed by justification. Irony too is a displacement of idealism which (as in *The Jacobite's Journal*) is misunderstood and so requires explanation. He is doing something under powerfully compelling circumstances, which does not mean what it appears to mean. On a large scale, the same sort of displacement informs John Cleland's *Memoirs of Fanny Hill* (published just as *Tom Jones* appeared), which was England's contribution to pornography. Translated, adapted, and imitated on the Continent, it became a genuinely and proverbially "English" book.[23] Fanny uses her frantic whoring as an outlet for her frustrated feelings for her lost love Charles; in retrospect, she has enjoyed and utilized her life as a whore as pure experience with low life, preparing her for her true love Charles's return as her husband. It is as if Tom Jones had let himself go with one Molly Seagrim after another, until, at the end, he was reunited with Sophia. Although Cleland omits the elaborate verbal justifications, something similar can be discerned in Fanny's periphrastic style and in the structure of the plot itself. He has explained Fanny's slumming.

Fanny Hill preaches behavior according to the model of the low. Fanny points out that the low have the ability to give sexual pleasure that raises them high above the "loftier qualifications of birth, fortune, and sense." Sexual enjoyment is "purer," closer to nature itself in "a character in low life" (like the servant Will) than "amongst the false ridiculous refinements" of the upper classes. Like Hogarth's Harlot, she is caught in her affair with Will by her rich keeper, who dismisses her. But unlike the Harlot, she then joins a "little Seraglio" (Mrs. Cole's) run along Cadogan's lines of the natural, rural life, enlivened by "the pure native charms" of country maids, which functions as a reaction equally against the modesty of the middle class and the "force, or constraint" of the upper.[24]

As an "English" pornographic fiction, *Fanny Hill* exalts personal freedom, in this case in the elemental metaphor of sexual freedom—the right to develop oneself freely. The rise of literary pornography in the late seventeenth century (partly at least a vehicle for libertine philosophy) contrasted the natural impulse of sexual desire with the falsities of society. But Fanny's cry of "Truth! stark naked truth," like Cadogan's advice to unbind children, is a stage between Hogarth's Nature having her skirt lifted (in *Boys Peeping at*

Nature) as a prelude to *A Harlot's Progress* and the metaphoric stripping of Nature bare by Rousseau and the French revolutionaries.

Richardson is the alternative case, for his paragon, the ideal Clarissa, seemed (to many readers) to have been replaced by, or become, the real flesh-and-blood woman who falls in love with Lovelace, who is himself on some level sincerely attracted to her. Then Richardson has to explain away this substitution, in his case by claiming it did not exist—by actively tampering with his text as well as explaining it. He begins at once, in the second edition (Apr. 1749), to make additions: footnotes and a long index summary of the novel, placed at the beginning of the text. These were to correct serious "errors" of reading, which questioned Clarissa's heroic virtue. The third edition (1751) weaves two hundred pages of footnotes and "suppressed" letters and passages into his text to explain what he really meant—the meaning his readers were missing; and this amounted to the exemplary status of Clarissa. So important did Richardson consider the "restorations from the original manuscripts" that he also published them separately for the use of the readers of the first edition. All of these were additions to superimpose a public meaning and to repress a private one which he all too clearly felt himself to have unconsciously let slip, and which was being picked up by unwary readers. But if a reader of the first edition understood anything of the novel it was that such a judgment cannot be easily made, that the characters are themselves playing roles and creating fictions about themselves in their letters, and that this is what the novel is really about.[25]

Fielding's procedure is only a more self-aware version of Richardson's. Much closer to *Tom Jones* was the model of Pope, who to begin with knows that as a poet he cannot be Virgil, cannot write an epic; he cannot even be Horace in the Age of Walpole (as George II cannot be Augustus), and so he writes satire of a sort that can be said to set off or, by contrast, redefine the Virgilian or Horatian ideal. And this substitute Horace requires justification. It is the difference or disjunction that he constantly represents in his poetry. The example to take is *The Dunciad*, where over a number of years he added important elements: in the second edition the prefatory matter, the notes, and the appendices, which serve two functions. One is to further anatomize the nature of the dunces, but this seems almost incidental beside the explicit purpose of explaining why Alexander

Pope (whose identity is now first revealed) was compelled to write such an unpleasant howl of anger, such a scandalous poem, sink to so low a level (instead of writing a true epic) as to write *The Dunciad*.

In short, the displacement of a good and gentle poet's ideals into the excesses of satire is justified much as is Tom Jones's displacement of his love for the ideal Sophia to the temporary physical presence of Molly Seagrim or Jenny Waters.[26] For their very different (though at bottom related) reasons, both Pope and Fielding give priority to the low, the poor and untended, the natural and instinctual response to a complex experience. The difference is that Fielding demonstrates a process of demythologizing. But he knows that there can be no demythologizing without a remythologizing. This is already apparent in Cadogan's return to the nursery and the metaphor of a general unbinding, which is based on a displacement of value to an unideal object, the poor, followed by much explanation to justify the notion. Fielding's process of remythologizing is far more sophisticated, for he is also demonstrating and puzzling over the fact that no person can be understood as nakedly himself. Tom or Sophia can only be known by being translated into something else, approached in terms of a contrary (perhaps low as well as high), and therefore by being interpreted and explained.

6. The '45 and
Bonnie Prince Charlie

WHAT THE PARABLE OF THE GOOD SAMARITAN and Fénelon's *Telemachus* meant to *Joseph Andrews* the historical Rebellion of '45 means to *Tom Jones*. And this fact indicates a fundamental difference between the narrative modes of the two novels, the one based on a literary and the other on a historical nexus. In 1745, perhaps early in the year, Fielding began writing *Tom Jones*.[1] The rebellion broke out in the summer, and in November he began to produce *The True Patriot*, an alarmist propaganda organ for the government, and at the same time wrote A *History of the Present Rebellion in Scotland*. Three years later, with the '45 quite dead but the unpopularity of the Hanoverians growing and with the need to defend the Pelham ministry's policies at home and abroad, he spent the year 1748 issuing weekly attacks on opponents from the right and left who, he claimed, sought a change in the sovereign. The journal he published for this purpose was called *The Jacobite's Journal*; reading through its pages today, one must be impressed by the coincidence of concerns with the great novel Fielding was finishing at the same time.[2] It is instructive to watch the historical situation of the *Journal* carried over into the novel and made its central paradigm.

The satiric designation "Jacobite" was perhaps not so purely propagandistic as has sometimes been thought: for every five portrait prints advertised of Charles I in 1747 there was one of William III and none of George II. *The Jacobite's Journal* spends much of its time contrasting the Jacobite mythology with the plain historical facts of 1688, 1715, and 1745. For Fielding, this myth becomes the embodiment of the larger controversy, in which his work and Hogarth's were embroiled, of the foreign, Roman Catholic, hieroglyphic iconography that had replaced the original object or sign with a second

190

system of signs, and perhaps a third, which totally obscured the original truth.

A number of English works had appeared which attempted in various ways to get back to the original truth through historical research and linguistic etymology. Among the English scholars the pivotal figure was Joseph Spence, who in 1747 published *Polymetis*. He has Polymetis, his spokesman in the dialogue, argue that we should not need to carry around with us copies of Ripa's *Iconologia*; we should require no scholarly sources in the sense of medieval/ Renaissance commentary on a text, idea, or image. Supporting the *Polymetis* in this respect was a letter Spence wrote a year later to Samuel Richardson, after reading *Clarissa*, in which he summons up a dream vision of a beautiful woman (Nature = the art work, *Clarissa*) attacked by a French milliner who cuts away half her dress (Art = critics and interpreters). *Clarissa*, he warns Richardson, should not be tampered with by forces external to itself—whether "outside" critics or even Richardson himself.[3]

Spence's demystifying, which attempts to clear away the accretions of the commentators and return the observer's eye to the object in its original historical meaning, is a later stage of Shaftesbury's attack on "hieroglyphic" or hermetic signification in his *Tablature of the Judgment of Hercules* (1713). Around the same time, Addison had said, apropos of shop signs, that we should use or develop "a Sign which bears some Affinity to the Wares in which it deals."[4] Probability (Shaftesbury's concept) demands that we rationalize those improbable combinations that began as erroneous puns. The willful separation of word from thing led to the catastrophic, independent progress of the word, ever further removed from truth and reality. The sequence of argument is complete if we add Addison's *Dialogues upon the Usefulness of Ancient Medals* (1726), which offers coins as the source for a historical grounding of mythological signs; Thomas Blackwell's analysis of the classical myths as poetic metaphors, *Letters concerning Mythology* (1748), immediately after Spence's *Polymetis*; and Hogarth's *Analysis of Beauty* (1753), which extends Spence's argument to aesthetic principles and conventions of genre and style. The intermingling of the two traditions, the antiquarians who sought the original, undefiled object (Bentley to Winckelmann) and the commentators (Ripa, Alciati, Valeriano), comes to a head in England at least in the 1740s. In the poetry of Pope, for example, a case can be made for his return to an original *Aeneid* and equally for his continuing reliance on the Renaissance commentaries for its meaning. With his younger colleague, John Gay, a little further along the road, we are approaching Hogarth and Fielding. While Spence sought to demystify the references of Ripa's *Iconologia* altogether, Hogarth and Fielding sought to discredit the learned tradition, if necessary by reaching down to the most popular forms and traditions, but without sacrificing the intellectual and aesthetic play to which the commentaries so notably contributed. They were, in a way, continuing Pope's practice of satirizing learned commentary in his footnotes while at the same time using it to forward his own satiric meaning.

For the linguistic theorists who distrusted the conventionality of the relation between words and things (the equivalent of the commentators' interpretation of Virgil), historical etymology was the only way to trace back the conventions as expressed in usage and language derivation, and from the process of change assign certain possibilities (or limits) of meaning to the word.[5] John Free's *An Essay towards a History of the English Tongue* (1749) tries to relate the development of the English language to English history and argues that etymology demonstrates the language to be closer to the Saxon tongue than to French, imposed after the Conquest. Free's argument, Murray Cohen notes, was another "contribution to the conflict between Hanoverian and Jacobite" raging at the time.[6] But Benjamin Martin's *Institutions of Language* (1748) also sought the "original and genius of our tongue" and traces back the meaning of words. The etymological approach depends on an awareness that there *is* an original meaning and, consequently, the need to justify the present meaning—or make it explicit—and correct the errors of the superimposed meaning. In the same way, Spence wished to get back to the original meaning of visual iconography by wiping out the intermediary interpretations of Ripa and the others.

In practice, however, all the grammarians and linguists could do was use etymology to record and collect the linguistic differences created by custom as indications of the true English character (and so interesting for their own sake). Their discoveries were not meant to be prescriptive; even though they might seek out the "best and most approved language," it was in fact to demonstrate the fullness and variety of the English language.[7] There could not, should not, writes

Benjamin Martin, be an attempt at "fixing a standard to the purity and perfection of any language," and it would be "utterly vain and impertinent" to try. For "more than a just account of the original, progress, and present state of our tongue, I know nothing that can be done."[8] Johnson's *Dictionary* of 1755 uses etymology to produce a partial record of English social, political, and intellectual history, but in the "Preface" he says he hopes "the spirit of English liberty" will prevent any prescriptive academy from arising. This was a view expressed by Hogarth in the early 1750s, opposing a state academy of art.[9]

As with Johnson and Hogarth, the xenophobic bias was evident. Knowledge of classical or foreign languages was not necessary for a better command of English, was no longer necessary to the linguistic theorist; in fact could "interfere with the effectiveness of teaching by introducing irrelevant analogies."[10] As in manuals on nursing, so even in cookbooks the tendency was to recoil from the elaborate French recipe to the common English practice. William Ellis' *Country Housewife's Family Companion* (1750) offers recipes for common bread and apples as plain English fare, the object being health based on the model of country life (though also, perhaps, on the model of the Horatian retirement poem). Hannah Glasse's *Art of Cookery, Made Plain and Easy* (1755) points out that "if a Gentleman will have French Cooks, they [sic] must pay for French Tricks," such as using six pounds of butter to fry a dozen eggs when half a pound is sufficient. "So much is the blind Folly of this Age, that they would rather be imposed on by a French Book, than give Encouragement to [the practice of] a good English Cook."[11]

In all of these fields two principles emerge: (1) If we cannot have an ideal, an unchanging model language (such as those universal systems seventeenth-century theorists like Bishop Wilkins sought), then we must take what there is. (2) The scholar, instead of accepting custom, should engage in historical and comparative studies, valuable because the examples of usage they examine have been evolved in England by Englishmen. Thus the normative elements are now national and popular, a matter of the sheer collection of examples. Fielding, like these writers, knows that you cannot get back to an original meaning by wiping out the intermediary usages. But he begins by exposing the false encrustation in the manner of Spence. *The Jacobite's Journal* begins with the mythology of the Stuart family as a type of falsification, but then goes on to all kinds of verbal misunderstandings.

Some readers take his ironic mask of a Jacobite sympathizer literally; the Opposition press casts lies and slanders at him and his ministerial friends, analogous to the Jacobite lies about Stuart genealogy and the succession. The *Journal*'s essays obsessively treat such subjects as slander (nos. 8, 26, 28) and personal attacks on Fielding (from serious slanders to the comic mimicry of Samuel Foote [nos. 20, 22]) and on his friends (e.g., no. 18 on Lyttelton). The equation between the slandering of the man and his writing, which Fielding develops so strikingly in *Tom Jones*, from the chapters on "mixed character" in Black George and Tom (VIII, i, and X, i) to the defense of the Good Book with some blemishes against the attacks of "critics" (XI, i), is already laid out in *The Jacobite's Journal*. The application Fielding makes is equally to a *Paradise Lost* and to a Socrates or Brutus: "to condemn a Work or a Man as vicious, because they are not free from Faults or Imperfections," is contrasted to the alternative, a paragon or "faultless Monster" (no. 8) of the sort treated in the apparent paragon of, say, Blifil.

False history is the subject of *The Jacobite's Journal*, and so it is of *Tom Jones*, where Jacobite rumors lead to the identification of Sophia Western with Jenny Cameron, the Young Pretender's mistress, and the Jacobite rumors act as a kind of acute sympton for the chronic fabrications that surround Allworthy, Partridge, and especially Tom, re-creating "character" in the forms of the personal fantasies of the rumor mongers.[12] By book VIII (pp. 432–33), rumor has Tom getting a servant maid with child, breaking Thwackum's arm, snapping a pistol at Blifil, and beating a drum while Squire Allworthy is sick. Book VIII continues with Partridge's story of a man's fight with a ghost (a drunk encountering a white-faced calf) and ends with the Man of the Hill's conclusion that men must be mad to entertain the possibility of the Stuarts' return. The climax, of course, is Upton, where, we are told, "they talk, to this Day, of the Beauty and lovely Behaviour of the charming *Sophia*, by the Name of the Somersetshire Angel" (X, viii, 554); and at the Bull's Head at Meriden, the rumor is that 10,000 Frenchmen have landed in Suffolk and that Sophia is Jenny Cameron (XI, iii). In this atmosphere, Rumor herself appears, and a toast to Sophia becomes a toast to the Pretender (p. 441). The Liars' Club's lie that

Tom has been killed in a duel (XV, iii) is only the last and most perfectly unfounded rumor.

The narrator of *Tom Jones* is himself in the limited, though privileged, position of a historian who is trying to extricate the true from the false. In VIII (i), as he nears the center of the narrative, he talks about the historical origins of fictions, telling us that remarkable deeds of humans "gave Birth to many Stories of the Antient Heathen Deities (for most of them are of poetical Original)" (p. 397). It was the poet who carried out this transformation, whereas "the Historian will confine himself to what really happened, and utterly reject any Circumstance, which, tho' never so well attested, he must be well assured is false" (p. 401).[13]

The source for the historiography employed in *The Jacobite's Journal* is Abbé Banier's *Mythology and Fables of the Ancients, Explain'd from History* (translated 1739–40). Fielding singles out Banier's volumes (republished in 1748) for praise in the "Court of Criticism," and we know that he owned a copy himself.[14] Banier's euhemerist analysis of myths is the basic methodology Fielding brings to bear on the Jacobites' constructions in nos. 6 and 12, first as a parallel or comparative mythology linking the story of Bacchus to the Jacobite ethos of hunting, drinking, and dipping into politics, and second as a pursuit of the sources or motivations for such fabulating (vanity, illiteracy, the lies of travelers, etc.).

Fielding cites Banier by name only once in *Tom Jones* (XII, i, 619), but, as in the passage I cited from VIII (i), Banier's approach is discernible in much of the historical analysis that is carried on. There is, of course, a close relationship between euhemerism or the reducing of mythology to history and the travesty mode Fielding had practiced in the 1730s. Banier's explanation, "that the *Minotaur* with *Pasiphae*, and the rest of that Fable, contain nothing but an Intrigue of the Queen of *Crete* with a Captain named *Taurus*" (I, 29), could almost, but not quite, have appeared in *Tumble-down Dick*.[15] The difference is between finding the source of the god in a great man and in a bumpkin. The latter is the strategy of Gay's lines in *The Shepherd's Week* (1714):

> Now plain I ken whence *Love* his Rise begun.
> Sure he was born some bloody *Butcher*'s Son,
> Bred up in Shambles, where our Younglings slain,
> Erst taught him Mischief and to sport with Pain.[16]

The real Mars here is a butcher and Eros the butcher's son. But we also see Gay's melancholy speaker, Sparabella, mythologizing her unhappy love affair.

The euhemerist Banier, to "fully unravel the History of this God" Mars, relates him to several possible sources: first to the king Belus (the scriptural Nimrod), "to whom *Diodorus* attributes the Invention of Arms, and the Art of marshalling Troops in Battle," or perhaps Ninus or Thutas; second to an ancient king of Egypt; third to a king of Thrace named Odin; fourth to a Greek named Ares; and finally to a Roman named Mars, a brother of Amulius Numitor (II, 316). His researches seek a correspondence in dignity to the god, which would explain the magnitude of the fable; no discrepancy is sought, though one of course emerges; and the mode is scholarship of the historian, not travesty of the satirist.[17] Unlike travesty (or its sister, mock heroic), this mode is concerned with causality and historical relationships, in some sense genealogy and etymology: How *did* the historical ur-Tom become the rake, the Adonis, the "Angel from Heaven," or the "murderer"? And what exactly is the relationship, and does it tell us something about the reality, or is it an element without which the reality itself does not signify?

Let us take two battle scenes, Joseph Andrews and the fox hounds (III, vi) and Tom Jones and the attackers of Molly Seagrim in the graveyard (IV, viii). In the first, Fielding is merely demonstrating the inadequacy of heroic analogues as literary forms to characterize the real heroism of Joseph: he tells us that no simile, no figure from literature, is "adequate to our Purpose," that Joseph is himself a simile for heroism (p. 241). Tom's battle against Molly's attackers begins as a travesty: Echepolus is in fact a Somersetshire sow gelder and Myrdon is Kate of the Mill; but there is an additional dimension, already established by all the lies and fabrications that from the start have surrounded Tom, Allworthy, and the others. There is no longer the same kind of adverse comment on the heroic level itself. For there to be, Tom and even Molly would have to be acting foolishly to fight, and they are not (except insofar as Tom is deceived about his relations with Molly); only perhaps the villagers, these pious folk who are outraged by the sight of Molly in Sophia's finery and flaunting her pregnancy in church, retain something of the pretensions we associate with the mock heroic. But the villagers are primarily (like Gay's Sparabella) myth makers, and the narrator is showing that this local scuffle in a graveyard is "the real truth" or "what really happened" under the stories the villagers will spread, as under the Homeric description of the Greeks and Trojans in battle. Mars is really Alexander the Great, or the bull is really Captain Taurus; Achilles is a mythologized version, fabricated by the villagers to assuage their wounded self-esteem, of Tom Jones in the graveyard fighting off the mob that is after Molly; and the real Tom can only be known through the myths surrounding him. We are seeing history in the making and in the process of being mythologized, as earlier, in a more literal way, when Partridge's battle with Mrs. Partridge was promptly mythologized by their neighbors. What distinguishes such a scene from those in *Joseph Andrews* is the sense of a myth being simultaneously created and analyzed.

The analogy with war engendered by the skirmish in the graveyard leads directly to the real war with the Pretender's army. On his way with the troops to meet the Pretender's army, Tom and some soldiers are supping at an inn (VII, xii, 372–76). Tom compares these soldiers to the Greeks on their way to Troy; Ensign Northerton shows his ignorance of the classical allusion; and one of the soldiers identifies the Greeks and Trojans as "dey fight for von Woman." Shortly after, Tom toasts Sophia, Northerton mythologizes her into a notorious whore (the truth about Helen), Tom calls him a rascal, and he knocks Tom senseless with a bottle: "The Conqueror perceiving the Enemy to lie motionless before him, and Blood beginning to flow pretty plentifully from his Wound, began now to think of quitting the Field of Battle, where no more Honour was to be gotten." Sophia has been turned into a kind of Helen and the inn table into a "Field of Battle." The effect is very different from that of Joseph's battle with the hounds, but it is an extension of Tom's with Molly's attackers, and so quite naturally the battle of Upton is based on "no very blameable Degree of Suspicion" among the people at the inn as to Tom's relations with Mrs. Waters, who is a "poor unfortunate Helen, the fatal Cause of all the Bloodshed" (IX, iii, 504).[18] The battles progress toward the single combat of Tom and Mrs. Waters at the dinner table at Upton, introduced by an allusion to Pasiphae and the bull (a memory perhaps of Banier's amusing euhemerist account), which is presented as an elemental struggle that will be mythologized as a battle—and is literally mythologized in the conversation of the servants in the kitchen.

Banier offers Fielding something the proper historian like Hume does not, and that is the distinction between poet, historian, and mythologist. Banier's title, recall, was *The Mythology and Fables of the Ancients, Explain'd from History:* a title which would apply to *The Jacobite's Journal* and *Tom Jones* if we substitute for "Ancients" the word "Jacobites" or "Moderns." The fundamental point Banier makes is that the stories of the gods are not fables, "Tales of mere Invention," but "ancient Facts" (or "Truths of Importance") "embellished" with "numbers of Fables" (I, 21, 26). The form he describes is "ancient Histories, mix'd with several Fictions": "those which speak of *Hercules, Jason,* &c. instead of telling us in the simple way, that the latter went to recover the Treasures which *Phrixus* had carried to *Colchis,* they have given us the Fable of the Golden Fleece" (I, 30). The poetic fable does not rule out other kinds—philosophical, allegorical, moral—but all carry with them a historical truth, and so consist of two elements: fable *and* truth.

Important inferences can be made from this methodology, both for the narrative mode of *Tom Jones* and for the ontology of its characters. We have noticed the emphasis on history in the introductory chapter of book VIII; book IX returns to "this historic kind of Writing." Though not like the "historical Writers" who "draw their Materials from Records" (Banier identifies inscriptions on monuments as one source of "ancient Facts"), the author has "good Authority" for his characters from "the vast authentic Doomsday-Book of Nature" and so believes his work entitled "to the Name of History." By "genius," he explains, he means the powers of the mind "capable of penetrating into all Things within our Reach and knowledge, and of distinguishing their essential Differences"; and by "invention" he means not "a creative Faculty," as that of fabulists and romance writers, but rather "Discovery, or finding out; a quick and sagacious Penetration into the true Essence of all the Objects of our Contemplation."

Compared with the comic-epic-in-prose writer of *Joseph Andrews,* the historian's is a difficult role. As Banier describes it, however much "the Truths of ancient History . . . may be disguised by the great number of Ornaments mixed with them, it is *not absolutely impossible* to unfold the historical Facts they contain" (I, 20; italics added):

The most perplexing Difficulty in the way of a Mythologist consists in unravelling the Intricacy of different Opinions about one and the same Fable, which is told in so many ways, and so different from one another, that it is impossible to reconcile them all. [I, 18]

For example, the fable of Tom, Black George, and Molly, as told by Thwackum, Square, Blifil, and Tom, and interpreted by Allworthy, the narrator, and the reader—or by the critical, judicious, or good-natured reader—is a complex knot perhaps never completely capable of being untied.[19] The method "observed by our best Mythologists," says Banier, is never to adopt a fable "without having first enquired what might have given rise to it" (I, 18), and in both *The Jacobite's Journal* (e.g., no. 12) and *Tom Jones* Fielding's emphasis falls upon the searching out of motives. The awareness of difficulty and uncertainty carries from Banier to *The Jacobite's Journal*, where Fielding writes on the articles of the peace of Aix-la-Chapelle:

Whether we are to impute these Articles (if they are true) to the Intervention of Providence, to the reasonable Disposition of our Enemies, or to the Wisdom and Watchfulness of our own Ministers, I will not determine. [P. 278]

In *Tom Jones*, the "Whether . . . or . . . I will not determine" construction, an example of the classical figure of *aporia* or the doubtful, becomes a virtual refrain of historical probability.[20]

As opposed to the Hume who tries to present demythologized facts for history, or his opposite, the Christian weaver of the providential pattern, the Banier sort of euhemerist requires three roles.[21] The poet mythologizes historical facts, the historian tries to establish what really happened, and the mythologist analyzes the myth in the light of history. The product is a rich complex of the three stages with the emphasis on the process itself. This is a stage well beyond the role of the travesty-poet, "to strip it of the Marvellous" (I, 17), which in *Tom Jones* is conveyed by repeated phrases like "This was the true Reason why," "To say the Truth," "the real Truth," or "what really happened." But Fielding is showing the simultaneous construction and explanation of myth, showing how it is produced by poets out of historical events.[22]

The historical fact does not exist without its embellishment in fable. Banier asks "What would the *Aeneid, Iliad,* or *Odyssey* be, was it not for the . . . perpetual mixture of Truths of small concern, with the most interesting Fictions?" (I, 39). The "truth of small concern,"

that Ulysses and his crew loiter debauching at Circe's court, is augmented by the "interesting Fiction" that Circe is a sorceress who
transforms men into swine. Thus we may regard such fictions "as so
many Metaphors and figurative Ways of speaking," and the distinction applies equally to imaginative leaps like the connecting of Captain Taurus (a name only) with a bull. In general, Banier is describing what Cassirer calls the "mythico-religious Urphenomenon" in
which the primitive man is confronted by a new and strange thing,
and to come to terms with it *names* it, designates it metaphorically,
perhaps calling it a god or a spirit. The function of this activity in
Tom Jones is both instrumental and ontological, partly to express the
vanity and other motives of the fabulator and partly to approximate
the thing's essential being in the only way possible. I mean that there
is a sense in which Sophia *is* Jenny Cameron, just as there is one in
which Black George *does* love Tom, and Tom *is* both "so terrible a
Rake" and "an Angel from Heaven" (as Enderson calls him [p. 720]).

"We can only *conceive* being, sidle up to it by laying something
else alongside. We approach the thing not directly but by pairing, by
opposing symbol and thing." I am quoting Walker Percy in "Metaphor as Mistake," where he explores examples "of an accidental
blundering into authentic poetic experience . . . in folk mistakes . . .
for what light they may shed on the function of metaphor in man's
fundamental symbolic orientation in the world," but I could be quoting a great many contemporary linguistic theorists who see the metaphor's lie as "not a vagary of poets but a specific case of that mysteri-
ous 'error' which is the very condition of our knowing anything at
all."[23]

We come to understand Tom Jones or Sophia Western by a
number of "errors," much as we do the beautiful soaring "Blue
Darter Bird" by the mistake of "Blue Dollar Bird" or a woman having
an affair with a Captain Taurus by the story of Pasiphae and the bull.
What Fielding has in *Tom Jones*, that was only glimpsed in *Joseph
Andrews*, is the knowledge that the reality of Tom or of Molly in the
graveyard, or of Sophia–called–Jenny Cameron, is the historical figure plus the poeticized one plus the mythologist's relation of the two.
Any one of these is inadequate without the others.

Roughly speaking, we can say that Fielding presents the following types of mythologizing: (1) The true character of Tom (perhaps
ultimately unknowable) is related to the fables of his enemies and

others, reaching from the extreme cases of mistakes (Mrs. Fitzpatrick's thinking he is Blifil) to the gradual equation of him with "so terrible a Rake," "so very fine a Figure," or "an Angel from Heaven."

(2) "Fables of the Historical Kind," writes Banier, "are easily distinguished, because mention is made in them of People we know elsewhere" (I, 31). One such group would include Lady Ranelagh, painted by Kneller, and the duchess of Mazarin by Lely, who are given to us by Fielding as approximations of what Sophia looked like; Hogarth's Bridewell warden for Thwackum, the old lady in *Morning* for Bridget, and the servant woman in *Harlot's Progress* (plate 3) for Mrs. Partridge. Fielding may have recalled Banier's statement that

> the Painters working upon Poetical Fancies, may be reckoned instrumental in propagating some Fables. . . . They have even frequently promoted the Credit of fabulous Stories, by representing them with Art; a thing so true . . . that the Pagans owed the Existence of many of their Gods, to some fine Statues, or Pictures well done. [I, 44]

Ultimately we come to the scene or character that has no precedent, and he can only specify: "O, Shakespeare, had I thy Pen! O, *Hogarth*, had I thy Pencil!" (p. 555). This is not the exclamation of the author of *Joseph Andrews*, demonstrating the discrepancy between the real and the literary, but an attempt to approximate as best one can the unformulable.

(3) On another level are Ralph Allen and Lord Lyttelton, the actual historical figures of whom Allworthy is a poetic version; Charlotte Cradock Fielding for Sophia; and perhaps Fielding himself for Tom. Fielding is creating his own myth as he analyzes those of others, while at the same time admitting the fabrication. The public dimension of "historical truth" shades off into the private, and this applies especially to the '45 itself, the ultimate fact in process of being mythologized by the Jacobites. The confusion of Tom and Sophia wandering about searching for each other in the wilderness, of families broken up, lovers separated, and allegiances mixed, is the historical reality of the '45.[24] *The Jacobite's Journal* and Abbé Banier come together in Partridge, the garrulous, superstitious Catholic-Jacobite, who believes in the Jacobite "Mysteries" (that a popish king would defend a Protestant church) as he believes in prodigies and old wives' tales; and although he concludes of Tom's own story "that the whole

was a Fiction" (p. 427), he proceeds to construct his own on the basis of his fecund self-interest. As in the *Journal*, the time is one of rumors and lies and myths, the greatest being concerned with the virtues of an absolute monarchy (vs. a constitutional or mixed form of government) and an absolute paragon (vs. at best a "mixed char- acter," at worst a scoundrel).

We are reminded of the parallels from the outset with the two heirs to Paradise Hall, both as ambiguous as "the famous [Jacobite] Story of the Warming-Pan" and as "the no more unaccountable Birth of *Bacchus*" Fielding tells in his *Jacobite's Journal* parody of Banier (p. 125). Tom is a bastard, but Blifil is himself conceived out of wedlock, though technically born within. What is clear is that Blifil, despite his technical claim to inheritance, is morally disquali- fied from his right to carry on the Allworthy-Western line, while Tom demonstrates his right to the title of successor. As any English- man knew, the Act of Settlement of 1701 had given the reversion of the crown to the Protestant electress of Hanover and her children, rejecting Jacobite claims of divine right and hereditary succession. The parallels extend from the elaborate lies and plots of Blifil to his behavior after his exposure, which recalls that of the Stuart prince reported by unsympathetic observers during the rout of Culloden.[25]

(4) Another kind of myth is also in process of construction by Fielding the narrator. The similes from book V onward push unob- trusively toward the materials of country folklore. In the second battle scene, with Tom defending Molly from the interruption of Blifil and company (V, xi, 259–60), the simile links Tom's response to the ritual mating of a stag in "the Season of Rutting," and Tom becomes the defender of a "frighted Hind": "fierce and tremendous rushes forth the Stag to the Entrance of the Thicket; there stands the Centi- nel over his Love, stamps the Ground with his Foot, and with his Horns brandished aloft in Air, proudly provoks the apprehended Foe to Combat." The simile remains implicit in the battle that follows, modifying the stated epic terms, and thereafter extends from Par- tridge's story of the drunk's encounter with a white-faced calf that grows into a battle with a ghost, to the simile with which book X (ii) opens, with frolicking hares, hooting owls, a half-drunk clown in terror of hobgoblins and robbers on the prowl while watchmen are asleep: "in plain English it was now Midnight." We have left behind alien classical similes and are in the world of native English country

superstitions and folklore, where the absence of Punch and Joan in the puppet show is noticed and the presence of the gipsies' encampment comes as no surprise. This is the world of jests, practical jokes, and skimmingtons; of the people who turn Tom and Sophia into heroes that are versions of the upper-class heroes, the king, his generals, courtiers, and magistrates.

It is in this world that the major characters also function most suggestively. As Pasiphae's bull was a captain named Taurus, so God is in fact a benevolent country squire named Allworthy who lives in Paradise Hall. By Allworthy's errors and pomposities, Fielding makes it clear that he is *not* God; but mythologically the relationship is meaningful. We might say that Fielding never loses sight of the historical reality while mythologizing him—just as his neighbors also mythologize him as atheist, old fool, father of Tom, persecutor of Jenny Jones, and so on. Besides Allworthy of whom God is the fable, there is Tom of whom Adam (expelled from Eden and sent out, in Milton's words, into the world) is the fable, and Sophia of whom Wisdom is the fable, and so on to Molly, the latter-day Eve, and Blifil, associated with the Devil.[26]

In the case of Tom, all the contemporary "poetry" to the effect that he is the son of Jenny Jones and Partridge is swept away and we are left with the fact that he is the son of Bridget (Allworthy) Blifil and, as it happens, a man named Summer. Bridget herself, as her alliance with Hogarth's old woman in *Morning* and Fielding's identification as "an Emblem of Winter" suggest, is as real and yet projective of myth as her early lover named Summer, who is remembered by Mrs. Waters (Tom's supposititious mother, whose own married name has the same ambience) as "a finer Man, I must say, the Sun never shone upon" (XVIII, vii, 940).[27] Blifil, on the other hand, is the son of Winter—and whatever we are to make of the swarthy, rough, calculating, ungrateful, melancholic Captain Blifil. Fielding uses as his example, in the opening chapter on "contrast" (V, i, 212), "Thus the Beauty of Day, and that of Summer, is set off by the Horrors of Night and Winter," and this is roughly the scheme of the novel's own myth: the vigor and fertility in the native Englishman of somewhat confused blood lines—his release of erotic energy in a repressed civilization—versus the paragon of melancholy—the saturnine, self-enclosed, and scheming Blifil—as the historical reality of the whole imbroglio of 1745.

The hero as nature deity had been broached more straightfor-
wardly in Joseph Andrews, who is employed to serve as scarecrow to
keep off birds, "to perform the Part the Antients assigned to the God
Priapus." His cathexis is as ambiguous as Priapus' for his voice
"rather allured the Birds than terrified them," as do his protestations
of chastity to Lady Booby (I, ii, 21). Tom at times recalls one of the
gods analyzed by Banier. To take, not quite at random, the one
Fielding himself analyzes in *Jacobite's Journal* (no. 6), we notice that
Bacchus too came of an obscure liaison: "the Antients had formed a
Design to throw a Veil of obscurity over the true History of this
Prince's Birth and Education," and what follows (II, 437–53) is the
analysis of whether he comes of a human or immortal father, and
after that of the myths of Bacchic celebration—all those women
dancing "to celebrate the Memory of his Conquests" and carrying
aloft the phallus. The main point of debate, indeed, is the nature and
meaning of the strange ceremonies that accompanied him wherever
he traveled, characterized by "Debauchery, Lewdness, and Prostitution being carried to the greatest Extremity." Bacchus was "commonly represented like a young Man, without a Beard," rendered
enthusiastic by too deep a use of the vine, and known for his generosity—spreading his mysteries to the world, especially to women. He
carried about with him "a Kind of ambulatory Seraglio," Banier wrily
remarks. Tom, there can be no argument, attracts both men and
women of all kinds, and only repulses sterile figures like Blifil.

I use Bacchus (whose *Jacobite's Journal* caricature is the Jacobite
country squire) only as a referent to underline the observation that
Fielding has reversed the "popular" characteristics of the Jacobite
myth, making Tom the life force which Bonnie Prince Charlie was
portrayed as being, while Blifil has all the Hanoverian-Whig traits
attributed by the Jacobites—as by many objective Englishmen. It is
certainly the case that the names with which Jacobite pamphlets com-
memorated Charles Edward—the Wanderer, the Young Adventurer,
the Young Chevalier, and Ascanius (pamphlets with which Fielding
was very familiar)—apply to Tom, not to Blifil.[28] The sort of song the
loyalists were singing about Prince Charles (parodying a Jacobite song)
is a song that Blifil and his friends might have sung about Tom:

> Over the water and over the lea,
> And over the water to Charley.

> Charley loves good ale and wine,
>   And Charley loves good brandy,
> And Charley loves a pretty girl
>   As sweet as sugar candy.[29]

Fielding himself had had a difficult task demythologizing the prince in 1745, first in *The True Patriot* and then in his *History of the Present Rebellion in Scotland*. In the latter, where we can juxtapose passages from newspapers and contemporary accounts, what Fielding did was to turn the dashing prince into a Blifil, the spontaneity and expansive gestures into calculation, prudence, and vanity.[30] When the real prince leads his soldiers across the Forth, his Rubicon, dashing ahead into the historic waters, Fielding's prince does it to show off:

> Here Charles attempting to give an extraordinary Instance of his Bravery by passing the Water first, and mistaking the Ford, very narrowly escaped drowning, from which he was preserved by Lieutenant *Duncan Madson*, who at the Hazard of his own Life rescued him from the Waves.[31]

Fielding's most egregious fabulating of the '45, however, had been in the pages of *The True Patriot*, where he exaggerated the dangers of rape, burning, looting, and terror to the civilian population. And yet even there, true to his own character and preoccupations, Fielding carefully distinguished by headlines between "The Present History of Great Britain" and an "APOCRYPHA. Being a curious Collection of certain true and important WE HEARS from the News-Papers." And once the rebellion was over, in his final apology for his work on *The True Patriot* (no. 33) he expressed something of a sense of guilt:

> For the Paper principally intended to inflame this Nation against the Rebels, was writ whilst they were at *Derby*, and in that Day of Confusion which God will, I hope, never suffer to have its equal in this Kingdom.

His valedictory was to urge not justice but mercy, human understanding, and a spirit of tolerance toward the defeated—sentiments echoed in his attitude toward Tom throughout the narrative and in Tom's toward Blifil and Black George at the denouement.[32]

I would like to know more about Fielding's response to the undeniably romantic boy who landed in a remote corner of the

Kingdom with only a few men to win back his father's crown. Whether Tom or Prince Charles Edward came first is, I suppose, an academic question; Fielding may have begun *Tom Jones* before the prince's landing. But without Squire Western nearby as the pure Jacobite country squire, Tom might have reminded readers of the prince. Either Fielding is turning the myth upside down, or he finds that, in an ironic way, the myth of the gallant young prince is closer to the one he had already sketched in *Joseph Andrews,* and for that matter to his own story, or one aspect of it. That is not to suggest that he is in any way more sympathetic with the prince's cause than he was in *The Jacobite's Journal,* but only that a common myth of alienation from one's true home and wandering as exile or fugitive tie these two heroes together. Perhaps Tom is the true historical figure beneath the Jacobitish myth, as Sophia is beneath Jenny Cameron.

In any case, Fielding the etymologist knows he must retain the encrustations and work out a meaning that includes them. He knows that Tom exists in terms of Bacchus and Bonnie Prince Charlie, while being something quite different, and that the linguistic differences created by custom are interesting for their own sake. One seeks neither the unchanging model language nor the original one, now long lost, but rather demonstrates the change and variety in the reality, which is Tom as *all* of the things said about him, or Sophia as including not-Sophia, elucidated in the grubby variety of Molly, Jenny, and Lady Bellaston. This is what history actually means to Fielding—and to Hogarth.

It should be added that Fielding ends his *History of the Present Rebellion in Scotland* with the rout of Colonel James Gardner's dragoons prior to the Jacobite victory at Preston Pans. This is in fact the focal encounter of his *History,* and he even includes a list of casualties. This also happens to be the event Hogarth alludes to through the signboard of "Giles Gardner" (the "Adam and Eve" nursery) in *The March to Finchley,* which is the historical event he too chose to represent: the '45 as seen in *Tom Jones.* Rouquet takes time off in his essay on *The March to Finchley* to devote a paragraph to *Tom Jones,* which he praises in the same terms as Hogarth's works. For both Fielding and Hogarth the '45 is a metaphor for a clash between ideals of order and stability in the Jacobite's absolute monarchy and the relatively disorderly but very English parliamentary system of government staggering along under the Hanoverians. Absolute and limited (constitutional) monarchies represent the same oppositions that appear on the level of character in the contrasts between a theoretical paragon and Tom Jones, between Sophia and the Mollies and Jennies, or in the judgment of characters between law and mercy. These are the same poles upon which Hogarth constructs his *March to Finchley*, and they take the form of the same historic struggle that sundered families, confused loyalties, and led to egregious misunderstandings. Like Fielding's, Hogarth's context is not the patriotism of 1745–46 but the later discontent in an unhappy England ruled by an unpopular foreign family and swarming with dissident elements; and more immediately for Hogarth, the Treaty of Aix-la-Chapelle (1748), from which England had gained little or nothing, and the current attempt by the victor of Culloden (also known as "the Butcher") to bring the British army up to a German standard of order and precision. An English "liberty" and disorder are juxtaposed with the imposed order of the Mutiny Bill.

The old mythology of Continental history painting and heroic behavior, of the Jacobites *and* the Hanoverians, is replaced in *The March to Finchley* by a new one based on English folk skimmingtons and charivaris and their particular brand of disorder. This is Hogarth's etymological attempt to go back to what really happened when the troops marched north to meet the Young Pretender—not the Jacobite or Hanoverian myths of it. But the "natural" actions of these people are only meaningful in relation to the polite metaphors, models, and paradigms—with which the painting swarms—of the Good Samaritan, Hercules at the Crossroads, Adam and Eve, and Madonna and Child.

Illustrations

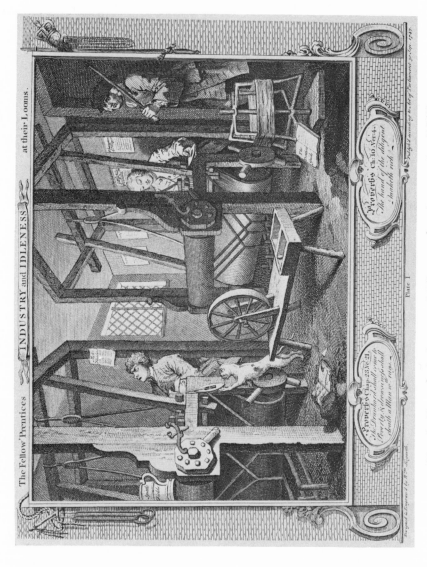

Fig. 1. Hogarth, *Industry and Idleness*, plate 1, engraving (1747)

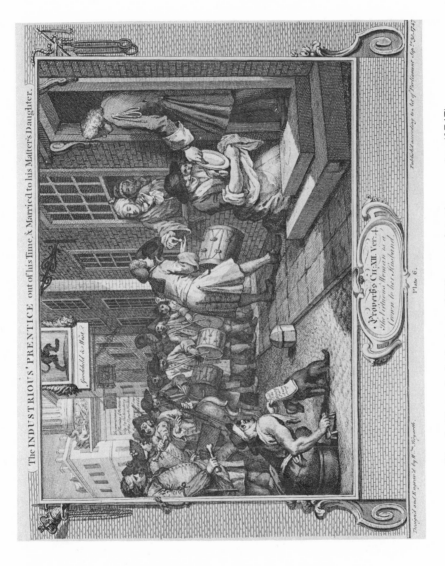

Fig. 2. Hogarth, *Industry and Idleness*, plate 6, engraving (1747)

Fig. 3. Hogarth, *Industry and Idleness*, plate 8, engraving (1747)

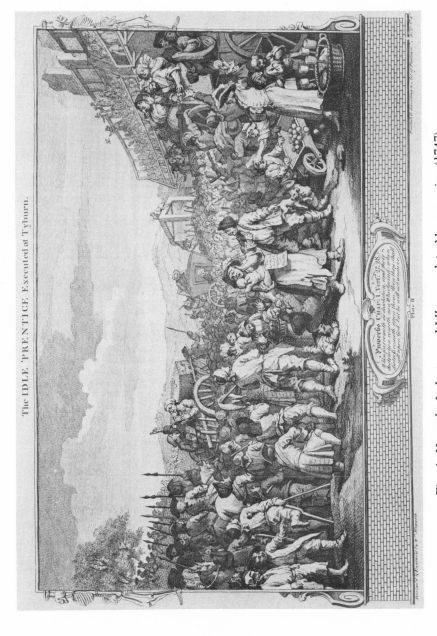

Fig. 4. Hogarth, *Industry and Idleness*, plate 11, engraving (1747)

213

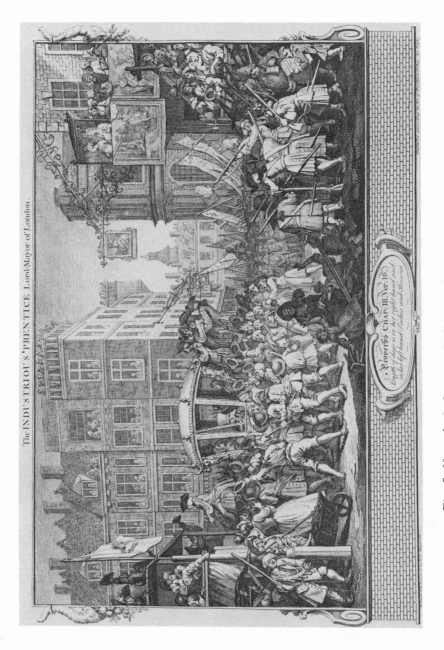

Fig. 5. Hogarth, *Industry and Idleness*, plate 12, engraving (1747)

Beer, happy Produce of our Isle
Can sinewy Strength impart,
And wearied with Fatigue and Toil
Can cheer each manly Heart.

Labour and Art upheld by Thee
Successfully advance,
We quaff Thy balmy Juice with Glee
And Water leave to France.

Genius of Health, thy grateful Taste
Rivals the Cup of Jove,
And warms each English generous Breast
With Liberty and Love.

Fig. 6. Hogarth, *Beer Street*, engraving (1751)

215

Fig. 7. Hogarth, *Gin Lane*, engraving (1751)

While various Scenes of sportive Woe
The Infant Race employ,
And tortur'd Victims bleeding shew
The Tyrant in the Boy.

Behold! a Youth of gentler Heart,
To spare the Creature's pain
O take, he cries–take all my Tart,
But Tears and Tart are vain.

Learn from this fair Example–You
Whom savage Sports delight,
How Cruelty disgusts the view
While Pity charms the sight.

Design'd by W. Hogarth   *Published according to Act of Parliament Feb.1.1751.*   *Price 1.*

Fig. 8. Hogarth, *The Four Stages of Cruelty*, plate 1, engraving (1751)

217

The generous Steed in hoary Age
'Subdu'd by Labour lies;
And mourns a cruel Master's rage,
While Nature Strength denies.

Designed by W. Hogarth.

The tender Lamb o'er drove and faint,
Amidst expiring Throws;
Bleats forth it's innocent complaint
And dies beneath the Blows.

Publish'd according to Act of Parliament Feb. 1 1751.

Inhuman Wretch! say whence proceeds *Price 1.s*
This coward Cruelty?
What Intrest springs from barbrous deeds?
What Joy from Misery?

Fig. 9. Hogarth, *The Four Stages of Cruelty*, plate 2, engraving (1751)

218

Fig. 10. Hogarth, *The Four Stages of Cruelty*, plate 3, engraving (1751)

Price 1.ˢ Designd by W. Hogarth.

Behold the Villain's dire disgrace!
Not Death itself can end.
He finds no peaceful Burial-Place;
His breathless Corse, no friend.

Torn from the Root, that wicked Tongue,
Which daily swore and curst!
Those Eyeballs, from their Sockets wrung,
That glow'd with lawless Lust!

His Heart, expos'd to prying Eyes,
To Pity has no Claim:
But, dreadful! from his Bones shall rise,
His Monument of Shame.

Published, according to Act of Parliament Feb.1.1751.

Fig. 11. Hogarth, *The Four Stages of Cruelty*, plate 4, engraving (1751)

Fig. 12. Hogarth, *The March to Finchley*, engraving (1750)

Fig. 13. Hogarth, *Hudibras Encounters the Skimmington*, engraving (1726)

Fig. 14. Hogarth, *Burning the Rumps at Temple Bar*, engraving (1726)

Fig. 15. Hogarth, *A Harlot's Progress*, plate 2, engraving (1732)

224

Fig. 16. Hogarth, A *Harlot's Progress*, plate 3, engraving (1732)

225

Fig. 17. Hogarth, *The Times of the Day*, plate 2 (Noon) engraving (1738)

Fig. 18. Hogarth, *Nobody*, drawing (1732) (London, British Museum)

227

Fig. 19. Hogarth, *Somebody*, drawing (1732) (London, British Museum)

Whoever makes a DESIGN, without the Knowledge of PERSPECTIVE, will be liable to such Absurdities as are shewn in this Frontispiece.

Fig. 20. Hogarth, *Satire on False Perspective*,
engraving (by Luke Sullivan) (1754)

Fig. 21. Hogarth, *Marriage à la Mode*, plate 4, engraving (1745)

230

Fig. 22. Hogarth, *The Strode Family*, painting (c. 1738)
(London, Tate Gallery)

Studious he sate, with all his books around,
Sinking from thought to thought, a vast profound!
Plung'd for his sense, but found no bottom there;
Then wrote, and flounder'd on, in mere despair.

DUNCIAD, Book I, line 111.

Fig. 23. Hogarth, *The Distresed Poet*, engraving (1736)

232

Gulielmus Hogarth.

Fig. 24. Hogarth, *Self-Portrait with Pug,* engraving (1745)

233

THE BRUISER, C.C. CHURCHILL (once the Rev.d) in the Character of a Russian Hercules, Regaling himself after having kill'd the Monster Caricatura that so forely Gall'd his Virtuous friend the Heaven born WILKES.

— But he had a Club this Dragon to Drub.   Or he had ne'er don't I warrant ye .——— Dragon of Wantley

Design'd & Engrav'd by W.m Hogarth Price 1.6."   Publish'd according to Act of Parliament August 1 1763.

Fig. 25. Hogarth, *The Bruiser*, engraving (1763)

234

Fig. 26. Rowlandson, *Kew Bridge*, drawing (c. 1790) (Henry E. Huntington Library and Art Gallery)

Fig. 27. Hogarth, *The Beggar's Opera*, painting (1728) (W. S. Lewis Collection)

Fig. 28. Hogarth, *The Beggar's Opera*, painting (1729) (Yale Center for British Art)

237

Fig. 29. Hogarth, *The Good Samaritan*, painting (1736–37) (London, St. Bartholomew's Hospital)

238

Fig. 30. Hogarth, *The Pool of Bethesda*, painting (1735–36)
(London, St. Bartholomew's Hospital)

239

Fig. 31. Hogarth, *A Rake's Progress*, plate 3, engraving (1735)

Fig. 32. Hogarth, A *Rake's Progress*, plate 4, engraving (1735)

241

Fig. 33. Hogarth, A *Rake's Progress*, plate 8, engraving (1735)

242

Notes

Preface

1. See E. P. Thompson, *The Making of the English Working Class* (London, 1963), and Christopher Hill, *The World Turned Upside Down: Radical Ideas during the English Revolution* (London, 1972).

2. Thompson, op. cit. (New York: Vintage ed., 1969), p. 59.

3. Thompson, *Whigs and Hunters: The Origin of the Black Act* (New York, 1975), p. 17.

4. Cf. Thompson, "Patrician Society, Plebeian Culture," *Journal of Social History*, VII (1974), 396–404; and Thompson's most recent statement, which appeared after this manuscript was completed: "Eighteenth-Century English Society: Class Struggle without Class?," *Social History*, III (1978), 145. For Thompson's argument for the relatively unified subculture of the eighteenth century, as opposed to the fragmented subcultures of the sixteenth and seventeenth centuries, see his "Anthropology and the Discipline of Historical Context," *Midland History*, I (1972), 51–55, and Keith Thomas' reply in "An Anthropology of Religion and Magic," *Journal of Interdisciplinary History*, VI (1975), 104–5n., with Thompson's further reply in "Eighteenth-Century English Society," pp. 156–57.

5. *Art of Cookery*, pp. 22, 18; see Joan Owen, "Philosophy in the Kitchen; or Problems in Eighteenth-Century Culinary Aesthetics," *Eighteenth-Century Life*, III (Mar. 1977), 77–79.

6. See Edmund Leach, *Culture and Communication: The Logic by Which Symbols Are Connected* (Cambridge, 1976), p. 35.

7. A good example is C. J. Rawson, *Henry Fielding and the Augustan Ideal under Stress* (London, 1972).

8. Mintz, "Foreword," in Norman Whitten and John F. Szwed, eds., *Afro-American Anthropology: Contemporary Perspectives* (New York, 1970), pp. 9–10.

9. "The Moral Economy of the English Crowd in the Eighteenth Century," *Past and Present*, no. 50 (Feb. 1971), pp. 109ff.

10. *Biographia Literaria*, chap. XVII, ed. J. Shawcross (Oxford, 1907; 1973 ed.), II, 40. See also p. 31 on More and the Bible.

11. In particular, cf. Davis' remarks about "the social creativity of the so-called inarticulate" and "the way in which they seize upon older social forms and change them to fit their needs" ("The Reasons of Misrule: Youth Groups and Charivaris in Sixteenth-Century France," *Past and Present*, no. 50 ([Feb. 1971], p. 74).

12. See J. Meier, *Kunstlied und Volkslied in Deutschland* (Halle, 1906) and H.

Naumann, *Primitive Gemeinschaftskultur* (Jena, 1921); cf. on a two-way flow, which is obviously closer to the truth, e.g., R. Redfield, *Peasant Society and Culture* (Chicago, 1956), p. 42. On the whole problem, see Peter Burke's excellent *Popular Culture in Early Modern Europe* (London, 1978), pp. 58–63. Burke's book appeared too late for me to utilize in any general way.

13. See *Religion and the Decline of Magic* (London, 1971); Penguin ed., 1973), a work I have found especially useful.

14. Thompson's argument is that while conservative in their forms, plebeian manifestations are rebellious in their content. This is "a rebellious traditional culture," he says, which "resists, in the name of 'custom,' those economic innovations and rationalizations (as enclosure, work-discipline, free market relations in grain) which the rulers or employers seek to impose" ("Eighteenth-Century English Society," p. 154).

15. *The New Art: A Critical Anthology* (New York, 1973), p. xviii.

16. I will give precise references in the relevant footnotes.

The Criminal

1. See Malvin R. Zirker, Jr., *Fielding's Social Pamphlets* (Berkeley and Los Angeles, 1966). Caroline Robbins can still call Fielding "the most radical of the Whigs of George II's reign" (*The Eighteenth-Century Commonwealthman* [Cambridge, Mass., 1959], p. 287).

2. *Enquiry*, 1st ed., p. 4.

3. Fielding belives that the underlying cause is the working-class's succumbing to the vice of "luxury," or simply wanting more than it needs. The whole concept of luxury or *luxuria* was a traditional and upper-class one. See Fielding's *Enquiry*, pp. 4–12, and John Sekora, *Luxury: The Concept in Western Thought, Eden to Smollett* (Baltimore, 1977), pp. 91–92.

4. *Enquiry*, pp. 22–23.

5. Cf. Fielding's *Champion* for 16 Feb. 1739/40, where he divides the poor into five categories. His irony cuts against the first, the affluent who "by following their Superiors into Luxury, in order to support, as they call it, the Figure of Gentlemen, reduced themselves into Distress and Poverty." His irony supports the other four: the younger sons who have opposed Walpole and so lost preferment; those reduced by misfortunes and unavoidable accidents to want; the unlucky ones who have no powerful friends; and the oppressed. The problem of the degree of his irony comes to rest on the "streets"—"whose begging Inhabitants deserve Punishment more than Relief, and are a Shame not to the Legislative but the Executive Power of our Land." He adds: "However as I may possibly dedicate a whole Paper to the Provision of the Poor, I shall say no more of them here."

6. *Enquiry*, p. 37. St. Giles Parish, in the Seven Dials area, had one of the highest crime rates in London and every fourth house was a gin shop (see George Rudé, *Hanoverian London, 1714–1808* [Berkeley, 1971], p. 91; George Clinch, *Bloomsbury and St. Giles* [London, 1890], pp. 73–75).

7. The sentimental exception was Fielding's treatment of prostitutes. As Bow Street magistrate, he was a scourge of the pimps and bawds, not of the girls themselves; and this was probably related to his faith in the innocence of Elizabeth

Canning (against the exploiters whom she accused of having kept her prisoner). Fielding, like Hogarth, saw women not as the culpable agents of man's downfall but as the victims of men. He probably also saw them in the New Testament light of Christ's treatment of publicans and sinners versus the scribes and Pharisees. See Edward J. Bristow, *Vice and Vigilance: Purity Movements in Britain since 1700* (Dublin, 1978).

8. T. G. Coffey, "Beer Street: Gin Lane: Some Views of 18th-Century Drinking," *Quarterly Journal of Studies on Alcohol*, XXVII (1966), 669–92, esp. 673–76, 690–91; see Sidney and Beatrice Webb, *History of Liquor Licensing in England* (London, 1903), pp. 20–22, 29; and Brian Inglis, *Forbidden Game: A Social History of Drugs* (London, 1975), p. 67.

9. E. P. Thompson, "The Moral Economy of the English Crowd," p. 91. From the perspective of Thompson and his school we get a Hogarth quite different from the "reformer" who tries to save the lower classes by attacking their gin drinking, let alone the simple case of the rising bourgeois, in Frederick Antal's naive Marxist interpretation (*Hogarth and His Place in European Art* [London, 1962]).

10. Place, corrected proofs of *Drunkenness*, BM. Add. MSS. 27825; quoted in Lawrence Stone, *The Family, Sex and Marriage in England, 1500–1800* (New York, 1977), p. 638. See also Keith Thomas, *Religion and the Decline of Magic*, pp. 22–23, on gin as solace for the poor.

11. There is the question of how many of the "working class" actually saw Hogarth's popular prints. From *Industry and Idleness* (1747) through the prints of 1751 Hogarth reduced his price from 3 or 4 shillings per print to 1 shilling (for those printed on higher quality paper he charged 1s. 6d.). A shilling was still a sizable sum for the poor, but Hogarth's gesture extended his audience to the small artisans and journeymen if not to apprentices. Moreover, his prints were displayed in taverns, coffee houses, and other public places, so that for each purchaser dozens of others who could not afford to buy the prints saw them.

12. "The Tyburn Riot against the Surgeons," in *Albion's Fatal Tree: Crime and Society in Eighteenth-Century England*, ed. Douglas Hay et al. (New York, 1975), p. 115. Linebaugh links these feelings "with attitudes of class hatred." The upperclass audience might have seen the print as graphically reminiscent of the tradition of dissection scenes in high art (see W. H. Heckscher, *Rembrandt's Anatomy of Dr. Nicolaus Tulp: An Iconological Study* [New York, 1958], pp. 102–6).

13. See John Ireland, *Hogarth Illustrated* (1791), II, 72n. However, given Freke's appearance and his specialty (eye surgery), it seems as likely that he is the man gouging out Nero's eye. See the bust in the Library Gallery, St. Bartholomew's Hospital (reproduced, *St. Bartholomew's Hospital Journal*, vol. LIX [Aug. 1955]). The Act for Preventing the Horrid Crime of Murder (25 George II, c. 37) was introduced in spring 1752 and signed 25 March (Linebaugh, op. cit., pp. 76–78).

The Apprentice

1. Thompson, *Making of the English Working Class*, p. 60.

2. Fornication, for example, is to be avoided because of the "lewd Women" it brings one in contact with, "who have been the Bane and Ruin of many an hopeful [i.e., potentially successful] young Man"; but matrimony is equally redolent of "fatal

Consequences" because of the offspring that will inevitably follow to drain away resources before a stable economic situation has been secured (ed. A. D. McKillop, Augustan Reprint [Los Angeles, 1975], pp. 4–5). For background, see Steven R. Smith, "The London Apprentices as Seventeenth Century Adolescents," *Past and Present*, no. 61 (1973), pp. 149–61; Stone, *Family, Sex and Marriage*, p. 376. For another work exploring a subculture, see Susan Eckstein, *The Poverty of Revolution: The State and the Urban Poor in Mexico* (Princeton, 1977), which examines the working-class society of "downtown" Mexico City, which has its own slang and local heroes, who are nationally known boxers, sometimes criminals.

3. Davis, "The Reasons of Misrule: Youth Groups and Charivaris in Sixteenth-Century France"; Merchant Adventurers, Minutes, 13 Dec. 1704, quoted in O. J. Dunlop, *English Apprenticeship and Child Labour* (London, 1912), p. 184.

4. *Emblem and Expression: Meaning in English Art of the Eighteenth Century* (London, 1975), pp. 58–78; Hogarth, *Analysis of Beauty* (1753; ed. Joseph Burke [Oxford, 1955]), p. 45; and *Spectator*, no. 315. The whole series of twelve plates of *Industry and Idleness* is reproduced in *Emblem and Expression*, also in Paulson, *Hogarth's Graphic Works* (New Haven, 1965; rev. ed., 1970) and *Hogarth: His Life, Art, and Times* (New Haven, 1971).

For the middle-class feeling about industry and idleness, see *The London Magazine* of 1747 (XVI, 221): "It is our Industry that changed the Face of this Country from what it was, and proved thereby the Source of our Liberty and Property; it is our Industry that is the Basis of domestick and foreign Trade, and consequently the sole Fountain of our Riches; in short, it is our Industry that must maintain us, enable us to do Justice to others, and to live happily ourselves; for without it we can do neither." Industry therefore "ought to be as much encouraged as possible, and . . . everything capable of lessening it, ought to be the object of Censure." On the social stigma of idleness and popular recreations, and on the force of labor discipline, see Robert W. Malcolmson, *Popular Recreations in English Society 1700–1850* (Cambridge, 1973), Chap. 6, esp. pp. 90–93.

5. Cf. Richardson, *Vade Mecum*, p. 4: "In the *first* Place, it is hardly possible that such a one should marry upon advantageous, or even *equal* Terms, since it must necessarily be done in a private and clandestine Manner, contrary to the Rules of Prudence, contrary to Duty, and express Stipulation."

6. In *Hogarth's Graphic Works*, cat. no. 173 (I, 197), I distinguished these as states 2 and 3, remarking of the latter, "Being informed that the senior partner's name should come first, Hogarth reversed the names on the sign to read: 'West and Goodchild.' " I see no reason why these could not have been alternative versions, distributed to different buyers, as Hogarth did later with the subscription ticket for *An Election Entertainment* (see cat. no. 197), and indeed with the different versions of *Paul before Felix*.

7. S. T. Coleridge, on the "Reading Public" in *The Statesman's Manual*, in *Collected Works*, ed. R. J. White (London, 1972), VI, 39. There are many analogues for the phenomenon I am describing; for example, the Balinese murals which illustrate stories central to their culture are interpreted in opposite ways by the different castes of the society. In a battle between dogs and a bull and lion, the low caste sympathizes with the dogs, whereas the high caste sympathizes with the bull or lion. (Pointed out by the anthropologist Anthony Forge in a lecture at the University of California, Berkeley, in Jan. 1978.)

8. See Isaiah 11:1–4. The story of David and Saul is in 1 Samuel 16.

9. Michal also appears with David in the picture of the Ark of the Covenant on

the wall of *Harlot's Progress*, plate 2 (fig. 15). Here their presence remains enigmatic. But in the context of the *Industry and Idleness* plate we recall the difficulties David went through to obtain her, and wonder at Hogarth's obsession with the story. On the day of David's greatest triumph, when he brought in the Ark of the Covenant to Jerusalem, Michal turns on him, despises him, and drives him from her bed. The only reason given is her anger that he "uncovered himself to-day in the eyes of the handmaids of his servants, as one of the vain fellows shamelessly uncovereth himself" (2 Samuel 6:20–23). We have now passed beyond the area devoted to the "readers of greater penetration" and into one given over to Hogarth's private impulses, with a personal allusion to David–Hogarth, Michal–Jane Thornhill, Jonathan–John Thornhill, and Saul–Sir James Thornhill, which looks ahead to the triangle of Sigismunda–Tancred–Guiscardo (Jane–Sir James–Hogarth) in his late painting *Sigismunda* (see *Hogarth: His Life, Art, and Times*, II, 274, and below. p. 37).

10. *Ways of Seeing* (London, 1973), pp. 15–16. For the aristocratic version of the middle-class ethic represented by Goodchild, see Lord Chesterfield's *Letters to His Son* (publ. 1774), where he defines idleness, "the mother of all vices," as not doing anything—by which he means not being "constantly employed either in amusements or in study" (30 Sept. 1738).

11. Looking back from Blake's radicalism, David Erdman has noticed the contrast between the industrious apprentice's "devouring good beef and ale among fat aldermen while the gaunt poor await their leavings" (*Blake: Prophet against Empire* [Princeton, 1954; rev. ed., 1969], p. 119). The feasts on the Lord-Mayor's Day were proverbial for the gluttony of the aldermen (see Pope, *Dunciad*, I, 90, vs. the starving poet in his garret); anon., *Bath* (1748), p. 18; and George Lyttelton, *Dialogues of the Dead* (1760), p. xix.

12. "The Sea," Richardson tells us, is "the best Choice for such as cannot comport to orderly Rules; and better at first than at last" (*Vade Mecum*, p. 51). The memory of Whittington remains in Idle's shabby ambience as only a scrawny cat (see pl. 9).

13. And in plate 1 another document, "A Full and True Account of yᵉ Ghost of Tho: Idle," is being hawked.

14. See Linebaugh, "The Ordinary of Newgate and His Account," in J. S. Cockburn, ed., *Crime in England, 1550–1800* (London, 1977), pp. 246–69, 348–52. The ordinary's pamphlets were titled *The Ordinary of Newgate: His Account of the Behaviour, Confession, and Dying Words of the Malefactors Who Were Executed at Tyburn*. John Villette, an ordinary of later years, edited a number of the earlier accounts in *The Malefactors' Register: Or the Annals of Newgate* (4 vols., 1776). If Hogarth's ordinary is a portrait, it would have to be Thomas Purney (who was ordinary until 1746) or possibly Samuel Rossell or John Taylor (who followed Purney within the year).

15. Thompson delivered this as a lecture at Yale University in the spring of 1976, and so far as I know it has not yet been published.

16. See Lawrence Stone, "Literacy and Education in England, 1640–1900," *Past and Present*, no. 42 (1969), pp. 69–139. Cf. Thompson, "Eighteenth-Century English Society," p. 155; Thompson argues that there is no simple distinction: "the illiterate hear the products of literacy read aloud in taverns and they may accept from the literate culture some categories, while many of the literate employ their very limited literate skills only instrumentally (writing, keeping accounts) while their 'wisdom' and customs are still transmitted within a pre-literate oral culture."

17. This is quoted by Gershan Legman, *The Rationale of the Dirty Joke* (New York, 1968, p. 66), but revised in the light of my own memory of the joke. Robert Darnton tells me that in France at any rate boys were given a nickname when they became apprentices (e.g., "Bonne-main" or "Clumsy").

18. Similar treatment of authority figures can be found in the satiric tradition, or at least in its popular roots, but to see the difference we need only compare the satire of Swift or Pope, which attacks those who *pretend* to possess authority without in fact doing so. Even Fielding, if he shows a bad clergyman, is sure to insert a good one also, a Parson Adams for a Parson Trulliber. But Hogarth's Methodism (as in *Industry and Idleness*, pl. 12) is a polarity of the Anglican, not a corrective, as we see by contrasting the two congregations—the "sleeping" Anglican one in *Sleeping Congregation* and the ranting Methodist in *Enthusiasm Delineated*.

19. See below, pp. 160–63. Hogarth's one Old Testament subject is *Moses brought to Pharaoh's Daughter*, another scene illustrating charity.

20. *The Age of Reason* (1795; London, 1937), p. 4.

21. See Hill, *The World Turned Upside Down* and *Milton and the English Revolution* (London, 1977).

22. See Stone, *Family, Sex and Marriage*, esp. pt. V.

23. *Autobiographical Notes*, in *Analysis of Beauty*, ed. Burke, p. 226; also on *Industry and Idleness*, p. 225. I have regularized the text.

24. See Robbins, *The Eighteenth-Century Commonwealthman*, p. 48, and Paulson, *Hogarth: His Life, Art, and Times*, chap. 2.

25. Eric Foner, *Tom Paine and Revolutionary America* (New York, 1976), p. xvi, where Paine is described as one who "did not simply change the meanings of words, he created a literary style designed to bring his message to the widest possible audience."

26. Herbert Marcuse, *Eros and Civilization* (Boston, 1955 [1974 ed.]), esp. pp. 161–70.

The Crowd

1. Rouquet's *Description du Tableau de Mr. Hogarth, qui représent la Marche des Gardes à leur rendez-vous de-Finchley* presumably appeared in 1750; the story about George II is from John Ireland, *Hogarth Illustrated*, II, 141–42. For the Hogarth–Wilkes friendship, see *Hogarth: His Life, Art, and Times*.

2. See Davis, "Reasons of Misrule: Youth Groups and Charivaris in Sixteenth-Century France." As Davis concludes, carnival "can evolve so that it can act both to reinforce order and suggest alternatives to the existing order" (p. 74). See also Thompson, "Rough Music: 'Le Charivari Anglais,' " in *Annales E.C.S.*, XXVII (1972), 285–312; Stone, *Family, Sex and Marriage*, p. 145; E. Shorter, *The Making of the Modern Family* (New York, 1975), pp. 188–97. For eighteenth-century cartoons of skimmingtons, see *British Museum Catalogue of Satiric Prints*, nos. 441, 1703, 2149. For the Wilkite crowd itself I am especially indebted to John Brewer, *Party Ideology and Popular Politics at the Accession of George III* (Cambridge, 1976), chap. 9, pp. 163–200. Brewer's essay, "The Number 45: A Wilkite Political Symbol," in Steven Baxter, ed., *From the Restoration to the American Revolution* (Los Angeles, forthcoming), further elucidates the popular use of calendar festivals. It is

well to remember, as Thompson remarks: "But if Wilkes acted the role of the crowd's 'fool,' he never ceased to be a *gentleman*-fool" ("Eighteenth-Century English Society," p. 163 n.).

3. Thompson, "Patrician Society, Plebeian Culture," *Journal of Social History*, VII (1974), 396; he likes the first sentence so well he repeats it verbatim on p. 402. Thompson treats the "countertheater" of the crowd in greater detail in "Rough Music." The other two forms of popular action he describes are anonymous letters (treated in greater detail in his essay in *Albion's Fatal Tree*) and swift, evanescent direct action (treated in "Moral Economy of the English Crowd"). For my purpose (and I think for Thompson's) "countertheater" can be said to include the other two: the crowd is anonymous and its theatrical play often slips over into direct action, especially against property.

4. Standard Words, XVIII, 15–17.

5. Thompson, "Patrician Society, Plebeian Culture," pp. 400, 400–404.

6. *Enquiry*, p. 7.

7. The ordinary of Newgate (see p. 15) was another conspicuous figure of the crowd, a bridge between the two cultures. Always present at Tyburn Fair in his official capacity, he was an unwilling protagonist in the theater of the crowd and usually the butt of its humor, subject both to mockery and parody. The ordinary was also ridiculed by the genteel culture; in the satires and novels of the period he appears as a failed literatus, a middleman between high and low cultures and societies.

8. *Artisans and Sans-Culottes* (London, 1968), p. 11.

9. "Realism as a Comic Mode: Low-Life Painting Seen through Bredero's Eyes," *Simiolus*, VIII (1975–76), 115–44; also "Brueghel's Festive Peasants," *Simiolus*, VI (1972), 163–76. In the first scene of the *Election*, the crowd (seen through a window) is specifically rioting, as historically the London crowd did, to preserve the "Eleven Days" the government stole from them by changing the calendar, and to overturn the "Jew Bill," which allowed naturalization of non-native Jews. In the second scene the mob is rioting against the Excise. For the riot that most seriously impinged on Hogarth in his youth, see Geoffrey Holmes, "The Sacheverell Riots," *Past and Present*, no. 72 (Aug. 1976), pp. 55–85. The cry then was "Sacheverell and High Church," as opposed to the later "Wilkes and Liberty," and the mob invaded St. John's Square, near Hogarth's family's house, to burn the Dissenter chapel, threaten Bishop Burnet's house, and scale the walls of Sir Edmund Harrison's house (a wealthy London merchant and leading Presbyterian).

10. It is surely significant that the Prince of Wales is prominent on the balcony overlooking the procession in *Industry and Idleness*, plate 12. Is he, in the context of Goodchild's triumph, the son inheriting from *his* father?

11. Thompson, *Making of the English Working Class*, pp. 62–63. This view conforms to Hogarth's imagery in *Election* (4), where the swine allude to the devils (or madness) that possessed the Gadarene swine as well as the crowd (Matthew 8:28, Mark 5:1–14, Luke 8:26–34), presumably the "devils" of electioneering politics.

The Signboard and Its Painter

1. Behind Hogarth's kite is the sort of popular wisdom found in John Newbery's *Little Pretty Pocket Book* (1744?), on "Flying the Kite":

Upheld in Air, the gaudy Kite
High as an Eagle takes her Flight;
But if the Winds their Breath restrain,
She tumbles headlong down again.

The "scolding woman" can be documented from *Joe Miller's Jests*, for example, no. 6.

2. See Matthew 23:37 for the biblical allusion.

3. In the learned context of the Garden of Eden, the withered dead tree on the right balances the Tree of Knowledge on the left, which withered after Adam and Eve ate the forbidden fruit (and from which the wood of the cross came, thus restoring its life through the sacrifice of Christ).

4. Bryant Lillywhite finds the "Bell" a sign of uncertain derivation, but he notes that a number of them are spelled—or misspelled—*belle* (*London Signs: A Reference Book of London Signs from Earliest Times to about the Mid-Nineteenth Century* [London, 1972], p. 3 [nos. 106, 110, 2795, 2804, 2925]). A bell sign is reproduced by F. G. Hilton Price in *The Signs of Old Lombard Street* (London, 1902), opp. p. 97, and by Ambrose Heal in *The Signboards of the London Shops* (London, 1947), p. 161.

5. *British Museum Catalogue of Satiric Prints and Drawings*, no. 2106 (hereafter *BM. Sat.*); first noted by G. C. Lichtenberg (1794), *The World of Hogarth: Lichtenberg's Commentaries on Hogarth's Engravings*, tr. I. and G. Herdan (Boston, 1966), p. 78.

6. For these and other examples, see Aubrey Williams, "The 'Fall' of China and *The Rape of the Lock*," *Philological Quarterly*, XLI (1962), 412–25.

7. See Jacob Larwood and J.C. Hotten, *The History of Signboards* (London, 1908), p. 3. As Arthur Charles Fox-Davies remarks: "In fact, far the larger proportion of the older coats of arms, where they can be traced to their real origin, exhibit some such derivation" (*A Complete Guide to Heraldry* [London, 1949 ed.], p. 5; see also p. 80). On signboards, see also *Catalogue of the Guildhall Museum* (2d ed.; London, 1908), pp. 252–53 and plates; Miller Christy, *The Trades Signs of Essex: A Popular Account of the Origin and Meanings of the Public House & Other Signs Now or Formerly in the County of Essex* (Chelmsford and London, 1887); G. J. Monson-Fitzjohn, *Quaint Signs of Olde Inns* (London, 1926); and A. P. Walton, *London Signs, Tablets, etc. Sketches by A. P. Walton* (Museum of London, n.d.). Brian Hill's *Inn-Signia* (London, 1949) tells of the exhibition of signboards held in London in 1936, and Whittoney Block's *What Innsigns Tell* (London, n.d.) finds Indian and other mystic symbolism in shop signs.

8. John Nichols and George Steevens, *Genuine Works of William Hogarth* (1808), I, 416–19.

9. *Notion of a Draught of the Tablature of the Judgment of Hercules* (1713).

10. See below, p. 113.

11. By implication, all Gin Lane's world of hunger and want is rejected in Beer Street, as the verses under Brueghel's print emphasize: "Beat it, Thinman! Though you are hungry, you are wrong. / This is Fat Kitchen here, and here *you* don't belong!" I do not know to what extent we can extrapolate the content from the model in this case; Brueghel's prints cannot have affected Hogarth's popular audience. But they do draw our attention to the extremes of fat and thin, of eating and starving in Hogarth's plates.

12. The act to improve the streets (2 George II, c. 2) was passed in the spring of 1762 and signed into law on 2 June. The signs began to come down in November,

and perhaps earlier. See *Journal of the House of Commons*, XXIX, 349, and *History of Signboards*, pp. 28–29.

13. The first announcement followed the notice of the Society of Arts Exhibition (*St. James's Chronicle*, 16–18 Feb., 18–20 Mar. 1762). The Sign Painters' Exhibition ran from April to June in Thornton's chambers in Bow Street. For evidence of the crowds, see *Public Advertiser*, 5 May 1762. A series of advertisements for such an exhibition had appeared the year before, but it is not clear whether these were by Thornton (they probably were) or whether an exhibition was more than a satiric fiction at that time (see *Hogarth: His Life, Art, and Times*, II, 334–38). We should not forget Wilkes's role in the movement of the artists to seek independence, and his presidency of the Society of Artists back in the crucial year of 1759 when they decided to seek a place to exhibit.

14. For the evidence of the anti-Hogarth prints, see *BM. Sat.*, 3841, 3842, 3999. There was a "Hogarth's Head" in Cheapside, facing Wood Street (1752), and a "Hogarth's Head and Dial" (1755), both for print sellers. See Lillywhite, p. 283, no. 8785, and p. 283, no. 8786.

15. George Vertue, *Notebooks* (Oxford: Walpole Society, 1934–55), III, 156.

16. M. D. George, *London Life in the Eighteenth Century* (London, 1925; 1966 ed.), p. 163. See also ibid., pp. 162–63, and Thompson, *Making of the English Working Class*, p. 236.

17. The first announcement of 18–23 Mar. 1763 (*St. James's Chronicle*) says that the sponsors "shall be obliged to any Gentleman who will communicate to them where any curious Sign is to be met with in Town or Country, or any Hint or Design for Signs, suitable to their Exhibition." But they were probably supplied by sign painters' shops, where large stocks of signs were kept (George, *London Life*, p. 164; *History of Signboards*, p. 37). The catalogue was dispensed with the ticket of admissions. An annotated transcription of the catalogue is in the *St. James's Chronicle* (24–27 Apr. 1762), reprinted in *History of Signboards*; a copy of the catalogue itself is in the Chiswick Public Library. For the general background, see *Hogarth: His Life, Art, and Times*, II, 334–38, 345–53.

18. The names of the sign painters, with the exception of "Hagarty," were those of the journeymen printers in Baldwin's office, where the catalogue was printed (*History of Signboards*, p. 512).

19. See Robert Southey, ed., *Works of Cowper* (1836–37), I, 37. There was, alas, no sign of a "pavior" in the exhibition. Hogarth may have painted the *Pavior's Sign* (Yale Center for British Art), and it could be from the time of the exhibition. Lillywhite lists a "Paviour's Arms," a tavern sign (p. 402, nos. 11236–41), surmising that it arose in the eighteenth century with the paving of London. St. Martin's Lane, near where Hogarth lived, was one of the first experiments in 1742, and the 1762 act included the paving of all the main streets.

20. See *European Magazine*, LI (1807), 43n., which claims that a picture of "The Harlot Blubbering over a Bullock's Heart" was shown in the Sign Painters' Exhibition to ridicule Hogarth. I suspect that the story is a conflation of accounts of the 1761 exhibition and the "Hagarty" picture "The Light Heart" (no. 6) and of the anti-Hogarth print of 1763, *A Brush for the Sign-Painters* (*BM. Sat.*, 3841).

21. *History of Signboards*, p. 457.

22. *The Author's Farce* (1730), air VII, to the melody of "The Black Joke." See Charles Mitchell's edition (Oxford, 1952) and *Hogarth: His Life, Art, and Times*, I, 293–98.

23. Lillywhite, p. 459. There was still a Three Loggerheads at 57 Virginia Road,

London, E.2, in 1966, built in the 1820s; and a drawing of one in Shoreditch by Walton, no. 52 of his series of shop signs, is in the Museum of London.

24. Cf. the jest in *Mother Brunch's Merriments* (1604) about the country fellow who asks a scrivener in his shop, "I pray you, master, what might you sell in your shop, that you have so many ding-dongs hang at your dore?" "Why, my friend," replies the scrivener, "I sell nothing but loggerheads." "By my fay, master, you have a fair market for them, for you have left but one in your shop, that I see." David Garrick, one of the proprietors of the *St. James's Chronicle*, may also have had a hand in the annotations.

25. For Hogarth and *The Beggar's Opera*, see below, p. 121. For the other "Hagarty" signboards in the exhibition, see *Hogarth: His Life, Art, and Times*, II, 347–48. For example, no. 30, "The Dancing Bears," seems built upon Hogarth's image in *The Analysis of Beauty* (pl. I) of the Grand Tour tutor with his bear-cub tutee; no. 40, "Welcome Cuckolds to Horn Fair," sounds like a development of *The South Sea Scheme* and *Times of the Day: Evening*, with a strong element of the *Skimmington*. No. 64, "View of the Road to Paddington, with a Presentation of the Deadly-Never-Green, That Bears Fruit All the Year Round," may be related to the view of Tyburn in *Industry and Idleness*, (pl. 11); and no. 67, "Death and the Doctor," probably alludes to the scene in *Harlot's Progress* (pl. 5), with the two doctors quarreling over their dying patient.

26. Said of *Childe Harold's Pilgrimage*, canto 4, in *Complete Works of William Hazlitt*, ed. P. P. Howe (London, 1933), XIX, 36. See also XVII, 33: "like the objects in Hogarth's Rules of Perspective, where every thing is turned upside down, or thrust out of its well-known place."

27. Lichtenberg (p. 86) refers to the earl's characteristic pose in plate 1 as "a sort of magnificent coat-of-arms." See *Boutell's "Heraldry,"* ed. C. W. Scott-Giles and J. P. Brooke Little (London, 1966), and L. G. Pine, *Heraldry and Genealogy* (Edinburgh, 1957).

28. The "Bear and Ragged Staff" appears, in Hogarth's time, in signboards of taverns and inns (Lillywhite, pp. 28–29, nos. 2733–44; reproduced in Monson-Fitzjohn, p. 25).

29. For an analysis of Zoffany's *Sharpe Family* along these lines, see Paulson, "Ensor and Zoffany," *Georgia Review*, XXXI (1977), 508–9.

30. Fox-Davies, op. cit., pp. 301–2, fig. 556. The Reynolds portraits of great men as children (John the Baptist, Samuel Johnson) are in fact metaleptic images of the grown man or woman: the man in his origin.

31. For graphic examples see Fox-Davies, fig. 754, p. 541, or figs. 757 and 758, p. 545.

32. Fox-Davies, p. 542. Often a painter adds a new quartering after the painting is finished—a new child (as in Hogarth's *Ashley-Cowper Family*, Tate Gallery), or he represents a dead father or mother by a figure with an angel flying over his/her head or a portrait elevated on the wall (*Cholmondeley Family*, Houghton).

The English Dog

1. *Structure of Complex Words* (London, 1951), pp. 158–74.
2. Roger Fulford, *George the Fourth* (London, 1935), p. 19.
3. James Boswell, *Life of Johnson*, ed. G. B. Hill (New York, 1889), I, 123.

4. See H. W. Janson, *Apes and Ape Lore* (London, 1952); in our period, Edward Young, *Conjectures on Original Composition* (1759), p. 43: "Why are Monkies such masters of mimickry? Why receive they such a talent at imitation? Is it not as the *Spartan* slaves received a license for ebriety: that their Betters might be ashamed of it?"

5. Diogenes' context was Socrates' assertion in *The Republic* that "your dog is a true philosopher" (II, 376). Because, Socrates explains, his only criterion for attacking a stranger and welcoming an acquaintance, neither of whom has done him good or harm, is knowing and not knowing, the test of knowledge and ignorance. Rabelais, on the other hand, cites Plato but explains that what proves the dog "the most philosophical" is the way he goes after the marrow of a bone (*Gargantua and Pantagruel*, prologue to bk. I).

6. For the Pope poems, see *Minor Poems* (Twickenham ed., London, 1954), VI, 372, 366–71.

7. Pope to Henry Cromwell, 19 Oct. 1709, in *Correspondence*, ed. George Sherburn (Oxford, 1956), I, 74 (73–74 on dogs).

8. See Donald Posner, *Watteau: A Lady at Her Toilet* (London, 1973), pp. 77–83.

9. The Fragonard is in the Alte Pinakothek, Munich, where one also sees Veronese's *Cupid with Two Dogs:* Cupid is holding them on leashes, restraining the animal appetite of love. See also Spranger's *Venus and Adonis* in the Kunsthistorisches Museum, Vienna, with Adonis' dog in the lower right corner glaring at the viewer, parallel to the Cupid above. For the dog as surrogate lover, see Steen's *Love-Sick Woman*, in which the doctor is taking her pulse while she holds a love letter, and the nearby dog represents the absent author of the love letter; or Tintoretto's *Vulcan's Discovery of Mars and Venus*, in which the dog is barking at the concealed Mars (both in the Pinakothek, Munich).

10. But Pope's Shock is an alternative, a rival, rather than a surrogate of the lover who (we later learn) lurks in Belinda's heart. The illustration for canto 3 (1714 ed., presumably made with Pope's approval) shows Shock barking at the baron as he triumphantly holds up the severed lock. This dog appears again in Hogarth's *Before* and *After*, where he barks at his mistress's seducer before but is his exhausted surrogate after, and may have been seconding his natural impulses.

11. See below, pp. 160, 269 n.7.

12. One is reminded of the Wilkites around that same time marking the symbolic "45" on everything in sight; but also of Hogarth's *removal* of his shop sign, "Van Dyck's Head," after his disappointing picture sale.

13. For example, cf. the dog in George Stubbs's *The Prince of Wales' Phaeton* (Royal Collection) or in Zoffany's conversations, where he is frequently the artist's dog and his surrogate.

14. Rowlandson's dog is usually both the cause of disorder and the surrogate for the woman's lover, as in *The Milk Sop* (London, V & A), where he fulfills both functions, paralleling the lover in the window as he laps the milk out of the milkmaid's pail, reminding us of reality as he did in Hogarth's *Distressed Poet*.

15. Quoted, Burton Stevenson, *The Home Book of Proverbs, Maxims and Familiar Phrases* (New York, 1948), p. 613.

16. Burke, *Enquiry*, ed. J. T. Boulton (Oxford, 1958), p. 67.

17. See Herbert M. Atherton, *Political Prints in the Age of Hogarth* (Oxford, 1974), p. 103.

18. *Craftsman*, 13 Sept. 1729. "In all baiting sports the testing of a dog's skill

and courage was one of the principal points of the exercise" (Robert W. Malcolmson, *Popular Recreations in English Society*, p. 47, referring to dogs in bull or badger baiting).

19. The print alluded to is *The Gallic Cock and English Lyon or a Touch of the Times* (1729–30); (*BM. Sat.*, 2437, Atherton, pl. 26).

20. Edwards, pp. 4–5. Cf. the dog and his master in Hogarth's *Good Samaritan* (fig. 29).

21. *BM. Sat.*, 3469.

22. David C. Itzkowitz, *Peculiar Privilege: A Social History of English Foxhunting, 1753–1885* (Hassocks, Sussex, 1977).

23. An old harrier complained of the fox hunt: ". . . and for what?—to gratify a few gentlemen, who think it more manly to ride after a poor animal turned out of a sack, because they can go home, and say they have been foxhunting, than to find a hare well, and hunt her well, and kill her well, though much more congenial to the feeling of themselves and horses; and I am convinced these same gentlemen, if they will speak the truth, like hare-hunting best, laying aside the name, the noble sound of fox-hunting" (*Sporting Magazine*, LXI [Jan. 1823], 210).

24. Cf. the jokes about the Frenchman who does not understand fox hunting and congratulates the hunt master when his hounds capture the fox in his covert.

25. E. P. Thompson, *Whigs and Hunters: The Origin of the Black Act*, pp. 31–37 and *passim*.

26. Published in February 1751—by coincidence in the same month as Hogarth's *Stages of Cruelty*—was Coventry's *Pompey the Little*, with an equally SPCA message. The children, his masters, decided that Pompey was full of fleas: ". . . and then he was dragged thro' a canal till he was almost dead, in order to kill the Vermin that inhabited the Hair of his Body. At other Times he was set upon his hinder Legs with a book before his Eyes, and ordered to read his Lesson; which not being able to perform, they whipt him with Rods till he began to exert his Voice in a lamentable Tone, and then they chastised him the more for daring to be sensible of Pain" (Oxford English Novel, ed., ed. R. A. Day [Oxford, 1974], p. 49).

27. See Edwin de T. Bechtel, *Callot* (New York, 1953), p. 221.

28. Hogarth's *Stages of Cruelty* should be contrasted with Sarah Trimmer's children's book version of the same structure at the end of the century in *Fabulous Histories Designed for the Amusement and Instruction of Young People* (1786). Her message is that we can learn from our friends the animals; for example, "an unfaithful servant may be admonished by a dog and so on." Being kind to animals, she shows, is not only good in itself but in the end pays off as well. In the last chapter she sums up the ledger: the boys and girls who were good to animals have done well in the world and are respected by all. But the young boy who beat his animals and cared only for himself is now despised by all who know him, and finally killed by a horse he was beating—Hogarth's poetic justice caught at an earlier stage (pl. 2).

29. *Essay on the Picturesque* (1794), pp. 60–61.

30. *Mysteries of Udolpho*, Oxford English Novel ed., ed. Bonamy Dobrée (Oxford, 1966), pp. 95–96.

31. For the swaddling bands (which appear in Blake's "Infant Sorrow"), see below, p. 172.

The Joke and Joe Miller's Jests

1. I am not sure what significance can be made of the distinction between the words "jest" and "joke," which have become further confused in our time by Freud's

distinction between *Scherz* (jest) and *Witz* (joke) as pure and tendentious forms. Originally "jest," from the Latin *gesta* (deeds or exploits), shows the ultimate linguistic derivation of "Jestbook" from the *Gesta Romanorum* and the suggestive relationship between these *gestes* and those in the *Chansons de geste*. They are stories or recordings of actions which have become mock-serious *gestes*. "Joke" by contrast, is from the Latin *jocus*, with connotations of game, pastime, or sport; the verb is "to act upon" somebody, to "toy with" or "make game of" someone in an active and physical way. By the eighteenth century the words seem to have been interchangeable, both carrying the potential of either physical or verbal action (practical joke); but the collection was always called "jestbook." (For Freud, see Standard Edition, VIII, 129.)

2. *Tales and Quicke Answers*, no. 13. My text is *Shakespeare's Jest-Books, I. A Hundred Mery Talys, II. Mery Tales and Quicke Answeres*, ed. W. Carew Hazlitt (London, 1881). See also P. M. Zall, ed., *A Hundred Merry Tales and other English Jestbooks of the Fifteenth and Sixteenth Centuries* (Lincoln, Neb., 1963); F. P. Wilson, "The English Jestbooks," *Huntington Library Quarterly*, II (1939), 121–58; G. Legman, *Rationale of the Dirty Joke: An Analysis of Sexual Humor* (New York, 1968), p. 35 (on Poggio's *Facetiae*).

3. Preface to the 1836 edition, p. v.

4. Letter no. 144, 9 Mar. 1748 (first published in London, 1774).

5. For the argument against the saturnine Miller, see Evan Esar, *The Legend of Joe Miller* (San Francisco, 1957), pp. 15–17. No real evidence exists to disprove the claim of the 1836 edition. Miller's tombstone describes him as both a "facetious companion and an excellent comedian," and Mottley's title page even refers to him as a "facetious gentleman," but neither is inconsistent with his supposed gravity.

6. Appendix, "A List of All the Dramatic Authors" (on Mottley, by himself), in Thomas Whincop, *Scanderbeg, or Love and Liberty, a Tragedy* (1747). Poggio, author of the earliest jestbook (*Liber Facetiarum*, 1477), claims in his preface to have acquired his *facetiae* largely from conversations with friends, but they are mostly from classical sources. When Zall (op. cit., p. 2) writes that "*A Hundred Merry Tales* seems to have been compiled from jests circulated by word-of-mouth," his point is that this is more obviously an *English* jestbook than, for example, the *Quicke Answers*, with its many foreign references (and sources in Poggio, Erasmus, and Sebastian Brandt). The seventeenth-century English jestbooks, with some claims to originality based on talk of the town, were Dekker and Wilkins, *Iests to Make You Merie* (1607), and John Taylor (the Water Poet), *Wit and Mirth* (1629), *Bull, Bear, and Horse* (1638), and *Taylor's Feast* (1638), though many jokes are still traceable (see Wilson, "English Jestbooks," p. 127).

7. Mottley updated and rearranged with different order and numbers the jokes in *Peachum* and *Pinkethman*, adding a few contemporary jokes (Esar, pp. 21–24). The 109 jokes from *Peachum* appear among nos. 1–148 in *Miller; Pinkethman* contributes nine to the first 148, and most of the remainder. For *Pinkethman*, Mottley apparently uses the fourth edition of 1735. He did not use other jestbooks, like *Spiller's* (1730).

8. *Pinkethman* (2d ed., 1721), I, 110–20. The first collection of printed puns in English appeared in Robert Chamberlain's *Conceits, Clinches, Flashes, and Whimzies* (1639), though word play is also important in the Taylor collections and in Dekker and Wilkins' *Iests to Make You Merie*.

9. Osborn, "Introduction," in Joseph Spence, *Anecdotes* (Oxford, 1966), I, xxxii.

10. See Keith Thomas, "The Place of Laughter in Tudor and Stuart England," *Times Literary Supplement*, 21 Jan. 1977, pp. 77–81, for an opening up of the whole subject of popular, uninhibited humor in politics. A Tory joke in *Pinkethman* that has its teeth pulled by *Miller* tells of a farmer in Lincolnshire "who was sowing of hemp in the time of the Grand Rebellion: And a Party of the Parliament Soldiers passing by, one of them told him, They hoped to reap his Crop whatever it was. I am sowing Hemp Gentlemen (says He), and hope I have enough for you all." *Miller* removes all topical reference (no. 189).

11. Freud, Standard Edition, VIII, 68–69.

12. No. 596, 1836 ed. Even here the joke is printed long after his death. A bit closer is the one about George III's hatred of Wilkes: "So ungrateful was the sound of 'Wilkes and No. 45' (the famous number of the 'North Briton') deemed to be to a high personage, that about 1772, a Prince of the Blood (George IV) then a mere boy, having been chid for some boyish fault, and wishing to take his boyish revenge, is related to have done so by stealing to the king's apartments, and shouting at the door, 'Wilkes and 45 for ever!' and running away. It is hardly necessary to add, (for who knows not the domestic amiableness of George III?) that his majesty laughed at the thing with his accustomed good humour" (no. 53, 1836 ed.). Is there an ironic emphasis in "domestic" or in the whole parenthesis? A very subversive joke is the Alexander–Dionedes one (no. 380, 1836 ed.), which ends with Dionedes saying that he who plunders with one ship is called a pirate whereas Alexander, with a great army, is called a king. This is followed by: "This bold answer so pleased Alexander, that he set him at liberty"—when in a less bookish world Alexander must have realized that Dionedes was far more dangerous (as he was witty) than your usual pirate. One exception is the joke on Archibishop Laud, one of the recurring characters in the jestbooks, but long dead and not royal (no. 750).

13. Freud, VIII, 68.

14. Chesterfield, no. 144, 9 Mar. 1748. See also no. 155, 19 Oct. 1748, and (on jokes vs. wit) no. 190, 10 Aug. 1749. For the sort of relationship Chesterfield suggests between biological control of the body and civilization, see Norbert Elias, *Uber den Prozess der Zivilisation* (1936), tr. Edmund Jephcott as *The Civilizing Process: The History of Manners* (New York, 1978).

15. See Lucien Febvre and Henry-Jean Martin, *The Coming of the Book: The Impact of Printing, 1450–1800*, tr. David Gerard, ed. Geoffrey Nowell-Smith and David Wootton (London, 1977), who argue that while publication often gave life to works that might not otherwise have survived, it was essentially a conservative phenomenon, especially among the authorities who controlled production.

For one view on the relation between performance and text, see Burke, *Popular Culture*, pp. 66–67, 71–73, and in general chap. III.

16. Morris, pp. xii, xiv–xv, xviii, 12–13.

17. The passages are in Morris, pp. 5–7.

18. Fielding would have interpreted the dedication (nearly a third of Morris' text) as the idea of Walpole suddenly—in a series of illuminations—brought into conjunction with the real Walpole (as Fielding and many contemporaries saw him) to elucidate that real Walpole. Perhaps Morris should have specified Walpole's art collection; but it is impossible, reading passages like the following in dedication, not to recall Pope's "Epistle to Augustus" and its conclusion that undeserved praise is scandal in disguise: "For, my Lord, though the weightier Concerns of this Empire, and the daily Direction and Welfare of Millions, have demanded your Attention for a long Series, the *Belles Lettres* have never resigned their Claim to your Lordship.

The *politer* *Arts*, which bemoaned your Avocation from their Charms, have still constantly numbered you with their favorite Sons" (p. iv).

19. As an example of a pure pun, which fits Morris' definition, I offer *Miller*, no. 72: "A Gentleman eating some Mutton that was very tough, said, it put him in Mind of an old English Poet: Being asked who that was; *Chau—cer*, replied he."

20. Charles II keeps cropping up in *Joe Miller*, as in 195, 200, 203, and 209, but only as a vehicle; he is lodged somewhere in the jokester's consciousness, but none of the jokes one would expect about him appears, except in the displacement mentioned above. Rather, he presides over the jestbook as he does over Hogarth's *March to Finchley*. Thomas More jokes (nos. 21–23, the last about his execution) are followed by no. 24 about Sidney's execution. Most undisguised are the sequences about bad clergymen (nos. 30–32, the last the famous one about the "moving discourse"); also Lord Strangford, nos. 36–37, 183.

21. See Legman, *Rationale of the Dirty Joke* (p. 81), who discusses this sequence.

22. See Legman (pp. 81–82), who gives a modern version, "of an American in Paris who refuses the egg in his whiskey that will 'Put lead in his pencil,' on the grounds that he has 'no one to write to.' "

23. Legman, pp. 17–18; for the political jokes, see Thomas, "Place of Laughter," p. 80. For transmission of jokes—oral or written—see Legman, "Toward a Motif-Index of Erotic Humor," *The Horn Book: Studies in Erotic Folklore and Bibliography* (New York, 1964), pp. 454–93 (esp. pp. 462–70).

24. Cf. Legman's argument "that the punch-line, which is nowadays believed to be the heart & soul of the joke, is actually just a modern accretion, capable of a good deal of radical change. The important and universal elements of the joke have all be delivered before the punch-line is reached" (*Rationale*, p. 139; see also p. 230). Example: "A young man phones to cancel a date, explaining that he mashed his finger at work. 'the *whole* finger?' asks his girl anxiously. 'No, the one *next to* the hole finger.' " The joke is "on the castration theme, and it is that theme, and not the pun, that makes both examples meaningful to the teller" (pp. 230–31). The question seems still debatable.

25. Cf. Walter Benjamin on the "story," which always "contains, openly or covertly, something useful. The usefulness may, in one case, consist in a moral; in another, in some practical advice; in a third, in a proverb or maxim. In every case the storyteller is a man who has counsel for his readers" ("The Storyteller," *Illuminations* [New York, 1969], p. 86).

26. *Life of Johnson*, I, 493.

27. However, cf. John Brewer's explanation of the Wilkite rationale of the Wilkite jest, that "the virtue and rightness of the Wilkite cause naturally generated good humour and high spirits. How could Wilkites not be joyous when celebrating the sacred cause of freedom and liberty? The oppressed, those who lived in tyrannical regimes or breathed the corrupt air of courts, were naturally devious, shifty and sullen; Wilkites, *au contraire*, were bold, hale and hearty, ready and willing to laugh and *enjoy* their freedom" ("The Number 45: A Wilkite Political Symbol," in Steven Baxter, ed., *From the Restoration to the American Revolution* [Los Angeles, forthcoming]).

28. Hogarth may have conflated the joke with his memory of Gay's lines on the master beating his collapsed horse in *Trivia* (1716, II, ll. 233–35).

29. Freud, VII, 53; also pp. 80–81.

30. The joke appears in *Funny Stories, or the American Jester* (1795), the *Joe*

Miller of 1836 (no. 97), and in Bennet Cerf's *Try and Stop Me* (New York, 1944); cited in Esar, p. 18.

31. There are also such books as *The Female Jester; or, Wit for the Ladies* (1771–78), which takes jokes from Miller and elsewhere that relate to women or have a woman involved—not necessarily seen from her point of view.

32. Another line followed by the picaresque jestbook is from the distanced, symbolic, almost hieroglyphic gestures of *Wilkes' Jestbook*, relished by supporters and regarded indulgently by others, to Raspé's *Baron Munchausen* (1784), whose protagonist takes us from pun back to adventure/fantasy. Munchausen, who began as *Gulliver Redivivus*—Gulliver the *splendide mendax*—goes far beyond Wilkes's effect of discomfiting George III to an overthrow of all the laws of nature. Though called "adventures" and gathered together in chapters, *Munchausen* was essentially a string of jests rather than episodes, and the intersection posited by Morris was replaced by addition through hyperbole. The structure of each episode requires a horrible disorder in the world—a monumental snowstorm, horses halved by closing gates, alligators devouring men; and Munchausen "trumps" nature by an even more fantastic gesture which corrects the disorder, in a most unorthodox way reconstituting order. After he discovers that his horse has been divided by the town gate, he joins the two quivering halves and sews them together with sprigs of laurel. The laurel not only repairs the horse but grows into a bower to protect Munchausen from the sun as he rides along (chap. 5). The lie, the exaggeration, the fantastic elaboration or escalation expands the mere fact until it becomes lost in a fantasy that is pleasurable for its own sake because generated by its own rules. One thinks of analogies with the contemporary Gothic novel—certainly with Beckford's *Vathek*—as well as with the folk tale; and one wonders about the connection, if there is one of any sort, with the sense of the word "revolution" that was evolving, from a regular circular rotation to an irreversible change or progression that is totally destructive to the *status quo*, replacing what is with what was only dreamed of in the wildest imaginings of the order-seeking Munchausen. One direction taken after *Joe Miller* is from words back to actions, though actions still coded as words and exaggerated into harmless fantasy.

33. It is too bad that Pat Rogers' *Grub Street: Studies in a Subculture* (London, 1972), the one book that broaches the subject of hack-writers in a serious manner, does not go into the question of the subculture. For the commercialization of popular culture, see Burke, *Popular Culture*, pp. 248–49.

Card Games and Hoyle's Whist

1. To Sir Horace Mann, 27 Sept. 1767, in Yale Walpole, XXII, 555; echoing passages in letters to Thomas Brand, 19 Oct. 1765, and George Selwyn, 2 Dec. 1765.

2. Southey, *Letters from England, by Don Manuel Alvarez Espriella* (2d ed., 1808), III, 77–78; on whist's continuing popularity, p. 76.

3. *Compleat Gamester* (5th ed., 1734), p. 10; *Gentleman's Magazine*, LVIII (1788), 190, and Southey, III, 76–77. See also Samuel Johnson, *Dictionary* (1755), "Whist"; William P. Courtney, *English Whist and English Whist Players* (London, 1894), pp. 6–7.

4. It is used as an injunction to silence in Thomas Dekker's play *The Honest Whore* (1604, 1635 ed.), scene xi: "Whist! Whist! my Masters!"

5. William Pole, *The Evolution of Whist* (1895), pp. 23–24, also p. 42n.

6. Pole, p. 35. See also Daines Barrington (then eighty-six), "Observations on the Antiquity of Card-Playing in England," *Archaeologia*, VIII (1787), 134–46: "*Whisk* seems never to have been played upon principles till about fifty years ago [i.e., c. 1737], when it was much studied by a set of gentlemen who frequented the Crown coffee-house in Bedford-Row: before that time it was chiefly confined to the servants' hall with *all-fours* and *put*" (p. 145). An advertisement (cited by Pole, p. 35) for a pirated Dublin edition of Hoyle's *Treatise* in 1743 mentions Slaughter's, White's, and George's coffee houses as the chief centers of the game in London at that time.

7. See Edward S. Taylor, *The History of Playing Cards* (London, 1865), p. 18.

8. The earliest preserved English cards, from the seventeenth century, are already moving in this direction. Cf. a French king of c. 1567 and English of c. 1750, reproduced by W. Gurney Benham, *Playing Cards: History of the Pack and Explanations of Its many Secrets* (London, 1931), figs. 76, 77. The other basic works that deal with the images of card decks are Roger Tilley, *A History of Playing Cards* (London, 1973); H. T. Morley, *Old and Curious Playing Cards* (London, 1931); William S. Chatto, *Facts and Speculations on the Origin and History of Playing Cards* (London, 1848); and a Mr. Gough, "Some Observations on the Invention of Cards and Their Introduction into England," *Archaeologia*, VIII (1787), 152–74. For the most thorough coverage, see C. P. Hargrave, *History of Playing Cards* (Boston, 1930; 1966 ed.). Tarot cards do not appear in England until much later, when they were cherished for their antiquarian and romantic associations.

9. In *The Knave of Clubs, The Knave of Hearts, More Knaves Yet? The Knaves of Spades and Diamonds* (and so on), Rowlands complains of the limitations of card knaves as opposed to other knaves, whom he lists: "A Proud Knave; A shifting Knave; A lying Knave; A whoring Knave; A dissembling Knave; A hypocritical Knave . . ."

10. "The Bloody Game at Cards, as it was played betwixt the King of Hearts and the rest of his Suite, against the residue of the Packe of Cards, Wherein Is discovered where faire Play was plaid and where was fowle . . . Shuffled in London, Cut at Westminster, Dealt at Yorke, and Plaid in the open Field, by the Citty-clubs, the Country Spade-men, Rich Diamond Men and Loyall Hearted Men." The illustration appears in the ellipses (reproduced in Benham, fig. 63).

11. Benham, figs. 211, 212.

12. Major collections of card decks are in the British Museum, Museum of London, the Beinecke Rare Book Library, Yale (Cary Collection), and the Houghton Library, Harvard (Whitney Collection).

13. *Compleat Gamester* (5th ed., 1734), p. 113.

14. *Court Gamester* (1720), p. 3. It is also noted that the "Matadores," or "murderers," are "not oblig'd to pay obedience to an inferiour Trump," that is, to a king of trumps, but only to other matadores—Spadille, Manille, and Basto.

15. Pole, p. 14.

16. Cambridge, 1729; quoted in Pole, p. 14.

17. Pole, p. 20; *Compleat Gamester*, p. 3; Barrington, p. 145. On the games, see Charles Goren, *Goren's Hoyle: Encyclopedia of Games* (New York, 1961).

18. Pole, pp. 53–54. Barrington's summary of the new game was (loc. cit.): "To play from the strongest suit; To study your partner's hand as much as your own; Never to force your partner unnecessarily; and To attend to the score."

19. *Games and Gamesters of the Restoration*, ed. J. Isaacs (London, 1930), which reprints Cotton's *Compleat Gamester* of 1674 and Theophilus Lucas' *Memoirs*

of the Lives, Intrigues, and Comical Adventures of the Most Famous Gamesters and Celebrated Sharpers in the Reign of Charles II, James II, William III, and Queen Anne (1714).

20. It was divided into three parts: I. "The Court Gamester; or, The Games of Ombre, Quadrille, etc."; II. "The City Gamester," which explained the "true manner of playing the most useful games at cards—viz. Whist, all Fours, Cribbidge, etc."; and III. "The Gentleman's Diversion," which "dealt with Riding, Racing, etc." Cf. the divisions of a jestbook like *Tarlton's:* "1 His Court-witty Iests. 2 His Sound City Iests. 3 His Countrey-pretty Iests."

21. 1742 ed., pp. iii–iv. The full title: "A Short Treatise on the Game of Whist, containing the laws of the game; and also some Rules whereby a Beginner may, with due attention to them, attain to the Playing it well. Calculations for those who will Bet the Odds on any Point of the Scores of the game, then playing and depending. Cases stated to shew what may be effected by a very good player in Critical Parts of the Game, References to Cases—viz. at the End of the Rule you are directed how to find them. Calculations, directing with moral Certainty, how to play well any Hand or Game, by shewing the Chances of your Partner having 1, 2, or 3 certain Cards. With variety of cases added in the Appendix."

22. See Fielding's *Enquiry*, p. 29.

23. Of Hoyle's fifteen chapters, the first was "Some General Rules to Be Observed by Beginners" (37 rules); II adds particular cases, and III to XIII consist almost entirely of examples of typical cases or situations; XIV has further explanations of the play of sequences, and XV, on "Artificial Memory," advises on sorting and placing the cards in your hand for mnemonic purposes ("Artificial Memory").

24. The movement was from whist outward in Hoyle's subsequent editions, to backgammon (1743), piquet (1744), quadrille (1745), and brag (1751), grouped around or as addenda to the central matter, which was whist. The result was a compendium on the order of *Joe Miller's Jests*.

25. *The Humours of Whist, a Dramatic Satire, as Acted Every Day at White's and Other Coffee-Houses and Assemblies* (1743); Walpole to Sir Horace Mann, 4 Apr. 1743, Yale Walpole, XVIII, 204. Payne's *Maxims for Playing the Game of Whist, with All Necessary Calculations; and the Laws of the Game* (1770) was intended to redress the lack of arrangement in Hoyle, arranging the rules under the proper heads of "Leader," "Second Hand," "Leading Trumps," and so on. Payne's *Maxims* was incorporated into later editions of Hoyle, as was T. Mathews' (or Matthews') *Advice to the Young Whist-Player* of 1804—and so on down to *Goren's Hoyle* of 1961.

26. *Gentleman's Magazine*, XXV (Feb. 1755), 75. Cf. M. M. McDowell, "A Cursory View of Cheating at Whist in the Eighteenth Century," *Harvard Library Bulletin*, XXII (1974), 162–75. McDowell, an expert on cheating at cards, bases his argument on the *Gentleman's Magazine* article (a passing remark) and the satiric *Humours of Whist*—very slender evidence. He argues that Hoyle's *Treatise* actually increased cheating. He fails to distinguish, however, between the old and new games, the old treatises (which warn against cheating) and Hoyle's which tries to circumvent cheating. But it is possible that, as he believes, "the complications of Hoyle were ammunition for the knowledgeable, and only served to bewilder the unskilful and gullible" (p. 170). Hoyle's "Artificial Memory" may have blurred the line between skill and cheating, when a sharper could assume his opponent was using the mnemonic devices for arranging his cards that Hoyle had outlined for him.

27. *Tom Jones*, bk. XV, chap. iii, ed. Martin Battestin (Oxford, 1974), II, 791.

28. Anon., "Whistology," in *All the Year Round* (Mar. 1860); Courtney, op. cit., p. 305.

29. *Religion and the Decline of Magic* (London, 1971; Penguin ed., 1973), pp. 131, 24.

30. *Enquiry*, sec. 3 on gambling, p. 29.

31. *Man, Play, and Games*, tr. Meyer Barash (London, 1962), p. 44.

32. See below, p. 188. I can see the structure projected by cardplay as also related to what I have called elsewhere "the pictorial circuit" (see *Emblem and Expression*, pp. 132–36, and below, p. 111).

33. *Compleat Gamester*, 1734 ed., p. 59.

34. Pole, op. cit., p. 26.

35. Virginia and Harold Wayland, "John Lenthall: Purveyor of Playing Cards," *Journal of the Playing-Card Society*, I (Aug. 1972), 2–3; and in many subsequent issues other Lenthall series are discussed. The series does not seem to have originated in England. A similar game is supposed to have been invented to amuse and instruct the dauphin, later Louis XIV, and augment those sober manuals of instruction like Fénelon's *Telemachus*. Each card had, besides its own suit sign and value, a picture of a king of France (sometimes more than once, given the limitations of fifty-two cards), and thus Louis learned the names and images of his predecessors as he played loo or écarté.

36. An exception is a deck dated 1701 in the Cary Collection, Yale. The new card games of the nineteenth century originated sequences of their own, as in a "Family Game" of 1858, which has some suits that require a rigid order—vowels, meals, or days of the week, seasons or months of the year. The game, however, was largely based on matching cards rather than following sequences, suits, runs, or flushes. Other "families" included fire irons (tongs, poker, shovel), Great Britain (England, Wales, Scotland, Ireland), professions (divinity, medicine, law, army, navy), the senses, and even the suits of ordinary playing cards. Though there is a rough hierarchy that places England or divinity or perhaps hearts first, the arrangement is not intended as a sequence. Other card games were based on actual families or on professions or on the cries of London. Whole new ways of categorizing were undertaken, but were based on clearly defined sets, some of them ancient.

Bifocal Series

1. See M. F. Thwaite's facsimile of *A Little Pretty Pocket Book* (1767 ed.; London, 1966) and his introduction, pp. 1–49.

2. Anthony Burgess, "Murray and His Monument," *TLS*, 30 Sept. 1977, p. 1094. This is basically the freedom of play W. K. Wimsatt has shown to be at work in various poetic forms of the later eighteenth century ("Imitation as Freedom: 1717–1798," in *Day of the Leopards* [New Haven, 1976], pp. 117–39).

3. *Totem and Taboo*, Standard Edition, XIII, 95–96. Italics added.

4. See Murray Cohen, *Sensible Words: Linguistic Practice in England, 1640–1785* (Baltimore, 1977), pp. 90–93.

5. Boswell, *Life of Johnson*, I, 215.

6. Quoted in N. P. Stallknecht, *Strange Seas of Thought* (2d ed.; Bloomington, Ind., 1962), p. 39.

7. Langbaum, "The Evolution of Soul in Wordsworth's Poetry," *PMLA*, LXXXII (May 1967), 270.

8. "Literary Art in Defoe's *Tour:* The Rhetoric of Growth and Decay," *Eighteenth-Century Studies*, VI (1972–73), 154–64. I am also indebted in these pages to Joann Hackos' "Metaphor of the Garden in Defoe's *A Tour thro' the Whole Island of Great Britain*," in *Papers on Language and Literature*, XV (Spring 1979).

9. *Tour thro' the Whole Island of Great Britain*, ed. G. D. H. Cole (London, 1927), II, 643.

10. Ibid., p. 4.

11. Originally he had intended to make a circuit of the whole island by sea, tracing every harbor and bay, and claims to have hired a ship for that purpose. He wanted to see the whole of Britain—coastline, boundaries, as well as harbor and shipping installations—from the outside looking in, and then from the inside looking out. The plan fell through, but instead he designed the overlapping circuits.

12. See Paulson, *Emblem and Expression*, p. 27; Christopher Hussey, *English Gardens and Landscapes, 1700–1750* (London, 1967), p. 73.

13. In *Spectator* no. 476, on method, Addison takes his example, as if it were the natural thing to do, from gardening, and in the next *Spectator* (no. 477) he describe gardens themselves in terms of poetry and painting. One form (or lack) of method is like walking in a wood "that abounds with a great many noble Objects, rising among one another in the greatest Confusion and Disorder"; whereas when he reads a methodical discourse, "I am in a regular Plantation, and can place my self in its several Centers, so as to take a view of all the Lines and Walks that are struck from them." But in the next paper, comparing the gardeners of the second sort as Heroic poets, he compares himself to the Pindaric manner that runs "into the beautiful Wilderness of Nature, without affecting the nicer Elegancies of Art." He describes the experience as "walking in a Labyrinth of my own raising, not to know whether the next Tree I shall meet with is an Apple or an Oak, an Elm or a Pear-tree" (*Spectator*, ed. Donald F. Bond [Oxford, 1965], IV, 186).

14. *Sensible Words*, pp. 55, 64.

15. See Paul Alkon, "Critical and Logical Concepts of Method from Addison to Coleridge," *Eighteenth-Century Studies*, V (1971), 97–121.

16. The basic change recorded is of course from deductive to inductive reasoning, from one kind of order to another on all levels. It is from a syllogistic—that is, sequential—order to a kind of accumulation, which Lord Kames distinguished as synthetic and analytic: "The synthetic method descended regularly from principles to their consequences, is more agreeable to the strictness of order; but in following the opposite course in the analytic method, we have a sensible pleasure, like mounting upward, which is not felt in the other: the analytic method is more agreeable to the imagination; the other method will be preferred by those only who with rigidity adhere to order, and give no indulgence to natural emotions" (Kames, *Elements of Criticism* [2d ed.; Edinburgh, 1763], I, 32). Kames's key term in his examination of poetry is "connection," not order or method—"the adequacy of explicit transitions, not the sequence of those parts that are well or poorly joined." For Watts, see his *Logick* (8th ed., 1745), pp. 346, 363.

Life as Pilgrimage and as Theater

1. For the *Spectator*, see Bond ed., II, 351–54. This section appeared in a somewhat different form as "Life as Journey and as Theater: Two Eighteenth-Century Narrative Structures," *New Literary History*, VIII (1976), 43–58.

2. For Epictetus, see *Encheiridion*, 17; also Seneca, *Epistulas morales*, 77, 20, and E. R. Curtius, *European Literature and the Latin Middle Ages* (New York, 1953), pp. 138–44.

3. Addison includes, between the two metaphors I have mentioned, a third: life as an inn, "which was only designed to furnish us with Accommodations in this our Passage." This metaphor Addison seems to mix with life as journey (as does Fielding in *Joseph Andrews*, where some of the most elaborate scenes are in the inns along the path of Joseph's journey). Later, in the nineteenth century, drawing upon the tradition of the Symposium (and the satiric dinner parties in Horace and Petronius), writers begin to depict a weekend in a country house as a microcosm of life—a structure most clearly seen in the classical whodunits laid in an isolated house or railway carriage.

4. An alternative was rewards and punishments *at the end of the play*; but even here, as in Ralph Cudworth's use of the metaphor, the emphasis is on "at last," suggesting the Last Judgment. See Cudworth, *The True Intellectual System of the Universe* (2d ed., 1743), II, 879–80.

5. See also no. 483.

6. Plato, *Laws*, I, 644de; Palladas, *Greek Anthology*, X, 72; quoted in Curtius, p. 138. Elsewhere Addison tells us that discretion "is like an Under-Agent of Providence to guide and direct us in the ordinary concerns of Life" (no. 225). On "the theatre of the great" in contemporary society, see E. P. Thompson, "Patrician Society, Plebeian Culture," *Journal of Social History*, VII (1974), 382–405. On the more general rhetorical sense of role playing, which would include Jacques's speech, see Richard Lanham, *Motives of Eloquence: Literary Rhetoric in the Renaissance* (New Haven, 1976), esp. chaps. 1 and 2.

7. As Homer Brown nicely puts it, "the point is not that writers like Defoe tried and failed to write novelistic allegories but that life could not be reduced or raised to a spiritual meaning" ("The Displaced Self in the Novels of Daniel Defoe," *ELH*, XXXVIII [1971], 562–90). Moll Flanders is, of course, Defoe's most flamboyantly play-acting heroine, accompanying new roles with costumes as well as gestures, and in the preface to *Moll Flanders* (1721) Defoe makes one of his infrequent allusions to the stage (as an analogue to his defense of the portrayal of vice in his novel). In a large sense, we could say that Defoe himself is "impersonating" his protagonists—if we wished to limit "impersonate" to the theatrical metaphor ("dramatic monologue").

8. 2 Corinthians 3:18, cited in Sacvan Bercovitch, *The Puritan Origins of the American Self* (New Haven, 1975), p. 14. One has to recall the way Hogarth deals with threats to his own identity, as in the replacement of his face with Charles Churchill's in *The Bruiser*. For the problem of the Harlot as the Virgin Mary, see above, p. 19.

9. In the first plate of *Marriage à la Mode*, a *Martyrdom of St. Agnes* after Domenichino omits the heavenly host and Christ crowning the martyr. In *"Rake,"* plate 5, divinity has been expunged from the church, only the human-centered commandments remain; and in *The Sleeping Congregation*, *"Dieu"* is omitted from the royal motto on the wall, leaving in effect only *"et mon droit."* In *Marriage à la Mode* when a St. Luke appears in a picture above the murder of Earl Squanderfield, he is only a spectator, and can only stare but not intervene.

10. The only indication of providence in "modern moral subjects" is the lightning bolt aimed at White's Gambling House in *Rake*, plate 4 (which is shown burning in pl. 6), and this is an addition which is precisely balanced by a group of dice-playing boys and their game of chance. The parallelism is between White's and

Black's gambling establishments, of course, but as an addition the lightning bolt becomes a second kind of chance, parallel with the boys' game.

11. In plate 4, when consequences begin to descend, we read: "Approaching the poor Remains / That Vice hath left of all his Gains." No mention is made in plate 6, where there is a possibly providential figure, and the verses to plate 8 end admonishing the poor Rake to "cure they self, & curse they Gold."

12. One example among many is the *Plain Dealer* in 1726: "The *Painter* informs the Understanding, and warms the Imagination, by striking the *Sight* strongly, and giving it the Height of Pleasure; while all that can be done, of that kind, by the greatest Poet that ever liv'd is to make us merely *imagine*, that he sets Things before our Eyes" (collected ed. [1730], II, 26–27).

13. Hogarth frequently relates his works to the theater: "The figure is the actor / The attitudes and his actions together with which / The face works an expression and the words must speak to the Eye and the scene . . ."; "I have endeavourd to weaken some of the prejudices belonging to the judging of subjects for pictures, by comparing these with stage compositions [,] the actors in one suggesting whats to the spectator [in the other]"; "We will therefore compare subjects for painting with those of the stage . . ."; and, above all, "my Picture was my Stage and men and women my actors who were by Mean of certain Actions and expressions to Exhibit a dumb shew" ("Autobiographical Notes," in *Analysis of Beauty*, ed. Burke, pp. 203, 211, 209). The recognition of Hogarth's use of visual structures in terms of theatrical conventions was immediate among his contemporaries. Aaron Hill compares his art with the stage as early as 1736, praising him as a reformer; unlike his "rival theatre-managers," he gives purpose and propriety to his "dramas" (*Prompter*, 27 Feb. 1736); see also Arthur Murphy in *The Gray's Inn Journal* (9 Mar. 1754) and Reynolds in his *Fourteenth Discourse*.

14. See J. V. Guerinot and Rodney D. Jilg, eds., *The Beggar's Opera, Contexts* (New Haven, 1976), pp. 118–41.

15. The subject of the relationship between Fielding's rehearsal plays and his novels has been dealt with in my *Satire and the Novel in Eighteenth-Century England* (New Haven, 1967), pp. 85–99; see also J. Paul Hunter, "Fielding's Reflexive Plays and the Rhetoric of Discovery," *Studies in the Literary Imagination*, V (1972), 65–100, reprinted in *Occasional Form* (Baltimore, 1975), pp. 48–75.

16. Fielding's history of Mr. Wilson, for example, is the progress of Hogarth's Rake up to the point of despair and madness; but Fielding has the truly Christian Harriet Hearty intervene, which awakens the would-be rake to the errors of his ways, and converts him. In Hogarth's progress there is only the ineffectual version of Harriet, Sarah Young, and no chance of reprieve.

17. Blackwell, p. 70. On sight, empirical evidence, and stage presentation as opposed to history painting, see p. 32. Blackwell should also be considered in the context of Banier's *Mythology*, for which see below, pp. 195 ff.

18. Hume, *Treatise*, ed. A. D. Lindsay (London, 1959), I, 239–40.

19. For Partridge's reaction to Garrick's Hamlet, cf. *Miller's Jests*, no. 188, where the yokels at the London theater are enjoying all the goings on, from music to orange wenches, until the curtain goes up and three actors begin the play—"upon which one of them cry'd to the other, Come, Hodge, let's be going, ma'haps the Gentlemen are talking about business."

20. In this chapter Fielding quotes from Samuel Boyse's poem *Deity* (1740), which calls the world "the vast Theatre of Time": "Perform the parts Thy providence assign'd, / Their pride, their passions, to Thy ends inclin'd"—emphasizing the Epic-

tetus version. (He also quotes from the poem in *The Champion*, 12 Feb. 1739/40.) For one view on Fielding and divine providence, see Martin C. Battestin, *The Providence of Wit: Aspects of Form in Augustan Literature and the Arts* (Oxford, 1974), chap. 5. I do not want to suggest an exclusive causal relationship between Fielding's novels and *The Beggar's Opera*. The metaphor of the theater is, of course, central to part II of *Don Quixote*—in the theatrical performance for Sancho on his island, in the puppet show, and in the role playing carried on for Don Quixote's benefit. It continued in the more specific terms of a troupe of actors in Scarron's *Roman comique*. The relationship between journey and theatrical performance was already implicit in one strain of the picaresque.

21. Arthur Friedman, ed., *Collected Works* (Oxford, 1966), IV, 135.

22. Battestin, op. cit., chap. 7.

23. K. Eichenberger, *Oliver Goldsmith, das Komische in den Werken seiner Reifeperiode* (Bern, 1954), p. 78; see also Sven Bäckman, *This Singular Tale, a Study of 'The Vicar of Wakefield' and Its Literary Background* (Lund, 1971), pp. 94 and 131 n.33.

24. The primrose is also, of course, used by Goldsmith in *The Deserted Village* to suggest rural innocence and simplicity; but even here it is "Sweet as the primrose peeps beneath the thorn" (l. 330 [*Works*, IV, 299]).

25. Thompson (in "Eighteenth-Century English Society," p. 157) sees the "plebeian culture" as essentially "picaresque"—"not only in the obvious sense that more people are mobile, go to sea, are carried off to wars, experience the hazards and adventures of the road. In more settled ambiences—in the growing areas of manufacture and of free labour—life itself proceeds along a road whose hazards and accidents cannot be prescribed or avoided by forethought; fluctuation in the incidence of mortality, of prices, of employment, are experienced as external accidents beyond any control. . . ." My own definition of picaresque depends on the shifting relation of a servant to a master—to the moments of stability sought (or imposed) on the wanderer. The moments of stability tend to assume that relationship, which of course leads to theatrical impersonation. See my *Fictions of Satire* (Baltimore, 1967).

Instruction and the Family

1. My text is the London edition of 1720 in twenty-four books. This chapter is a condensation of my essay "The Pilgrimage and the Family: Structures in the Novels of Fielding and Smollett," published in *Tobias Smollett: Bicentennial Essays Presented to Lewis M. Knapp*, ed. G. S. Rousseau and P. -G. Boucé (New York, 1971), pp. 57–78. For the remarks on *Telemachus*, see below, p. 269, n.1.

2. "Discourse upon Epick Poetry; Particularly on the Excellence of the Poem of Telemachus," in *Telemachus*, I, xxx.

3. J. Paul Hunter has noticed a relationship between Fielding and the *Telemachus*, but only in *Tom Jones* (*Occasional Form: Henry Fielding and the Chains of Circumstance*, pp. 133–35). His observation is that the original version of the *Telemachus* (tr. 1699) was in eighteen books, divided as *Tom Jones* is (rather than twelve or twenty-four, the usual number). Like *Tom Jones*, it falls into three equal parts: books 1–6, Telemachus and Calypso; 7–12, his "banishment," wanderings, and battles; 13–18 (or 18–24 in the later twenty-four-book version), his descent into the

underworld and return home. Telemachus, he argues, "becomes attached to three earthly ladies, and one of them dominates each of the three sections, as Molly, Mrs. Waters, and Lady Bellaston occupy Tom in the country, on the road, and in the city" (p. 135). I do not know to what lady he refers in the second part; but Calypso much more strongly resembles Lady Booby vis-à-vis Joseph than does Molly Seagrim vis-à-vis Tom.

4. *Telemachus*, I, 144, 146.

5. The parallel here is with Antiope, daughter of Idomeneus, whom Telemachus is destined to marry *after* he has delivered Penelope from the suitors, and so Mentor stands between them, despite her father's stratagems. The point of the temptation of Antiope, Fénelon tells us, is that "he was not now the same Telemachus who had been such a slave to a tyrannical passion in the island of Calypso" (II, 312).

6. The theme of education is also supported by the tradition of epic commentary, which interprets the thematic or allegorical structure of the classical epics as a hero's education.

7. See Dick Taylor, Jr., "Joseph as Hero in *Joseph Andrews*," *Tulane Studies in English*, VII (1957), 91–109, and Jessie R. Chambers, "The Allegorical Journey in 'Joseph Andrews' and 'Tom Jones' " (doctoral dissertation, Johns Hopkins University, 1960), chap. 3.

8. For the background of *Telemachus* and English educational theory of the period, see Jay Fliegelman, "The American Revolution against Patriarchy, 1720–1800" (doctoral dissertation, Stanford, 1977). Fliegelman's focus is on the popularity of *Telemachus* in the American colonies in the 1770s and '80s, based on its usefulness as a paradigm for the relationship of the colonies with the fatherland.

9. As Minerva says, at the end (bk. XXIV), "The best precepts of the wise Ulysses would instruct you less than his absence, and the suffering which, while you sought him, you have endured."

10. *Locke on Politics, Religion and Education*, ed. Maurice Cranston (New York, 1965), p. 181.

11. Garland reprint of the 1708 edition, p. 7.

12. *Devil on Two Sticks*, p. 22. All the exposed evil has been balanced with two long romantic tales of ideals that win out but are clearly romances, fictions, rather than what Cleofas has *seen*. In a roughly structural way, the two tales correspond to the antiromantic tales that interrupt the narrative of *Joseph Andrews*.

13. My text of *Letters Written by the . . . Earl of Chesterfield to his Son* is the New York (1824) edition; letter CXXXIII, 11 Dec. 1747.

14. Ibid.

15. Fliegelman discusses the influence of Chesterfield's letters on the colonial propagandists of the 1770s (see note 8 above).

16. Letters CXV, 2 Dec. 1746; CXXIV, 30 July 1747; CXII, 4 Oct. 1746.

17. See C. J. Rawson, *Henry Fielding and the Augustan Ideal under Stress* (London, 1972), chap. 1, where Fielding and Chesterfield are compared.

18. See Stone, *Family, Sex and Marriage*, pt. III. Before leaving the subject, we should mention that by the time Chesterfield's *Letters* was finally published in 1774, Sir Joshua Reynolds had delivered and printed his first six *Discourses* in which he sought to instruct the students of the Royal Academy School in the principles of art. These lectures are structured to correspond to the stages in their education, progressing also from parental obedience to adult independence (and are appropriately glossed by the irreverent apprentice in Blake's marginalia). But the most obvious

materialization of the *Telemachus* model emerges as we hear Reynolds tell his students: "My present design is to direct your view to distant excellence, and to show you the readiest path that leads to it," and he urges them to follow "those great masters who have travelled the same road with success" (*Discourses*, ed. R. R. Wark [New Haven, 1975], pp. 27–28).

19. See *A Collection of the Moral and Instructive Sentiments, Maxims, Cautions and Reflections Contained in the Histories of Pamela, Clarissa, and Sir Charles Grandison, Digested under Proper Heads* (1755); also *Miscellanies for Sentimentalists* (1786), *The Beauties of Fielding* (1782), and *The Beauties of Sterne* (1782).

20. "Inquiry concerning Virtue," in *Characteristics of Men, Manners, Opinions, Times* (1711), bk. I, pt. III, sec. 3, para. 8.

21. *Thomas Paine: Key Writings*, ed. H. H. Clark (New York, 1961), p. iv.

22. The best case is Earl R. Wasserman, "Johnson's Rasselas: Implicit Contexts," *Journal of English and Germanic Philology*, LXXIV (1975), 16–19; but I have also discussed it in the essay referred to in note 1 ("Pilgrimage and the Family"), and there is a good account of Augustine and the Fortunate Fall in Robert A. Nisbet, *Social Change and History: Aspects of the Western Theory of Development* (New York, 1969), pp. 90–95. A parallel to Milton's story of the Fortunate Fall is to be found in Aeneas' adventures: the Trojans are expelled from Troy into the world, where they travel until they find a place where they can reconstruct their lost city in a great modern equivalent, Rome, out of the materials present (as well as fight off natives). Aeneas, of course, served as another Adam for the Christianizers of Virgil, who found prophecies of Christ's coming in the *Pollio*.

23. Bk. VII, chap. ii, p. 331.

24. The critical question of how to read *Tom Jones* is treated in an interesting way by John Preston in "Plot as Irony: The Reader's Role in *Tom Jones*," *ELH*, XXXV (1968), 365–80; reprinted in *The Created Self* (London, 1970).

25. Although Smollett accused Fielding of having borrowed characters and situations for *Tom Jones* from *Roderick Random*, it is perhaps safe to say that once the two novelists became aware of each other as the chief practitioners of the comic novel, strange parallels began to occur. In the long run, Smollett may owe more obvious debts to Fielding than the other way around: there are suggestive echoes of *Joseph Andrews* in *Roderick Random*, the opening of *Ferdinand Count Fathom* appears to derive from *Jonathan Wild*, and the idea of *Sir Launcelot Greaves* is perhaps related to *Don Quixote in England* and Fielding's other mediating versions of the Cervantean hero. But a much more interesting and profound parallel occurs in *Peregrine Pickle*, in which Smollett abruptly adopts the third-person narrator, after the peculiarly Smollettian effects achieved with the first person in *Roderick Random*—effects he did not completely recapture until his *Travels through France and Italy* and *Humphry Clinker*. Assessment, distancing, and a more discursive effect were among the qualities he achieved in his second novel, and in these he may have emulated Fielding's successful example.

26. Grizzle's urge to dominate is also hereditary, traceable back to "the mayoralty of her papa" who had arrived at this position of honor in London after "small beginnings," and with her in charge of the garrison, "in less than two hours, the whole economy . . . was turned topsy-turvy"; "in less than three months [Trunnion] became a thorough-paced husband." To consolidate her position she uses the same device Mrs. Pickle had used on her, though Grizzle's pregnancy proves a false one.

27. *Peregrine Pickle*, ed. J. L. Clifford (Oxford, 1964), chap. xi, pp. 74–75.

28. The difference, of course, is that while in *Tom Jones* they have different

fathers and the mother secretly likes Tom better, in *Peregrine Pickle* they have the same father, and the mother, consciously at least, prefers the docile Gam, who is physically and morally deformed.

29. See William M. Sale, Jr., "From *Pamela* to *Clarissa*," in *The Age of Johnson*, ed. F. W. Hilles (New Haven, 1949); reprinted in *Samuel Richardson: A Collection of Critical Essays*, ed. John Carroll (Englewood Cliffs, N.J., 1969), pp. 39–48; also Margaret Anne Doody, *A Natural Passion: A Study of the Novels of Samuel Richardson* (Oxford, 1974), chap. 8. Although I do not take it for a source, an interesting analogue to the cipher father and the unnatural mother who disowns her son can be found in Johnson's *Life of Mr. Richard Savage*, first published in 1744. Another curious mother–son relationship which bears a resemblance to that of Perry and his mother appears in Mary Davies' *The Accomplish'd Rake* (1727).

30. See below, pp. 174 ff.

31. Chaps. 28, 59, 82.

32. Partridge is, in fact, named after a bird noted for hatching other birds' eggs; when they are hatched, the young birds fly away to find their true parents (see, e.g., *The Bestiary*, ed. T. H. White [New York, 1960], p. 136).

33. The parallels of Joseph–biblical Joseph and Abraham Adams–biblical Abraham were first pointed out by Battestin in *The Moral Basis of Fielding's Art* (Middletown, Conn., 1959). He, however, regarded them as normative.

34. If Adams is an uncle figure in *Joseph Andrews*, the bad mother-Eve may be Lady Booby, to whom Joseph feels as a son and a servant, while she regards him as a potential lover. This is perhaps a concealed version of what emerges in *Tom Jones*, where Lady Booby, in her hypocrisy and lechery and ambiguous attitude toward Joseph, becomes Bridget Allworthy, Tom's real mother (Lady Bellaston, of course, is another somewhat refined version of Lady Booby). Although the threat of incest enters only momentarily when Joseph and Fanny appear to be siblings, the taboo hovers over the Lady Booby–Joseph as well as the Bridget–Jenny–Tom relationship, as perhaps it does around all relationships between older women and boys (as in the jestbooks). Incest is probably for Fielding another form of slight subversion, reflecting his belief that a repressive society is worse than sexual so-called sins, even when taboos like incest are violated; and so we can see him in a mild way participating in the tradition of Diderot and later Shelley.

35. I accept the notion that Tristram *may* not be Walter Shandy's son as yet another hint of unrelatedness in Tristram's world, not necessarily as proof that Tristram was a bastard. Conceived on the first Sunday in March (Walter's sciatica kept him chaste from December to February), Tristram was born 5 November, "which," he says, "to the area fixed on, was as near nine kalendar months as any husband could in reason have expected"; thus our attention is drawn to the matter and we notice that the period was only eight months. For other hints, as to the discrepancy in Walter's and Tristram's size, see *Tristram Shandy*, ed. James A. Work (New York, 1940), pp. 331 (IV, 30) and 437 (VI, 18). We should note that if Walter may be only a putative father, Yorick is the character who most resembles Tristram in temperament as well as stature. See also R. G. Collins, "The Hidden Bastard: A Question of Illegitimacy in Smollett's *Peregrine Pickle*," *PMLA*, XCIV (1979), 91–105.

36. Ed. Lewis M. Knapp (Oxford, 1966), pp. 8, 17, 48, 49.

37. Win Jenkins to Mary Jones, 14 Oct., p. 338.

38. *Rights of Man* (1791; Penguin ed., 1969), p. 64.

39. See Angus Fletcher, *Allegory, the Theory of a Symbolic Mode* (Ithaca, 1970 ed.), esp. pp. 25–69.

The Good Samaritan

1. The general gist of this chapter appeared as "Models and Paradigms: *Joseph Andrews*, Hogarth's *Good Samaritan*, and Fénelon's *Télémaque*," *Modern Language Notes*, XCI (1976), 1186–1207.

2. Sermon XVI in *Twenty Sermons* (London, 1755), p. 332; noticed by Battestin, *The Moral Basis of Fielding's Art*, p. 22. On Hoadly's unorthodox positions, see Robbins, *Eighteenth-Century Commonwealthman*, p. 84.

3. See Paulson, *Hogarth: His Life, Art, and Times*, II, 382–88; also *The Art of Hogarth* (London, 1975), pp. 46–49. The convention of using the Good Samaritan in funerary monuments seems to have begun around midcentury. See Nicholas Penny, *Church Monuments in Romantic England* (New Haven, 1977), p. 136.

4. This is also true of Hogarth's comic-history paintings and engravings. Compare the prefatory subscription ticket for *A Harlot's Progress* and the preface to *Joseph Andrews*, which show the author as a maker with clear choices which correspond to the relationships within the work itself of the traditional and the new, the decorous and the indecorous, the high and the low.

5. "Autobiographical Notes," in *Analysis of Beauty*, ed. Burke, p. 202.

6. *Twenty Sermons*, p. 320. See also sermon II, "Of the Divisions, and Cruelties, Falsely Imputed to Christianity" (1702), in *Sixteen Sermons Formerly Printed . . . to Which are Added Six Sermons upon Public Occasions* (London, 1758), p. 33.

7. Notice the dog in both panels: the wounded man's wounded dog licking its bloody leg, and the black dog in the other panel who leans over the edge to look at us or connect with the story of Rahere below. The dog has by this time become a Hogarth trademark, as we have seen (above, pp. 54–56).

8. The graphic sources for *The Pool of Bethesda* might include various versions of Murillo (National Gallery, London), Sebastiano Ricci (Ministry of Public Buildings), and Louis Laguerre (Chatsworth). But the graphic *model* Hogarth would have wanted the viewer to connect it with was Raphael's cartoon of *St. Peter and St. John Healing the Lame*. Yet for Hogarth himself the decisive model may have been a verbal one: Rembrandt's *Christ Healing the Sick* (the "Hundred Guilder Print"), which is not close visually but was described by his friend Jonathan Richardson in his *Essay on the Theory of Painting* (1715; 1725 ed., pp. 66–67). Richardson discusses it as the model for just the kind of historical composition Hogarth was projecting, insisting on variety in the delineation of different types of the diseased and crippled, and emphasizing Rembrandt's story-telling details: the Ethiopian, for instance, who shows how far Christ's fame had reached. For Hogarth, the point is the tension between visual and verbal sources—often the priority of a work *written about*, to be understood in its conceptual sense as *an example* of great history painting.

9. *Twenty Sermons*, p. 332.

10. *Apprentice's Vade Mecum*, ed. McKillop, p. 43.

11. See Paulson, *Hogarth: His Life, Art, and Times*, I, 183, 271–75; *Emblem and Expression*, pp. 39–40.

12. See below, p. 136.

13. *Telemachus*, pp. xxxvi, lx–lxi.

14. Cf. Fielding's *Champion*, 10 June 1740 (on Hogarth).

15. *Analysis of Beauty*, p. 82.

16. The painting is in the Tate, London.

The Iatrohydraulic System

1. William Cadogan, *Essay upon Nursing and the Management of Children, from Their Birth to Three Years of Age. By a Physician. In a Letter to One of the Governors of the Foundling Hospital* (1748; 3d ed., 1749), p. 5. Cf. William Buchan, *Domestic Medicine* (1772); M. King-Hall, *The Story of the Nursery* (London, 1958), and Stone, *Family, Sex and Marriage*, pp. 426–32.

2. Norbert Elias' *The Civilizing Process* (London, 1977) is also relevant here. Elias argues that bodily control characterizes civilization. See also Keith Thomas' review of Elias, *New York Review of Books*, XXV, no. 3 (9 Mar. 1978), 28–31.

3. Though, as Stone has remarked in conversation, there is no evidence to show that the poor (as opposed to the poor children treated by the Foundling Hospital) did not often imitate the rich in swaddling their infants.

4. Stone, op. cit., p. 426.

5. Before Joseph, there had been an ensign in Betty's life who "was the first Person who made any Impression on her Heart; he did indeed raise a Flame in her, which required the Care of a Surgeon to cool. . . . While she burnt for him, several others burnt for her." The principle is established with the ensign, and when that affair is over it continues with Joseph; and the metaphor is basically the same hydraulic one. But Betty is also (as the metaphor of Life as Theater emerges) miscast; we are told that she might have been controlled by a nunnery but could not be in "the ticklish Situation of a Chamber-maid at an Inn" (p. 86).

6. *Anatomy of Melancholy*, ed. Floyd Dell and Paul Jordan-Smith (New York, 1927), I, 203–5. Burton merely expresses in his inimitable way the old doctrines of Galen and others. For some examples, see Thomas Maresca, *Epic to Novel* (Columbus, 1974) on Bernardus Sylvestris, pp. 42–43; Stone, *Family, Sex and Marriage*, p. 497.

7. The iatrohydraulic dynamicists were firmly opposed by George Cheyne in *The English Malady* (1733), for example, pp. 4–5, and John Purcell, *A Treatise of Vapours, or, Hysterick Fits* (1702), chap. 2, esp. pp. 69, 72.

8. *The Remains of Thomas Hearne*, ed. John Bliss, rev. John Buchanan-Brown (Carbondale, 1966), p. 2. Cf. Freud's wolf-man (Standard Edition, XVII, 74–75).

9. See *Complete Poems of John Wilmot, Earl of Rochester*, ed. David M. Vieth (New Haven, 1968), pp. 37–40, 40–46, 60–61, 116–17, 54–55.

10. Ibid., pp. 102–3.

11. To his wife, in *The Complete Works of John Wilmot, Earl of Rochester*, ed. John Hayward (London, 1926), p. 288.

12. Stone, op. cit., p. 497. One fact Stone has exposed in his chapters on sexual practice in eighteenth-century England is the extent to which men of Fielding's class habitually repressed or displaced their orgasms. With the exception of their wives, they were restrained by the very real fear of venereal disease, the woman's pregnancy, and the inconvenience and discomfort of contraceptives. (Boswell was the great exception, with his seventeen cases of VD.) The result, Stone shows, was *coitus interruptus* and masturbation, but seldom penetration to orgasm. He sees a connection between this situation and, for example, the energetic empire building (especially in remote India), which he thinks was a sublimation of the repressed sexual urges.

13. To George Mantagu, 18 May 1749, Yale Walpole, IX, 84; also "Horace Walpole, Political Papers," fol. 48–50, in W. S. Lewis Collection.

14. St. Hildegard, *Causae et Curae*, ed. P. Kaiser (Leipzig, 1903), pp. 38, 143; cited in Raymond Klibansky, Erwin Panofsky, and Fritz Saxl, *Saturn and Melancholy: Studies in the History of Natural Philosophy and Art* (London, 1964), pp. 79–80.

15. See Maurice Johnson, *Fielding's Art of Fiction* (Philadelphia, 1961), pp. 119–22.

16. Though not in so schematic a form as in *Tom Jones*, the pattern is discernible in Hogarth's *Marriage à la Mode* (1745), where the fathers cut off the children's channels of sexual fulfillment and the result is what Sophia is indicating.

17. Morris, *Essay . . . of Wit*, p. 1, also pp. 1–12. For the "in tail" joke, see above, p. 68.

18. "The qualities of matter are not to be considered as sublime or beautiful in themselves, but as SIGNS or EXPRESSIONS of such qualities, as, by the constitution of our nature, are fitted to produce pleasing or interesting emotion" (*Essay on the Nature and Principles of Taste*, 1812 ed., II, 176).

19. Freud, Standard Edition, VIII, 99–100.

20. On "mixed character," see X, ii, 527. As Fielding says in *Joseph Andrews* (p. 5): "Mirth and Laughter . . . are probably more wholesome Physic for the Mind, and conduce better to purge away Spleen, Melancholoy and ill Affections, than is generally imagined."

21. Stone, p. 637. This emphasis makes it reasonable to mention the names of Freud, Reich, and Marcuse, especially the latter's *Eros and Civilization* (Boston, 1955).

22. For the *laissez-faire* position, see Nisbet, *Social Change and History*, pp. 139–58.

23. See David Foxon, *Libertine Literature in England 1660–1745* (New Hyde Park, N.Y., 1965), p. 45.

24. See William H. Epstein, *John Cleland: Images of a Life* (New York, 1974), pp. 102–3. On Cleland's use of *A Harlot's Progress* and *Moll Flanders* as his models, see Epstein, pp. 92–94. Epstein notes the publication in early 1749, just after *Fanny Hill*, of another plea for sexual freedom: Thomas Cannon's *Ancient and Modern Pederasty Investigated and Exemplified*.

25. William B. Warner has treated *Clarissa* from this point of view in his *Reading Clarissa: The Struggles of Interpretation* (New Haven, 1979). It is perhaps worth comparing Hogarth's and Fielding's bifocal readings with Richardson's words to Aaron Hill: "While the taste of the age can be gratified by a Tom Jones . . . I am not to expect that the world will bestow two readings, or one indeed, attentive one, on such a grave story as Clarissa" (12 July 1949, in *Selected Letters*, ed. John Carroll [Oxford, 1964], p. 126).

26. See Paulson, "Satire, and Poetry, and Pope," in *English Satire: Papers Read at a Clark Library Seminar* (Los Angeles, 1972), pp. 57–106.

The '45 and Bonnie Prince Charlie

1. See Battestin's arguments, *Tom Jones* (Wesleyan ed.), "Introduction," pp. xxxv–xxxix. This chapter appeared in a somewhat different form as "Fielding in *Tom Jones*: The Historian, the Poet, and the Mythologist," in *Augustan Worlds: Essays in Honour of A. R. Humphreys* (Leicester, 1978), pp. 175–87.

2. *The Jacobite's Journal and Related Writings*, ed. W. B. Coley (Wesleyan ed.; Oxford, 1974).

3. Spence to Richardson, 21 Jan. 1748, in Anna Laetitia Barbauld, *Correspondence of Samuel Richardson* (London, 1804), II, 319–27.

4. *Spectator*, no. 28. See above, p. 00.

5. Murray Cohen, *Sensible Words*, pp. 93–94.

6. Ibid., p. 130.

7. By the next generation the aim of linguistics was, in Cohen's words, "to preserve variety and avoid reducing composition 'to an insipid uniformity.' An academy for legislating the language would sacrifice what is living in language and would cramp English freedom" (quoting John Fell, *Essay towards an English Grammar* [1784], p. x; in Cohen, pp. 95–96).

8. Martin, p. 111; Cohen, pp. 130–31. See also V. J. Peyton's *History of the Engish Language* (1771), p. 29.

9. See Paulson, *Hogarth: His Life, Art, and Times*, chap. 21, and on etymology in this respect, cf. the concluding sentences in Paulson, *Emblem and Expression*, p. 231.

10. Cohen, p. 97.

11. Glasse, p. iv; see Joan Owen, "Philosophy in the Kitchen; or Problems in Eighteenth-Century Culinary Aesthetics," *Eighteenth-Century Life*, III (Mar. 1977), 77–79.

12. Fielding's concern with lies and fabrications appears in *Joseph Andrews* (I, iv) in Lady Tittle and Lady Tattle making up stories about Lady Booby and Joseph; but he makes no connection between their activity and the process of historiography.

13. Fielding pretty consistently refers to himself as historian (see, besides the title of the book, pp. 832 and 880). But his use of "history" was ambiguous and did not lose its older sense of mere "narrative," as in the titles of most of his books. For the poet–historian contrast, see the preface to *Journal of a Voyage to Lisbon (1754)*.

14. Baker catalogue, item no. 219. In the "Court of Criticism" it is ordered "that the said Mythology be strongly recommended to the Public, as the most useful, instructive, and entertaining Book extant" (no. 9, p. 146). I cite the 1739 edition. Cf. Thomas Blackwell's attack on Banier in his *Letters concerning Mythology* (1748), pp. 207–60.

15. Taken from, for example, Natale Conti, *Mythologiae sive explicationis fabularum libri decem* (1616 ed.), p. 305.

16. "Wednesday," ll. 89–92.

17. See Frank Manuel's explanation of the eighteenth-century euhemerist mode in *The Eighteenth Century Confronts the Gods* (Cambridge, Mass., 1959), p. 105; and on Banier, pp. 104–7.

18. By VII, iii, Fielding is beginning to show that the Blifil-Sophia "alliance" or "treaty" of marriage on the level of personal history is the equivalent of the alliances and treaties in the War of the Austrian Succession that in 1748 was just being brought to a close (p. 333). The myth maker is Mrs. Western, who sees the Blifil-Sophia negotiations in precisely this way (see p. 334).

19. The role of the audience in *Tom Jones* has usually been seen as participatory in the creation of the book's meaning. Certainly the indeterminateness is far less at issue than in *Tristram Shandy*. Fielding wants to create the impression of participation, but I suspect that the centrality of the audience is more nearly due to its part in the myth-making process. I am arguing that the central figure is in fact the historian-mythologist, who is set off somewhat from the audience and the other characters, who are themselves in the same general category of "poets" or myth makers.

20. For example, on Deborah Wilkins' searching out Tom's father (II, iii, 81) or

Partridge's not offering Tom any of his money (XIII, vii, 712). The either/or construction is also Fielding's version of the doubleness of causality stressed by Virgil in the *Aeneid*, as when Thymoetes urges the Trojans to take the horse into the city— "whether in treachery, or because / The fates of Troy so ordered," or when Laocoon's spear fails to break open the horse because "something / Got in his way, the gods, or fate, or counsel" (bk. II, Rolfe Humphries trans.). More generally, Aeneas tells us that "[Panthus'] words, or the gods' purpose, swept me on / Toward fire and arms."

21. I am suggesting an alternative meaning of "history" in *Tom Jones* to that offered by both Leo Braudy and Martin Battestin, the one based on Hume's *History of England* and the other on the pattern of divine providence. See Braudy, *Narrative Form in History and Fiction* (Princeton, 1970), esp. parts III and IV, and Battestin, *The Providence of Wit: Aspects of Form in Augustan Literature and the Arts* (Oxford, 1974), chaps. V and VI.

22. Characteristically, he also applies the historian's procedure to literary "rules." A writer does something well, critics then expand these nice details into "his chief Merit," and then to these "Time and Ignorance, the two great Supporters of Imposture, gave Authority; and thus, many Rules for good Writing have been established, which have not the least Foundation in Truth or Nature" (p. 211), and these are imposed tyrannically on subsequent writers. This passage points toward the analogy between the character Tom and Fielding's work *Tom Jones*.

23. *Message in a Bottle* (New York, 1975), pp. 72, 81.

24. See Battestin's essay, "Tom Jones and 'His *Egyptian* Majesty': Fielding's Parable of Government," *PMLA*, LXXII (1967), 68–77, and Manuel Schonhorn's convincing reply, "Fielding's Ecphrastic Moment: Tom Jones and His Egyptian Majesty" (forthcoming).

25. There are the stories that Elcho found Charles in a hut by the river Nairn after the battle "in a deplorable state," "prostrate and without hope, and surrounded only by his Irish friends," believing the Scots officers were going to betray him, and speaking to none of them, etc. See Chevalier de Johnstone, *Memoirs concerning the Affairs of Scotland* (London, 1820), p. 186 and n.; David Elcho, *A Short Account of the Affairs of Scotland*, ed. Evan Charteris (Edinburgh, 1907), pp. 94–95, 435–36. Fielding discusses Charles's behavior during and after the battle in *True Patriot*, no. 27, pp. 1–2. On the varying accounts, see Mariam Locke, ed., *True Patriot* (University of Alabama Press, 1964), pp. 222–23.

26. For Molly–Eve, see *Tom Jones*, IV, vi, 175.

27. The importance of names was of course equally thrust upon Fielding by the tradition of epic commentary with its etymological methods. See Maresca, *Epic to Novel*, pp. 33–35.

28. See *Jacobite's Journal*, no. 6, p. 125; Rupert C. Jarvis, *Collected Papers on the Jacobite Risings* (Manchester, 1972), vol. II, chaps. 16–18.

29. Iona and Peter Opie, *The Oxford Dictionary of Nursery Rhymes* (Oxford, 1951), no. 96, pp. 115–16.

30. Fielding's emphasis is on Charles Edwards' bigotry and such stories as how he executes a Protestant sheep stealer and pardons a Catholic rapist of an eleven-year-old girl. The refrain is "Such is the spirit of Popery" or "Such are the Terrors of arbitrary Power." See also Jarvis, II, 134.

31. *History* (London, 1745), p. 35; cited in Jarvis, p. 137.

32. See Locke, ed., *True Patriot*, p. 255. Cf., for example, no. 3, p. 35; cited in Jarvis, p. 137.

Index

Addison, Joseph: *Dialogues upon . . . Ancient Medals* (1726), 191; *Spectator*, 77, 122–23, 126, 127–28, 246, 272—life as an inn, 263; on metaphors of providence, 115–17; on method, 262; on shop signs, 33, 35, 36, 132, 191; theatrical metaphor, 121–24, 128
Aix-la-Chapelle, Treaty of, 207
Alciati, A., 11, 191
Alexander the Great, 69, 256
Alexander VI, Pope, 71
Alkon, Paul, 262
Allen, Ralph: in *Joseph Andrews*, 168; in *Tom Jones*, 201
Allison, Archibald, 183, 271
Alpers, Svetlana, 30, 249
Alphabet Books, x, 105–06
Anabaptists, 20
Anna Sophia, Electress of Hanover, 100
Anne, Queen, 99, 109
Antal, Frederick, 245
Ape, and dog, 51, 118–19
Apprentice: as subculture type, 8–23
Argyll, duke of, 73, 75
Armorial Bearings, 34–35, 42–46
Atherton, Herbert M., 253
Augustus, Emperor, 68–69, 71, 75, 188

Bäckman, Sven, 265
Bacon, Francis, 106, 114
Bailey, Nathan: *Dictionary*, 49–50, 52
Ballad of Jesse, The, 11–12, 13
Banier, Abbé: *Mythology and Fables of the Ancients* (1739–40), xv, 264, 272; and *Jacobite's Journal* and *Tom Jones*, 195–201
Barrington, Daines, 259
Bartholomew's Close, 22
Bassano, Jacopo: *Good Samaritan*, 55
Batcock, Gregory, xiv, 273
Battestin, Martin, 265, 268, 269, 271, 273
Beauties of Fielding, The (1782), 267
Beauties of Sterne, The (1782), 267
Bechtel, E., 254
Beckford, Peter: *Thoughts on Hunting* (1787), xi, 60
Beckford, William: *Vathek* (1786), 258
Beethoven, Ludwig van, xiii
Benham, W. Gurney, 259
Benjamin, Walter, 257
Bentley, Richard, 191
Bercovitch, Sacvan, 263
Berger, John, 12, 247
Bifocal Series: card games, 99–101, 105; dictionaries et al., 105–14
"Black Joke, The," 251
Black Laws, 61
Blackwell, Thomas: *Letters concerning Mythology* (1748), xv, 126, 191, 264, 272
Blake, William, 47, 63, 266
Block, W., 250
Blücher, Marshal, 88
Bolingbroke, Henry St. John, Viscount, and Johnson's *Dictionary*, 106
Book of Orders, xiii
Bosch, Hieronymus, xi
Boswell, James, 83: *Life of Johnson* (1791), 77–78, 252, 270
Boyse, Samuel, 264

275